PALESTINE
IS
COMING

BOOKS BY KERMIT ZARLEY
The Gospel
The Gospels Interwoven

FORTHCOMING
Babylon Is Coming
Christ Is Coming

PALESTINE
IS
COMING

The Revival of
Ancient Philistia

Kermit Zarley

Hannibal Books
Hannibal, Missouri

PALESTINE IS COMING
THE REVIVAL OF ANCIENT PHILISTIA

Library of Congress Cataloging in Publication Data

Zarley, Kermit, 1941-
    Palestine is coming: the revival of ancient Philistia
    Bibliography: p.
    Includes indexes.
    1. Palestine.   2. Israel.   3. Jewish-Arab relations.   4.
Bible prophecy (Christian eschatology).   I. Title.
ISBN 0-929292-13-8
Library of Congress Catalog Card Number: 90-082951

Edited by Marilyn Zarley.
Cover and design by Kermit Zarley and Harry Verploegh.

Hannibal Books
921 Center Street, Suite A
Hannibal, Missouri 63401

Printed in the United States of America

Contents

List of Maps

Preface

The troubled Middle East has been a powder keg ready to explode for decades. Looming in the forefront of Middle East turmoil is the prolonged Palestinian-Israeli conflict. How amazing it is that only a few million people and a tiny piece of real estate have been able to threaten the peace of the whole world. But then, the Jews are no ordinary people and the land under question is no ordinary land.

Palestine Is Coming is about land theology, one of the most neglected subjects in Rabbinic and Christian doctrine.[1] The concept of God's choosing a particular people and promising them a particular land is a primary theme of the Bible. Accordingly, this book defends the Israeli Jews' right to a portion of the land of Palestine. However, on the bases of the Jews' history and their own scriptures, it challenges Israeli leaders' repeated assertion that the Jews are entitled to all of Palestine.

This book presents more than a proposal for resolving the Palestinian problem; it is also a prediction of its outcome. From my study of biblical prophecy in 1981, I discovered that ancient Philistia would someday be revived. It appeared to me that a revival of Philistia could be the solution to the present Palestinian problem. This led to detailed studies not only of the scriptures (Chapters 11-14), but also of the histories of the land of Palestine (Chapters 1-4) and of the Palestinian problem (Chapters 5-9). Knowing the historical background of this complex problem is essential to an adequate understanding of it. Chapter 10, the proposed solution to the problem, is the highlight of the book.

I realize that countless statesmen have expended much effort toward resolving this dispute. My chief qualification for writing this book is that I have been a student of Bible prophecy for over thirty years. I want to share what I believe the Bible says about this subject. I am much indebted to my wife Marilyn, who collaborated with me and did extensive editing on this work.

Like so many writers on this conflict, I hope that *Palestine Is Coming* will make a positive contribution to the ongoing discussion of the Palestinian problem and to its resolution. I also hope that my viewpoint will be perceived as pro-Jewish, pro-Israel and pro-Palestinian.

Finally, it is my prayer that this book will influence spiritually uncommitted readers to seek to know the loving, just and foreknowing God of the Bible.

Kermit Zarley
Friendswood, Texas, USA

Part I

THE
ANCIENT
PAST

Chapter 1

THE PROMISED LAND

"To your descendants I will give this land" (Gen 12.7).

Every nation is entitled to a land of its own. The Jews regained theirs in 1948. The Palestinians are still waiting. Their land was seized by the Jews.

That the Palestinians have developed a national entity is now an indisputable fact. Like the Jews, they also deserve their own independent state. But the big question is, "Where should it be?"

Israeli leaders claim all of Palestine as the land of their forefathers. This is a mistake. The Hebrew Bible makes it clear: ancient Israel never really possessed the land of the Philistines. It is here, in ancient Philistia, where the Palestinian state should be located. Indeed, the word "Palestine" derives from "Philistine."

Moreover, the biblical prophets imply that the Palestinian state will be located in the Plain of Philistia as a revival of ancient Philistia.

But all of this is getting ahead of our story. To understand God's plan for nations like Philistia (Palestine), and especially for His chosen nation of Israel, we've got to go back to the beginning.

Nations as God's Will
Nations have always been God's plan for man. In the beginning God told man to "fill [populate] the earth, and subdue it" (Gen 1.28; 9.1). To accomplish this, God "made" the nations (Deut 26.19; Ps 86.9). Even in the Messianic kingdom, "nations" will come to Jerusalem to worship God (e.g., Isa 2.2; Zech 14.16). The concept of nations, however, does not justify the belligerent nationalism which sparks wars of conquest.

It has never been God's will for mankind to unite as one nation and one people on the earth. Soon after Noah and the flood, mankind tried to do this very thing. Noah's descendants journeyed from the region of Mount Ararat, in present eastern Turkey, and settled on the broad plain of present central Iraq. On the Euphrates River they began to build the famous city of Babylon with its Tower of Babel. They wanted its top to reach high into the sky, to "make for ourselves a name; lest we be scattered abroad over the face of the whole earth" (Gen 11.4). They were thwarting God's design to populate the earth and to establish nations.

Until then everyone spoke one language. "The LORD said, 'Behold, they are one people, and they all have the same language. . . . and now nothing which they purpose to do will be impossible for them' " (11.6). God had earlier said, "the intent of man's heart is evil from his youth" (8.21). The implication is that with one language and one nation, people would be able to accomplish every evil imaginable.

To restrain their bent toward evil, God confused their language and diverse human languages were born. By this means, "the LORD scattered them abroad from there over the face of the whole earth; and they stopped building the city" (11.8). Thus, God overthrew their designs; he forced them to spread out, populate the earth and subdue it.

Consequently, nations were formed according to families and languages. The oldest genealogical record in existence appears in Genesis 10. Called the "Table of Nations," it lists the nations according to the heads of families. Thus, the descendants of Noah spread out and settled "according to their families, according to their languages, by their lands, by their nations" (Gen 10.20, 31).

Moses recorded the first biblical testimony of the fundamental principle of the United Nations, that each nation is entitled to exercise sovereign control over its own land within specified borders. "When the Most High gave the nations their inheritance, when He separated the sons of man [by confusing their language], He set the boundaries of the peoples" (Deut 32.8). **It is therefore God's will that each nation have its own land**.

Yet the Bible warns that God may take a land away from its people if they persist in gross disobedience to Him. This is exactly what happened to the Canaanites, and later to that nation which overthrew them—Israel.

Curse on Canaan
Soon after the flood, Noah got drunk, shed his clothes and fell asleep. Ham "saw the nakedness of his father, and told his two brothers"

(Gen 9.22), who came and covered their father's nakedness. Without any further explanation, the Bible relates that when Noah awoke, he pronounced a curse on Ham's son, Canaan. Then Noah pronounced a blessing on Shem and Japheth for their part in covering his nakedness. Noah proclaimed what later came to pass,

> Blessed be the LORD,
> The God of Shem;
> And let Canaan be his servant (Gen 9.26).

Noah's prophecy was fulfilled in the history of the Canaanites and the Hebrews (Israelites). The Hebrews were descendants of Shem (Semitic). Centuries after the Canaanites became established in their land, the Israelites arrived, destroyed many of them and possessed their land. The remaining Canaanites became Shem's servants when the Israelites made them forced laborers (Josh 16.10; 17.13; Jud 1.17-35). But again, this is getting ahead of our story.

Where the Nations Settled
Noah's ark had landed in "the mountains of Ararat" (Gen 8.4). These are believed to be in eastern Turkey, where there is a very large Mount Ararat overlooking the Soviet border. From here Noah's offspring spread out and settled in the lands which came to bear their names (Gen 10).

The descendants of Japheth resided in present Turkey, then spread throughout most of the earth.

The descendants of Ham migrated southward, into Africa. On the way, Canaan and his descendants settled the important land bridge joining Africa with Europe and Asia. It included parts of present Syria and Lebanon, and all of Palestine.[1]

This "land of Canaan" was a good land, "flowing with milk and honey" (e.g., Ex 3.8). It was somewhat rectangular in shape, about 170 miles long and 50 miles wide. Its length was bordered by the Mediterranean Sea on the west and the Jordan depression on the east. Going north to south, the "territory of the Canaanite extended from Sidon as you go toward Gerar, as far as Gaza" (Gen 10.19). Vital trade routes were located there. Due to its position uniting three continents, this parcel has always been the most strategic geo-political region in the world.

The descendants of Shem traveled east and south from Mount Ararat to what is now Syria, Jordan, Iraq, Iran and the Arabian Peninsula. In this region lies a large fertile basin called Mesopotamia.

Watered by two great rivers, the Tigris and Euphrates, it became known as "the cradle of civilization" and "the breadbasket of the world." Together with the land bridge, the whole region is shaped in the form of the moon's crescent and called "the fertile crescent."

God Calls Abram

In 2,000 B.C., present southern Iraq was known as Chaldea. The prosperous city of Ur of Chaldea became a Semitic center for polytheism and idolatry. Here God called a man named Abram out of his father's house of idolatry (Gen 11.31; Ac 7.2-4):

> "Go forth from your country, . . .
> To the land which I will show you;
> And I will make you a great nation,
> And I will bless you,
> And make your name great;
> And so you shall be a blessing;
> And I will bless those who bless you,
> And the one who curses you I will curse.
> And in you all the families of the earth shall be blessed" (Gen 12.1-3).

A People and a Land

Obedient Abram took his family and left Chaldea. He apparently did not know his final destination (Heb 11.8). After a long stopover in

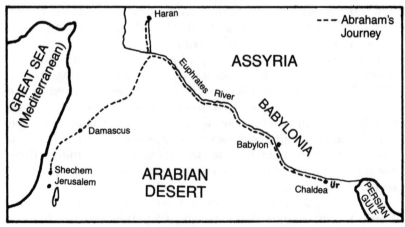

MAP 1: ABRAHAM'S JOURNEY

Haran, the family arrived in central Canaan at Shechem (present Nablus). It was here that "the LORD appeared to Abram and said, 'to your descendants I will give this land' " (Gen 12.7). It became known as "the Promised Land."

God confirmed this promise to Abram at nearby Bethel. As Abram looked around, God said, "All the land which you see, I will give it to you and to your descendants forever" (Gen 13.15). To the north there was Mount Carmel, the fertile Plain of Jezreel and the Galilee. Eastward lay the lush, green Jordan Valley and the land beyond. To the south was the Judean hill country and the Negev wilderness. Abram glanced west, where a long, fertile plain nestled alongside the calm, blue Mediterranean Sea. The southwestern portion was shaped like a rectangle, about 50 miles long and 15 miles wide, extending in a north-south direction. This corner of the Promised Land later became known as "the land of the Philistines." This piece of land is the major focus of this book.

God spoke to Abram on a third occasion and promised that his descendants would be as numerous as the stars in the sky (Gen 15.5). He later changed the patriarch's name to Abraham, meaning "father of a multitude of nations" (Gen 17.5). Thus, God promised to give Abram both a land and a people.

The first time God specified the northern and southern borders of the Promised Land appears in Gen 15.18: "On that day the LORD made a covenant with Abram, saying, 'To your descendants I have given this land, from the river of Egypt as far as the great river, the river Euphrates.' " Biblical scholars have differed on whether the southern border, the "river of Egypt," is the Nile River or the Wadi el Arish. Throughout much of antiquity the Wadi el Arish was recognized as the northeastern border of Egypt. Later biblical descriptions have "the brook of Egypt," which unquestionably identifies the wadi. It a seasonal stream located about twenty-five miles south of the present Gaza Strip. Most scholars believe that Gen 15.18 refers to the Wadi el Arish as the southern border of the Promised Land.

Conditional or Unconditional Covenant?
Understanding one fundamental principle is paramount in formulating a right attitude toward the Palestinian-Israeli conflict and to supporting a just resolution of it: **the Abrahamic covenant was conditional for each person**. The biblical record of God's covenant with Abraham is a gradually unfolding revelation. While the actual institution of the covenant does not stipulate any conditions to be met, later revelation does.

God instituted His covenant with Abraham according to a Chaldean custom (Gen 21.27). Abraham cut animal carcasses in half and placed them on the ground opposite each other. According to custom, two men would make a pact, recite predetermined oaths and walk together between the carcasses. The walk symbolized their unity and probably sealed it with the tacit confession, "let me be as these animal carcasses if I fail to keep my part of the agreement" (Jer 34.18 RSV). In God's covenant with Abraham, as darkness descended, the LORD signified His presence when "there appeared a smoking oven and a flaming torch which passed between these pieces" (Gen 15.17). But here there seems to have been a departure from the custom. Where was Abraham when the lights went out? Was the patriarch still asleep (v. 12)? Did he not pass between the carcasses? This detail is not made clear.

A very important question arises if Abraham did not walk between the carcasses. That is, will God keep His promise to give Abraham a people and a land without requiring either him or his descendants to fulfill any condition(s) whatsoever? Not so. Even if Abraham did not walk between the carcasses, this did not preclude him from the requirement of being faithful in order to receive the promise. In later encounters with the patriarchs, God explicitly affirms His covenant with Abraham as conditional.

Some biblical expositors think God's covenant with Abraham and his descendants is unconditional.[2] Focusing on the formal institution of the covenant in Gen 15, they deny that later revelation is a part it.

Relating the covenant to the present, does an unconditional Abrahamic covenant give the modern State of Israel a holy mandate for expanding its borders into southern Lebanon and/or Jordan in order to obtain more of the Promised Land? Put another way, have Israeli Jews been issued a divine edict to take the Promised Land by force at this time? This is what some Gentile Christian Zionists and hardline religious Israelis either advocate or would approve today because they believe the covenant was unconditional.

For God to make an unconditional covenant with sinful man raises serious questions. What if either Abraham or his descendants would turn away from God and His commandments and act very wickedly? Indeed, succeeding generations of the nation Israel did just that. Is God still obligated by His oath to bless the Israelites and give them the land?

Although it was not expressly stated at the time of its institution, God's covenant with Abraham depended on the patriarch's faithfulness and obedience.[3] This is evident even before the covenant was instituted. The reason God chose to make the covenant with Abraham in the first place was that He foreknew the patriarch's faithfulness. Ezra prayed concerning Abraham, "And Thou didst find his heart faithful before Thee, and didst make a covenant with him" (Neh 9.8). This view is quite prominent in ancient rabbinical literature, as well as in the Hebrew Bible.

Abraham's faith was evident from the beginning. At considerable sacrifice, and despite possible danger, God's model servant left his native land, took his family and went to a faraway, unspecified destination (Gen 12.1; Heb 11.8).

Soon after God instituted His covenant with Abraham, He appeared to the patriarch and declared, " 'I am God Almighty; walk before Me, and be blameless. And I will establish My covenant between Me and you, and I will multiply you exceedingly' " (Gen 17.1-2). There should be no doubt that God here adds a stipulation to His covenant with Abraham. God would only accomplish His covenant if Abraham remained "blameless," which does not mean the same as "sinless" (cf. Job 1.8; 2.3 and Lk 1.6 with Eccl 7.20).

God tested Abraham by commanding him to slay his son Isaac as a sacrificial offering. Abraham followed instructions and God stopped his hand at the last moment. Then God reaffirmed His promise to Abraham, explaining that He did so "because you have obeyed My voice" by offering Isaac (Gen 22.18). It must be concluded that if God, in His foreknowledge, had known that Abraham would refuse to offer Isaac, He would not have chosen Abraham with whom to make the covenant.

God later confirmed the covenant with Abraham's promised son, Isaac. God said He would multiply Isaac's descendants and give them the Promised Land, "because Abraham obeyed Me and kept My charge, My commandments, My statutes and My laws" (Gen 26.3-5).

God made clear His purpose for choosing the Israelites. Through Moses, He said they were to "be to Me a kingdom of priests and a holy nation" (Ex 19.6; cf. Deut 14.2). God required His Chosen People to "obey My voice and keep My covenant, then you shall be My own possession among all the peoples" (v. 5). Moses further explained that God "keeps His covenant and His lovingkindness to a thousandth generation with those who love Him and keep His commandments; but repays those who hate Him to their faces, to destroy them" (Deut 7.6, 9).

More particularly, Moses instructed the Israelites that their initial possession of the Promised Land depended on their keeping the Torah (essentially, the Law of Moses). Keeping the Law of God means respect for His commandments, which is reflected in the life. It does not signify absolute perfection. Moses commanded the Israelites to "do what is right and good in the sight of the LORD, that it may be well with you and that you may go in and possess the good land which the LORD swore to give to your fathers" (Deut 6.17-18; 4.1; 11.22-23; 27.3). Joshua later affirmed, "If the LORD is pleased with us, then He will bring us into this land, and give it to us" (Num 14.8).

The promise of the Land came before the giving of the Law. This sequence should not be construed to mean that the covenant had nothing to do with Israel's adherence to the Law. It is not as though there were no moral law of God before Sinai; it was simply further revealed and codified there. The Jews always connected the Torah with the covenant. **Nothing is more clear in the Hebrew Bible than this: the Jews' continued possession of their historic homeland has always been dependent on their adherence to the Law of God delivered to Moses at Mount Sinai.**

In his famous pronouncement of the blessing and the curse, Moses clearly warned Israel of their possible dispossession of the land (Lev 26; Deut 28). If the Israelites kept God's commandments, they would be greatly blessed. The nations would know it and fear Israel. God's primary method of manifesting Himself to the nations was by His treatment of the Jews (e.g., Gen 21.22; 26.28-29; Deut 29.22-28; Jer 22.8-9). But if the Israelites did not obey their God, He would send upon them the most frightful curses, resulting in much misery. Finally, they would be dispossessed and scattered throughout the nations of the earth. Moses' dreadful predictions have been repeatedly fulfilled in Jewish history:

> If you are not careful to observe all the words of this law. . . . The LORD will scatter you among all peoples, from one end of the earth to the other. . . . And among those nations you shall find no rest, and there shall be no resting place for the sole of your foot; but there the LORD will give you a trembling heart, failing of eyes, and despair of soul. So your life shall hang in doubt before you; and you shall be in dread night and day, and shall have no assurance of your life (Deut 28.58, 64-66).

The history of Israel's exiles from the land testify that God's covenant with Abraham is conditional. While God had obligated Himself to keep His oath to Abraham, Isaac and Jacob, He nonetheless did not keep it with certain wicked generations of Israelites, whom He judged severely. The Northern Kingdom was carried away in 722 B.C. by the Assyrians and the Southern Kingdom in 586 B.C. by the

Babylonians. The Romans completed the Jewish Diaspora in the 2nd century A.D.

Nevertheless, even though the covenant is conditional with each generation, God also promised to give the land of Canaan to Abraham and his descendants "forever," for an "everlasting possession" (Gen 13.15; 17.8; 48.4). The covenant is therefore both conditional and eternal. That is, it **will** be fulfilled when Israel repents nationally at the end of this age and turns to God. Then God will make a new covenant with Israel, a covenant which it will never break (Jer 31.31). How this is to be accomplished will be seen in the closing chapters of this book.

The Covenant Promise Through Isaac, Not Ishmael

Abraham's wife Sarah had been barren. Due to her unbelief, she insisted that Abraham bear a child by her maid, Hagar. Ishmael was born.

Years later God added the requirement of circumcision as a sign of his covenant with Abraham (Gen 17.10-13). Failing to circumcise would break the covenant: further evidence of its conditionality (v. 14). Abraham circumcised himself and his thirteen-year old son, Ishmael (Gen 17.25-26). When Isaac was born later to Abraham and Sarah, he was circumcised as well.

Some Muslim writers assert that, because of Ishmael's circumcision today's Palestinians are included in the covenant and therefore just as entitled to the Promised Land as the Israelis.[4] This view, however, is based on the popular but erroneous supposition that Arabs are descendants of Ishmael. (See Appendix B: Who are the Arabs?)

Furthermore, the covenant also required that Abraham circumcise the hundreds of male servants and slaves in his camp, which he did (Gen 14.14; 17.23). Then there were Abraham's six sons by his concubine, Keturah (Gen 25.1-6). Abraham's circumcising of them did not indicate they, like Isaac, were the "seed of promise" too.

Other Muslim writers even allege that Ishmael was the rightful heir because he was Abraham's firstborn son. But Ishmael was not born to Abraham's wife. Abraham did ask God to bless Ishmael (Gen 17.17-18). God replied, "As for Ishmael, I have heard you; behold, I will bless him, . . . and I will make him a great nation. But My covenant I will establish with Isaac, whom Sarah will bear to you" (vv. 20-21).

Thus, the covenant promise was clearly through Isaac, not Ishmael. Abraham's actions in later life affirmed Isaac as the rightful heir. Abraham "gave gifts" to the sons of his concubines—to Ishmael and to Keturah's sons—but he "gave all that he had to Isaac" (Gen 25.5-6).

God later repeated his covenant to Isaac (Gen 26.3-4) and to Isaac's son, Jacob (Gen 28.13-14), whom God renamed "Israel."

Moses and the Exodus
God did not give the Promised Land to Abraham's seed immediately. In the fourth generation, a famine forced the Hebrews (a term designating Abraham's descendants through Isaac and Jacob) to go to Egypt for food. They stayed there for some 400 years, were "fruitful and increased greatly, and multiplied, and became exceedingly mighty" (Ex 1.7).

During their sojourn in Egypt, God was fulfilling the first part of His covenant, to multiply His people Israel. At the time of the exodus, the Israelites numbered at least 2.5 million, based on Ex 12.37. The next part of God's covenant was to give them a land.

To do this, God chose Moses to lead the Israelites out of Egypt to the Promised Land. Surprisingly, they did not take the shortcut. "God did not lead them by the way of the land of the Philistines, even though it was near; for God said, 'Lest the people change their minds when they see war, and they return to Egypt.' Hence God led the people around by the way of the wilderness to the Red Sea" (Ex 13.17-18).

God, or Yahweh, as He was known by name to the Israelites (Ex 6.3), performed many miracles in the sight of His Chosen People. The ten plagues in Egypt and the parting of the Red Sea are well known. Then Moses received the Law at Mount Sinai amidst awesome divine revelation and power.

When the Israelites next drew near the land of the Canaan, God had told them to enter and take the land. But the congregation believed the spies' "bad report" (Num 13.32), and they refused to take the land. Yahweh punished the Israelites for this lack of faith by making them wander in the wilderness for 40 years. Except for the two faithful spies, Joshua and Caleb, God caused all the men of that generation to die without entering the Promised Land. **Here is more evidence that the promise to possess the land depends on Israel's obeying God.**

As the 40 years transpired, the Israelites came up the east side of the Dead Sea toward the Promised Land. God told them, "This day I will begin to put the dread and fear of you upon the peoples everywhere" (Deut 2.25). The inhabitants of the non-Canaanite lands of Gilead and Bashan (western Jordan) would not let them pass. So the Israelites defeated them and took their land. Upon their request, Moses gave these lands to the tribes of Reuben, Gad and the half tribe of Manasseh. (Deut 3.12-17). These lands will be included in the future Promised Land.

Finally, after 40 years, the Israelites arrived in the plains of Moab, near the southern extremity of the Jordan River, opposite Jericho. The time had come for them to cross the Jordan and dispossess the Canaanites. But earlier, Moses had committed a seemingly slight disobedience. For striking a rock in unbelief, God prevented Him from bringing the Israelites into Canaan (Num 20.8-12). **Again, God requires obedience to inherit the land.**

"Drive Them Out" or "Destroy"

Just before Moses died, God gave explicit instructions and warnings about taking the land of the Canaanites:

> If you do not drive out the inhabitants of the land from before you, then it shall come about that those whom you let remain of them will become as pricks in your eyes and as thorns in your sides, and they shall trouble you in the land in which you live. And it shall come about that as I plan to do to them, so I will do to you (Num 33.55-56).

The Israelites were to drive out or exterminate all the Canaanites because of their gross wickedness. Compared to other surrounding peoples (e.g., Deut 20.10-18), the Canaanites were the worst of sinners.

When God had promised Abraham this land, He had explained that "the iniquity of the Amorite [a prominent Canaanite nation] is not yet complete" (Gen 15.16). Not until their sins "reached up to heaven," over 400 years later, would God send Abraham's descendants to conquer the Canaanite nations and take possession of their land. Both archaeology and Scripture reveal that, by then, the Canaanites practiced idolatry, witchcraft, and every kind of sexual perversion, including homosexuality, incest, bestiality and cultic prostitution (Lev 18.21-27; 20.2-23; Deut 18.9-14). Moses said of them, "For every abominable act which the LORD hates they have done for their gods; for they even burn their sons and daughters in the fire to their gods" (Deut 12.31).

Moses warned the Israelites not to intermarry or make any covenants with the surrounding nations. They were to drive out or destroy all the Canaanites and destroy their idols and places of worship (e.g., Deut 7.1-8; 9.4).

Because of the vile wickedness and impenitence of the Canaanites, God was going to harden their hearts just as He had done to Pharoah.

They would resist the Israelites rather than flee from them (Josh 11.19-20). Whichever Canaanite cities resisted were to be "under the ban" for Yahweh. This meant that Israel was to annihilate all of the inhabitants of that city and not take any booty. The spoils were to be "devoted to God," i.e., utterly destroyed.

Many people are offended that the Israelites killed many thousands of Canaanites, including women and children. If so, they must also be offended at God's other judgments. Except for one family in each case, He drowned the entire earth's population with a flood and later burned up everyone in Sodom and Gomorah. The only difference now with the Canaanites was that God would destroy them by means of His Chosen People. God's design was that the Israelites take their place in the land as "a holy people" and "His own possession" (Deut 7.6).

But how could the Israelites be sure that God told them to destroy the Canaanites? There could be no doubt. Back in Egypt and in the wilderness, God had performed many signs and miracles which authenticated His word through Moses. Now, God confirmed His word through Joshua to destroy the Canaanites by stopping the waters of the Jordan and tumbling the walls of Jericho.

Today, there are Israelis who compare the Palestinians to the Canaanites, claiming that they, too, should be driven out of Israel. It is absurd to compare the Palestinians to the wicked Canaanites. Many unbiased observers today would argue that the Palestinians are no worse sinners than Israeli Jews. In fact, many Palestinians are professing believers in the God of Israel and in Jesus of Nazareth as His Messiah. Even Palestinian Muslims accept much of the Hebrew Bible as divinely inspired. Moreover, God has not raised up prophets to tell the Israelis to drive out the Palestinians, confirming such a message with genuine miracles as of old.

What Is the Promised Land?

Before Israel entered the land of Canaan, God designated the boundaries of the land that each tribe would inherit. Some of the place names and geography remain uncertain. Even the borders of the territories to be inherited by each of the twelve tribes cannot be accurately fixed.

The Hebrew Bible provides varying descriptions of the Promised Land. **Greater Israel** is the name often applied to the entire Promised Land described to Abraham. It extends "from the river of Egypt as far as ... the river Euphrates" (Gen 15.18; cf. Ex 23.31; Josh 1.4). **Canaan** identified the major portion of Greater Israel. "All the land of Canaan (Gen 17.8; cf. Ex 6.4) . . . extended from Sidon . . . as far as Gaza" (Gen 10.19). **The Tribal Inheritance** included Canaan plus land east of the Jordan River where the tribes of Reuben, Gad and the half tribe of Manasseh had settled (Num 34.1-15; Josh 13.8–19.48).

Jews have never decisively designated the borders of *Eretz Yisrael* (Hebrew for "the land of Israel"). Throughout their scriptures and ancient rabbinic literature, Eretz Israel "was never defined with geographical precision."[5] This condition remains today. When an Israeli leader asked U.S. President Johnson to recognize Israel's acquisition of the occupied territories, he retorted, "You are asking me to recognize your borders? You have never defined the borders of Israel."[6] Indeed, "the definition of what constituted the confines of Eretz Israel is one of the thorniest problems in Jewish literature."[7]

Jewish sources generally give three different designations of boundaries for Eretz Israel.[8] **Greater Israel**, again, refers to the larger, "ideal" territory promised to Abraham in Gen 15. **The First Commonwealth** identifies Israel's possession of land between the time of the conquest and the Babylonian exile. Its widest extent was during Solomon's kingdom. **The Second Commonwealth** describes the Jews' possession of a smaller land following the exile (537 B.C.), essentially a reduced Judah. Centuries later, however, during the Hasmonean era, it was much enlarged. Jews disagree on which territory can legitimately be claimed as that of the Second Commonwealth. This will be discussed in Chapter Two. In the last two designations, the term "Eretz Israel" is defined in a historical context.

Apparently, Israel's tribal inheritance is to be distinguished from Greater Israel. The northern border of the inheritance is usually given as a line extending from the vicinity of Sidon eastward toward Damascus. Yet according to Gen 15, the northern border of Greater Israel extends about 125 miles farther, to the Euphrates River.

There is a difference in the eastern border as well. We have just seen that the Torah included land east of the Jordan River as the Jews' ancient tribal inheritance. Several prophets confirm that Israel will indeed possess territory across the Jordan during the promised kingdom age. But Ezekiel expressly declares that the eastern border of Israel's tribal inheritance during the Messianic kingdom will be the Jordan River/Dead Sea (Eze 47.18). Yet concerning the same time, Ezekiel designates land east of the Dead Sea as "in Israel" (Eze 39.11). Will Israel's tribal inheritance during the Messianic kingdom be restricted to land west of the Jordan River/Dead Sea while land east will still be reckoned "in Israel"?

There is no problem with the western border of the Promised Land; it is always given as the Mediterranean Sea. Although Canaan extended from the vicinity of Sidon southward to the Gaza and its environs, many passages include the additional territory from Gaza to the Wadi el Arish in the Promise Land. **Therefore, all of the coastland, including Philistia and Phoenicia (present western Lebanon), were included in the Promised Land.**

During the patriarchs' sojournings, God specifically identified Philistia and included it in the Promised Land. When a famine occurred in Canaan, "Isaac went to Gerar, to Abimelech king of the Philistines" (Gen 26.1). God instructed Isaac, "Do not go down to Egypt; . . . Sojourn in this land . . . for to you and to your descendants I will give all these lands" (vv. 2-3). Later, Joshua allotted the Philistine cities and their territories, including the area extending to the Wadi el Arish, to the tribe of Judah (Josh 15.45-47). **Yet neither Judah nor the whole nation of Israel ever fully obtained Philistia.** And Phoenicia never came into Jewish hands.

Joshua Takes the Promised Land

Under Joshua's leadership, the sons of Israel obeyed Yahweh in dispossessing the Canaanites and taking much land. No king or any man was able to defeat Joshua in battle (Josh 1.5).

> So the LORD gave Israel all the land which He had sworn to give to their fathers, and they possessed it and lived in it. . . . no one of all their enemies stood before them; the LORD gave all their enemies into their hand. Not one of the good promises which the LORD had made to the house of Israel failed; all came to pass (Josh 21.43-45; cf. 11.23; 23.14).

The above passage and its parallels do not mean that Joshua took all of the Promised Land. The author of Joshua here affirms a major theme, which begins his book (Josh 1.3-5). It is Moses' earlier pronouncement, that "every place on which the sole of your foot shall tread shall be yours; . . . There shall no man be able to stand before you" (Deut 11.24-25; cf. Josh 14.9). In other words, during Joshua's lifetime God gave the Israelites all the land that they entered to possess.

The Unpossessed Land

Like Moses, just before Joshua died he exhorted the leaders of Israel to obey the Lord. His warning reveals they still did not possess all of their inheritance and that their attaining of it depended on their obedience:

> So take diligent heed to yourselves to love the LORD your God. For if you ever go back and cling to the rest of these nations, these which remain among you, and intermarry with them, so that you associate with them and they with you, know with certainty that the LORD your God will not continue to drive these nations out from before you; but they shall be a snare and a trap to you, and a whip on your sides and thorns in your eyes, until you perish from off this good land which the LORD your God has given you (Josh 23.11-13).

The unconquered territory included the southwestern portion of the Promised Land—"the land of the Philistines." The Israelites had entered Canaan from the east. They had kept largely to the hill country and away from the trade route along the coast, probably due to their lack of chariots.[9] As Joshua's career came to a close, "the LORD said to him, 'You are old and advanced in years, and very much of the land remains to be possessed. **This is the land that remains: all the regions of the Philistines . . . and all of Lebanon, . . .** I will drive them out from before the sons of Israel' " (Josh 13.1-2, 5-6; emphasis added).

Thus, when Joshua died, it was chiefly Philistia and Lebanon that remained to be taken for the tribal inheritance. And God intended to give them this land.

God had not promised to drive out all the inhabitants of the Promised Land at once. He spoke through Moses: "I will not drive them out before you in a single year, that the land may not become desolate, and the beasts of the field become too numerous for you. I will drive them out before you little by little, until you become fruitful and take possession of the land" (Ex 23.29-30; cf. Deut 7.22-23).

Philistia and Lebanon Withheld

After Joshua died, the sons of Israel grew strong and took more Promised Land. But did Israel or Judah ever take possession of the land of the Philistines? Here is a very important question relating to the present Israeli-Palestinian problem. It has thus far not received much attention. The subject first appears in the Bible in Jud 1.18-19, with mention of three of the five Philistine city-states:

> And Judah took Gaza with its territory and Ashkelon with its territory and Ekron with its territory. Now the LORD was with

Judah, and they took possession of the hill country; but they could not drive out the inhabitants of the valley [or "plain"] because they had iron chariots.

English versions reveal manuscript variance in these two verses. The above NASB translates the Hebrew Masoretic Text (MT). Most contemporary biblical scholars, however, agree with the Septuagint (LXX: Greek translation of the OT), which states that Judah did **not** take possession of these three major Philistine cities and their territories at this time.[10] Even if Judah did take possession then, Jud 3.1-3 reveals that it was very short-lived: "**Now these are the nations which the LORD left, to test Israel by them . . . the five lords of the Philistines**" and those nations in Lebanon.

The first failing of Israel was that when the tribes took additional territory, "they put the Canaanites to forced labor, but they did not drive them out completely" (Josh 17.13; cf. Jud 1.27-35). Contrary to God's command, they permitted them to live in their midst.

The angel of the LORD had guarded the Israelites during their journey to, and conquest of, the Promised Land (Ex 23.20-23; 33.2). **Now he appeared to Israel's leaders and announced: "I will not drive out [the nations] before you; but they shall become as thorns in your sides, and their gods shall be a snare to you" (Jud 2.2-3).**

As Moses had predicted, the Israelites and Canaanites intermarried. "Then the sons of Israel did evil in the sight of the LORD, and served the Baals, and they forsook the LORD, . . . and followed other gods from among the gods of the peoples who were around them, and bowed themselves down to them; thus they provoked the LORD to anger" (Jud 2.10-12).

Consequently, God gave His Chosen People into the hands of their enemies. During this period of the judges, the Israelites would repent of their sins, cry out to God and He would raise up a judge to deliver them. But when the judge died, they acted more corruptly than before (e.g., Jud 2.14-19). Thus, Yahweh swore in His anger,

> "I also will no longer drive out before them any of the nations which Joshua left when he died, in order to test Israel by them, whether they will keep the way of the LORD to walk in it as their fathers did, or not. . . ." **And they were for testing Israel, to find out if they would obey the commandments of the LORD** (Jud 2.21-22; 3.4; emphasis added).

Like the Philistines of old, today's Palestinians are testing Israel. Many Israeli leaders, such as prime ministers Menachem Begin and Yitzhak Shamir, have claimed that modern Israel is entitled to its present land plus the occupied territories because the Jews' forefathers possessed all of this in antiquity. It is surprising that this assertion has gone unchallenged. When Begin campaigned for prime minister in 1977, he opposed the Labor Party's Shimon Peres, who advocated trading part of the occupied territories for peace. Begin's Likud platform included the following statement: "The right of the Jewish people to the land of Israel is eternal and indisputable. . . . Judaea and Samaria will not be handed to any foreign administration; between the [Mediterranean] sea and Jordan [River] there will only be Israeli sovereignty." Begin has always included the entire Plain of Philistia in his designation, "land of Israel."

Ever since its beginning in 1948, modern Israel has included the major portion of the Plain of Philistia. The Gaza Strip represents a small portion of the Plain. **But ancient Israel's possession of the Plain of Philistia was so brief and partial, that this history does not warrant present Israeli claims to this land.** To this history we now turn.

Chapter 2

LAND OF THE PHILISTINES

"Have I not brought up Israel from the land of Egypt, and the Philistines from Caphtor . . . ?" (Amos 9.7)

The present Palestinian-Israeli conflict is basically a dispute over land. The Jews' primary argument for their claim to Mandate Palestine is one of historical precedent. They wish to reclaim the land their forefathers first possessed nearly 3,500 years ago, an occupancy which lasted for about 1500 years. Contrary to some Israeli and Christian claims and assumptions, the ancient Israelites never possessed the entire Plain of Philistia, and what part they did occupy was for only very brief periods. Certain passages in some English translations of the Bible seem to indicate otherwise. It is therefore necessary to examine these passages, as well as the overall history of the possession of Palestine. A related question will be addressed: Do the present Palestinians have any ethnic connection to the ancient Philistines?

"Philistine" and "Palestine"
The word "Philistine(s)" appears 283 times in the Hebrew Bible, "Philistia" occurs eight times. "Philistia" always refers to the southwestern coastal plain of what we call Palestine today. Philistia was often called "the land of the Philistines."

The term "Palestine" derives from "Philistine." Herodotus was the first known writer to apply the variant for Philistine—*Palaestina*—to the much wider region now called Palestine. Writing in the 5th century B.C., he was merely following usage by the Greek merchants and sailors who traded with the Philistines. By that time, during the Jews' exile to Babylon, both the term "land of Israel" and "land of Judah" had lost their significance.

No doubt the Philistines had expanded into the former Judean hill country, perhaps more so than Judah's other neighbors. If so, it would have become even more appropriate to apply the word *Palaestina*, as Herodotus did, beyond the historical borders of Philistia to include the former Judean hill country.

Later writers included present western Jordan, and even Lebanon, in their designation, *Palaestina*. Both Greek geographer Strabo and Roman scholar Pliny, who lived in the first century A.D., called the territory of Gaza and the Judean hill country northward through present Lebanon, *Palaestina*. Pliny included land east of the Jordan River in this designation.[1]

The Romans adopted this Greek usage. Later, land east of the Jordan River came to be called Eastern Palestine, and that west of the river was Western Palestine. Sometimes this entire area, along with Lebanon, was controlled by Syria and called Greater Syria. Not until the British Mandate in 1920 was the term "Palestine" restricted to land west of the Jordan River and south of Lebanon.

Confusion has recently emerged regarding the word Palestine, a word which the modern State of Israel refuses to use to identify any of its territory. In late 1988 the Palestine Liberation Organization (PLO) and its legislative body, the Palestine National Council (PNC), officially declared the existence of the State of Palestine—a state, however, without a land. For most people this creates confusion because the word "Palestine" is now used to refer both to a state and a geographic area, the two being unrelated. **If the word Palestine were applied according to its derivation, as in the Bible, it would identify only the Plain of Philistia**, the coastal plain south of Tel Aviv through the Gaza Strip.

Origin of the Philistines

In the past century, historians and archaeologists have devoted much attention to uncovering the origin of the Philistines and their material culture. Strangely, much remains hidden. No Philistine documents or monuments with writing have so far been found. The Philistines had their own language (cf. Neh 13.23-24), but apparently they did not commit it to written form.

The word Philistine means "migrant," signifying that the Philistines migrated to the southwestern coast of Palestine. There is uncertainty regarding both the place of their origin and the time of their migration. Most historians and archaeologists now maintain that the Philistines originated in the region of the Aegean Sea, where Greece and

Turkey are located. The predominant theory is that the Philistines, called "Sea Peoples," migrated from the mainland to the Mediterranean island of Crete. From there it is believed that they attacked Egypt by sea, were repulsed and settled for the first time in southwestern Palestine. However, some experts maintain that some, if not all, of the Philistines travelled by land from Turkey down the Mediterranean coast to settle in Palestine and later attack Egypt. Both views regard the Genesis accounts of the Philistines and their land as anachronisms. (See Appendix A: Early History of the Philistines.)

Philistines: A Geographic Designation

During their major attack on Egypt in the early 12th century B.C., the Philistines consisted of five different groups of people. In time these five groups apparently incorporated. Gleason Archer observes of the Philistines, that "biblical references show that they were a heterogeneous people including several distinct groups such as the Kaphtorim, the Keftim, the Cherethites, and the Pelethites."[2] Most scholars believe "Pelethites" was another term for Philistines.

"Cherethites," a name which may derive from Cretans, are mentioned ten times in the Hebrew Bible. In all of these passages "Cherethites" are either associated with "Pelethites" or used interchangeably with "Philistines." At first the Cherethites lived next to the Philistines, to the south. It is believed they eventually were subsumed by the Philistines.

Yohanan Aharoni claims the Philistines "enforced their rule upon the local Canaanite populace," and "their residents were absorbed by the Philistines with the passage of time."[3] Hanna Kassis alleges that excavation of Philistine cities confirms that although the Philistines conquered the Canaanites in southwestern Palestine,

> the culture of Philistia remained Canaanite and eventually subsumed that of the Philistines. The question that arises at this stage is: What does the Bible refer to when speaking of the "Philistines"? We shall argue that this reference is geographic rather than ethnic, and that the biblical term "Philistines" does not necessarily include ethnic or cultural implications.[4]

In conclusion, **many authorities support the contention that the term "Philistines" should not be reckoned as an ethnic (racial) group but only as a geographic designation. That is, they were Philistines because they lived in Philistia.**[5] (Again, see Appendix A: Early History of the Philistines.)

The Boundaries of Philistia

The early Philistines settled in the narrow Mediterranean coastal plain of southwestern Canaan. It is usually identified on Bible maps as the Plain of Philistia, Philistia or Land of the Philistines.

By the time the Israelites became established in their land, Philistia was somewhat rectangular in shape. Its width was 15 miles, extending from the Mediterranean Sea inland to the Shephelah ("lowlands"). The Shephelah was a strip of rising lowlands which separated the Philistine Plain from the Judean hill country to the east. Today, the Shephelah still has some towns and archaeological sites bearing Philistine names. These attest that the Philistines sometimes occupied valleys penetrating into the Shephelah.

During Israel's early history, Philistine territory reached farther northward to include Joppa. At that time its northern border was the Nahal Yarkon, just north of present Tel Aviv.[6] Throughout most of Israel's history, however, Philistia's northern border was farther south, at the Nahal Sorek, a seasonal stream which empties into the Mediter-

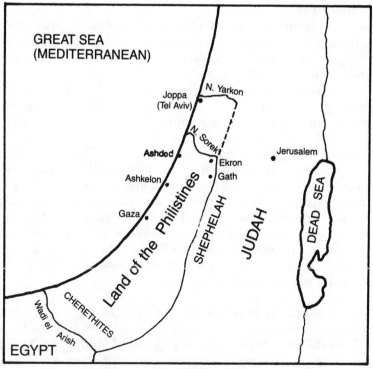

MAP 2: LAND OF THE PHILISTINES (PHILISTIA)

ranean Sea. The mouth of the Sorek is located nine miles south of the center of present Tel Aviv.

From the Nahal Sorek, Philistia stretched at least 50 miles southward to include the present Gaza Strip. Philistia's occupation often extended an extra 25 miles southward to the Wadi el Arish, the seasonal stream which represented Egypt's ancient northeastern border. Respected Israeli scholar Mordechai Gichon alleges, "From a geographical-historical point of view, the [Gaza] strip extends from El-Arish" northward.[7]

In addition, due to the Judean hills receding in the south, southern Philistia bulged eastward and farther inland, deeper into the Negev and the Sinai Peninsula.

During the early history of Israel, Philistia was known mostly for its pentapolis: the five well-administered city-states of Gaza, Ashkelon, Ashdod, Gath and Ekron. Gaza, Ashkelon and Ashdod were former Canaanite cities of early antiquity. Prior to the 12th century B.C., they were sometimes controlled by the Egyptians. The inland cities of Gath and Ekron were founded later, apparently by the Philistines.[8]

God-Given Land

As seen in Chapter 1, "When the Most High gave to the nations their inheritance, when He separated the sons of men, he fixed the bounds of the peoples" (Deut 32.8 NIV). In other words, it was God's plan for nations to have their own land.

In later times God gave other nations specific lands. For example, the Almighty destroyed the previous inhabitants of present western Jordan and gave these lands to relatives of Abraham—the Edomites, Moabites and Ammonites (Deut 2.9-22).

How did the Philistines get the southern coastal plain? It is written that "as for the Avvim, who lived in villages as far as Gaza, the Caphtorim who came from Caphtor, destroyed them and lived in their place" (Deut 2.23). The Philistines are called Caphtorim because they came from Caphtor, which many believe was Crete. Note the following comparison God made, "Have I not brought up Israel from the land of Egypt, and the Philistines from Caphtor and the Syrians from Kir?" (Amos 9.7). As He did with the Israelites and others, God gave the Philistines their land.

Rivalry Between the Israelites and the Philistines

Chapter 1 revealed that God withheld the lands of Philistia and Lebanon from the Israelites because they disobeyed Him in not driving out all of the Canaanites. He did this despite the fact that Joshua had previously allotted the entire Philistine territory to the tribe of

Judah (Josh 15.45-47). Yahweh left the Philistines and Lebanese "for testing Israel, to find out if they would obey the commandments of the LORD" (Jud 3.4).

From Joshua's time until the monarchy, Israel waged a long and arduous struggle with its chief enemy—the Philistines. Some of the most vivid and memorable stories in the Old Testament (OT) concern the rivalry between the Israelites and the Philistines. Take the story of Samson, who in his great strength repeatedly overcame the Philistines. They finally deceived him through the temptress, Delilah. Then there was David, who slew Goliath, the giant of the Philistines.

During the period of the judges (c. 1200-1020 B.C.), Israel existed as a loosely-knit tribal confederacy without a king. The Philistines frequently spread into Judean territory, "ruling over Israel" (e.g., Jud 14.4; cf. 10.7; 13.1; 1 Sam 4.10). Throughout this period of rivalry, the Philistines dominated the Israelites more than vice versa. For a while they even placed their own governors over Israel's southern tribes of Ephraim and Benjamin and exacted oppressive tribute. By establishing fortresses in the north, the Philistines controlled Megiddo and the Valley of Jezreel, as well as Geba of Benjamin (1 Sam 10.5; 13.3). They even extended their presence into the Jordan valley.[9] The Israelites suffered a severe psychological setback in the mid-11th century B.C., when the Philistines destroyed Shiloh, captured the ark of the covenant and removed it to Ashdod.

Until the time of David (late 11th century B.C.), the Philistines were the only opponents of Israel to remain unconquered.[10] The Israelites had not ventured into the Philistine plain. "South of Jaffa [later, Tel Aviv] the entire Coastal Plain remained the domain of the Philistines, who threatened to encroach on the territory held by the Israelites."[11]

It is frequently observed that this rivalry with the Philistines welded the tribes of Israel into a cohesive fighting force and nation. Today's Arab Palestinians have served the same function for modern Israel. This is one of many similarities between the warlike ancient Philistines and the Palestinians.

King Saul

Saul became Israel's first king in the late 11th century B.C. He spent most of his life fighting the Philistines, and that is how he died. "War against the Philistines was severe all the days of Saul" (1 Sam 14.52). He delivered Israel from its enemies, so that the Philistines retreated "to their own place" (1 Sam 14.46-48). Yet **King Saul never possessed any Philistine soil**.

King David

After David (reign: 1,011-971 B.C.) captured the strong fortress of Zion and Jebus (former Jerusalem), his fame as a warrior spread quickly among the Philistines. Twice they "spread themselves out in the valley of Rephaim" (2 Sam 5.17), near western Jerusalem, to challenge David and his forces. Both times he struck them down, the second time driving them all the way to Gezer, just outside the northeastern border of Philistia (v. 25).

Thus, King David defeated the Philistines, but not in their own territory. The effect of these victories was that David discouraged the Philistines from mounting further assaults upon Israel.[12]

Did David ever possess Philistine territory? Some Bible translations render 2 Sam 8.1 as if he did. For example, the NASB gives the following summary of the two battles: "Now after this it came about that David defeated the Philistines and subdued them; and David took control of the chief city from the hand of the Philistines." The Hebrew words, here translated "the chief city," are *metheg ammah*. The KJV, RSV and NIV do not translate, but render them as a placename, which is unknown. A footnote in the NASB provides the literal translation, "the bridle of the mother city." Most likely, *metheg ammah* should be translated "authority of the mother city,"[13] indicating that David exercised a general leadership there.[14]

The parallel passage in 1 Chron 18.1 reads, "David defeated the Philistines and subdued them and took Gath and its towns from the hand of the Philistines." The chronicler is surely not contradicting 2 Sam 8.1, written earlier, but clarifying its ambiguity. Both passages probably indicate the same accomplishment: David removed Gath and its territory from Philistine domination. Gath then served as a buffer zone between Israel and the Philistines.[15]

Scripture never indicates that David made the Philistines his servants or placed garrisons in their land. He only received silver and gold as tribute money when he initially subdued them (2 Sam 8.11-12; 1 Chron 18.11). In contrast, he made the Moabites and Edomites of present Jordan, as well as the Arameans of Damascus, his servants, putting garrisons in their land and regularly exacting tribute from them (2 Sam 8.2, 6, 14; 1 Chron 18.2, 6, 13).

The writer of 2 Sam 8.1 probably means that David pushed the Philistines back to their former territory of the coastal plain.[16] It is most unlikely that David would have attacked one of the three major Philistine cities of Gaza, Ashkelon and Ashdod without its mention in the Bible. Noted historian John Bright claims, "There is no evidence that [David] reduced the coastal cities of Ashdod, Ashkelon, and

Gaza."[17] Furthermore, some scholars believe that David avoided incursions into the Philistine plain because a newly-strengthened Egypt had by then regained control over the plain.[18]

In conclusion, although he extended his dominion all the way to the Euphrates River and beyond the Jordan, **King David did not rule over Philistia**, much less populate it with Israelites.[19]

King Solomon

But what about Solomon's reign? Surely he ruled the Philistines during Israel's Golden Age!

Under King Solomon (reign: 971-931 B.C.) Israel enjoyed unprecedented peace, prosperity and dominion never again achieved. "Solomon ruled over all the kingdoms from the River [Euphrates] to the land of the Philistines and to the border of Egypt; they brought tribute and served Solomon all the days of his life" (1 Kgs 4.21).

In 1 Kgs 4.21 the first preposition, "to," appears in italics in the NASB. This indicates it is not in the Hebrew text (MT), raising the question of whether Solomon ruled up **to** Philistia or **over** it. The parallel passage in 2 Chron 9.26 includes the preposition in the MT. The LXX includes it in both passages. The view that Solomon ruled **to** and not **over** the land of the Philistines is held by many biblical scholars. Solomon's dominion extended over vassal states all the way to the Euphrates River. Yet the Israelites continued to dwell within previous bounds. Only four verses later we read, "So Judah and Israel lived in safety, every man under his vine and his fig tree, from Dan even to Beersheba, all the days of Solomon" (v. 25; cf. Jud 20.1; 1 Sam 3.20). Dan was then a small region located just inside present southeastern Lebanon. Beersheba was located just east of Philistia. This expression says nothing about Israel's borders east and west. Israel was still bounded on the southwest by Philistia.

The Bible repeatedly mentions war between the Philistines and the Israelites in the days of Saul and David, but not Solomon. "Solomon conducted no serious military operations [anywhere,] that we know of."[20] Surprisingly, the Bible does not even mention the Philistines during Solomon's reign, which indicates peace with them, probably due to Egypt's dominion over the Philistines at this time. Indeed, Pharoah Siamun and his forces had to pass through all of Philistia to conquer the Canaanite city of Gezer, which Solomon obtained through a marriage alliance (1 Kgs 3.1; 9.16). This indicates both that Solomon did not control Philistia and that Egypt had reasserted dominance over it.[21]

Unlike his father, Solomon did not even control Gath. Two of Solomon's servants sought refuge from their master and "ran away to Achish . . . king of Gath," (1 Kgs 2.39).

The Scriptures do not include the Philistines among those nations which "brought tribute and served Solomon all the days of his life" (1 Kgs 4.21). Neither are they included among the list of peoples whom Solomon used as forced laborers for his ambitious building programs (1 Kgs 9:15, 17-21). The only possible conclusion from both secular and biblical evidence is that **Solomon never ruled over the Philistines**.

King Uzziah of Judah

As far as is known, Judah's King Uzziah was the first king of either Israel or Judah to possess any Philistine territory and place any Israelites in it. About 760 B.C. his powerful army invaded Philistia and broke down the thick casement walls of the Philistine cities of Gath, Jabneh and Ashdod. Jabneh and Gath were located near what was then Philistia's border. Uzziah afterwards "built cities in the area of Ashdod and among the Philistines" (2 Chron 26.6). This indicates that he did not capture Ashdod, only some of its territory. Israeli scholars Aharoni and Avi-Yonah remark, "It is difficult to assume that Uzziah ruled over Ashdod proper after this campaign, though he did reduce its borders, securing his conquests by building cities on lands formerly belonging to Ashdod."[22]

Thus, **during King Uzziah's reign Judah occupied a small portion of the land of the Philistines, but for only a few years.**

King Ahaz of Judah

At other times the Philistines sometimes penetrated and temporarily possessed Israelite territory. This happened under King Ahaz of Judah (reign: 743-727 B.C.). Because he "did not do right in the sight of the LORD" (2 Chron 28.1), "the Philistines also had invaded the cities of the [Shephelah] and of the Negev of Judah" and some in Judah itself (v. 18).

Assyrian King Tiglath-pileser III

In the second half of the 8th century B.C., the Assyrians waged several military campaigns in Palestine. In 734 B.C. Assyrian King Tiglath-pileser III came down the coastal plain, took all of Philistia and "afflicted" King Ahaz of Judah (2 Chron 28.20). The Philistine population, however, was left virtually intact. Philistia thus became a buffer between now powerful Assyria and Egypt.

King Hezekiah of Judah

The son of idolatrous King Ahaz of Judah was good King Hezekiah (reign: 715-687 B.C). Hezekiah "defeated the Philistines as far as Gaza and its territory, from watchtower to fortified city" (2 Kgs 18.8). Watchtowers were outlying territorial posts. "From watchtower to fortified city" may be an idiom meaning "everywhere." Or it could refer strictly to outlying Philistine towns and villages, excluding the fortified (walled) cities of the Philistine pentapolis.

Assyrian King Sargon II (reign: 721-705 B.C.) invaded and controlled Philistia in the late 8th century B.C. Thus, it is generally thought that Hezekiah did not vanquish the Philistines until after the Assyrian king's death in 705 B.C.[23] If so, **Hezekiah may have dominated Philistia for about three years,** until the Assyrians invaded the region again.

Assyrian King Sennacherib

Sargon II's son, Sennacherib, ascended the Assyrian throne. In 701 B.C. he waged a major military campaign in Palestine. For the first time, a foreign king "came against all the fortified cities of Judah and seized them" (2 Kgs 18.13), 46 in all according to Sennacherib's annals. After that, Philistine cities fell to him like dominos. Sennacherib threatened Israel's good King Hezekiah in Jerusalem because he had rebelled against Assyria by refusing to pay tribute and earlier attacking the Philistines (2 Kgs 18.7). Philistia had been controlled by the Assyrians. Sennacherib records concerning Hezekiah, "His towns which I had plundered, I took away from his country and gave them (over) to Mitinti, king of Ashdod, Padi, king of Ekron, and Sillibel, king of Gaza. Thus I reduced his country, but I still increased the tribute."[24] Thus, Philistine kings temporarily ruled over part of Judah.

The Assyrians never annexed Philistia. It remained a buffer between Assyria and Egypt. **In the 7th century B.C. control of Philistia went back and forth between Assyria and Egypt; Israel was no longer a contender.**

Post-Assyrian Philistine Existence

Some writers have incorrectly claimed that the Philistines ceased to exist after Sennacherib supposedly deported them *en masse* to Assyria. Actually, Sennacherib seems to have left the Philistine population quite undisturbed.

Whenever military conquerors made deportations of the local population, their purpose was to remove possible elements of rebellion.

Deportations therefore usually consisted of royalty and officials who might instigate an uprising. The large majority of the population was customarily left to cultivate the land and pay tribute. Even when a besieged city was conquered and its citizens deported, rural residents usually repopulated the city. Very rarely were wholesale deportations of cities or regions carried out. When they were, it nearly always resulted from an extraordinary rebellion or firm resistance. Sennacherib did not encounter such a situation with the Philistines.

There is abundant evidence that Philistines still inhabited Philistia centuries after the Assyrian conquests. In the mid-5th century B.C., Nehemiah returned from the Babylonian exile to rebuild the wall of Jerusalem. He discovered that many Jews who had escaped the exile "had married women of Ashdod, Ammon, and Moab; and half of their children spoke the language of Ashdod, and they could not speak the language of Judah" (Neh 13.24 RSV). The Philistine tongue was still spoken in Ashdod and beyond. Ashdod had become the chief Philistine city; its name probably identified all of Philistia.[25] The "women of Ashdod" were "Philistine women in general."[26]

As mentioned previously, during this period the Greeks called the entire region between the Mediterranean and the Jordan Depression, "Palaestina." This indicates that the Philistines not only still existed in their land following the Assyrian conquests, but had spread eastward and populated part of former Judah and perhaps Samaria.

Babylonian King Nebuchadnezzer
In the late 7th century B.C., Pharoah Necho of Egypt controlled and exacted tribute from Philistia, Judah, Samaria and Lebanon. But when Nebuchadnezzer (reign: 605-562 B.C.) became king of Babylon he attacked and defeated Necho's forces at Carchemish on the Euphrates River, driving all the way to the border of Egypt. Thereafter, the Babylonians controlled all of Palestine until Cyrus.

Persian and Hellenistic Periods
Babylon fell to the Persian King Cyrus in 539 B.C. For the next century, Persia dominated both Philistia and Judah.

The ascendancy of Greece brought another change of power. In 332 B.C. Alexander the Great besieged Gaza for two months and destroyed it. Though he purportedly killed 10,000 of its male citizens, this did not spell the demise of the Philistines in Gaza. "The city was soon repopulated with people from the neighboring areas."[27]

Following the death of Alexander, both Philistia and Judah came under the control of the Ptolemies of Egypt from 323 to 198 B.C.

The Seleucids of Syria controlled this territory throughout most of the period from 198 to 63 B.C.

Philistia During the Maccabean Era

Philistia did lose much of its significance as a nation after the Assyrian and Babylonian conquests. Nevertheless, although the Philistines absorbed Greeks, Nabatean Arabs and Egyptians over the centuries, they continued as a recognizable people. For example, writing in the 2nd century B.C., the author of 1 Maccabees refers to "the country of the Philistines," "Philistine territory," or the like, five times (1 Macc 3.25, 42; 4.22; 5.66, 68). He further relates that Philistia was **not** a possession of Judea (Greco-Roman name for Judah). Philistine temples, like those of Dagon at Ashdod and Marna at Gaza (1 Macc 10.83-84; 11.4), still existed at that time, substantiating the survival of the Philistines' religion. All of this reveals that in the mid-2nd century B.C., the southwestern coast of Palestine was still regarded as the land of the Philistines.

First century historian Josephus mentions Philistine cities several times. Although he does not call the inhabitants of these cities Philistines, he consistently refers to them as "people of Ashdod," "people of Gaza," etc., indicating non-Jews. Both Josephus and the authors of 1 and 2 Maccabees provide abundant evidence that Philistine cities were populated by non-Jews, and that the Jews did not possess them until the turn of the century.[28]

The Maccabees and the Hasmonean Kingdom

For a moment, let us leap forward in time to the 20th century. Following WWI the Jews presented the Allies with a proposal to establish their National Home in Palestine. They claimed the right to all of Palestine, southern Lebanon and western Jordan, citing for major support the occupation of this land by the Hasmonean Kingdom. Expansionists like Likud politician Ariel Sharon still claim this additional territory. Due to such claims, it is necessary to consider in some detail the Jews' land acquisitions during the Hasmonean era.

In 167 B.C. Syrian King Antiochus Epiphanes sought to rid Judea of its religion and culture and to Hellenize all of Palestine. He abolished the Jews' sacrificial system of worship, stopped their observance of the Sabbath and burned many copies of their scriptures. To the pious Jews, Antiochus' most heinous act was a two-fold desecration: he had an altar of Zeus placed upon the sacrificial altar in the temple at Jerusalem, and there he offered swine's flesh as an affront to the Jews.

Three years later, Mattathias, an elderly Jewish priest, courageously lead a revolt against Antiochus and removed the Syrian yoke. His five sons, "the Maccabees," reestablished Israel under what came to be called the Hasmonean Kingdom. It lasted for a century.

Both Judas and Jonathan Maccabaeus expanded Judah. Although they made military incursions into the Philistine plain, destroying a few villages and temples and once even burning Ashdod, they always withdrew from the plain. Then in 147 B.C. Macedonian King Alexander Balas awarded Jonathan "proprietary rights over Ekron with all its lands" (1 Macc 10.89). This control of Ekron, the northeasternmost region of Philistia, was the beginning of Maccabean expansion into Philistia. Simon Maccabaeus and John Hyrcanus led separate expeditions farther into the plain but withdrew (1 Macc 12.33; 16.10).

Both Michael Avi-Yonah and Yohanan Aharoni are distinguished Israeli Jewish scholars of archaeology and history of biblical lands. In all of their numerous and thorough maps in *The Macmillan Bible Atlas*, Philistia appears as a separate entity from Israel throughout Israel's entire ancient history until the reign of Alexander Jannaeus (reign: 102-76 B.C.).[29]

Alexander Jannaeus

Hasmonean King Alexander Jannaeus extended the kingdom of Israel to its farthest extent since the days of Solomon. He achieved considerable military success, mostly with foreign mercenaries.[30] In what is today's Gaza Strip, he besieged and took Raphia, the Greek-built city of Anthedon and Gaza. Gaza, the last to fall, was reduced to ruins in 96 B.C. following a one-year siege. Many inhabitants committed suicide rather than submit to their ruthless conqueror. Alexander Jannaeus "treated the [surviving] inhabitants of Gaza cruelly. He sold them into slavery and repopulated the city with people from the surrounding countryside."[31] Thus, Gaza was repopulated with Philistines from its own environs.

By this time Ashkelon had a reputation for conciliation and for making wise alliances. In the following centuries, Ashkelon was able to remain independent from both the Hasmonean Kingdom and the Roman Empire.

Except for an enlarged district of Ashkelon, which was allied with Egypt, Alexander Jannaeus subjugated the rest of the Plain of Philistia for the next twenty years. He also controlled the main caravan route from Gaza south to Rhinocoloura (modern El-Arish), on Egypt's northern border. **In all, Alexander Jannaeus subjugated southern Lebanon, southern Syria, western Jordan (which he later lost) and**

all of Palestine west of the Jordan River, including Philistia except for the enlarged Ashkelon district.

The Jewish people, however, did not profit from the Hasmonean territorial expansion.[32] Even more than with Antiochus Epiphanes, the Jews suffered drastically under the rule of their own king, Alexander Jannaeus.[33] Taking a Greek name signified his affinity for Hellenization, which he attempted to force on the populace. He was "autocratic, self-seeking and widely despised" among his own people.[34]

Alexander committed numerous atrocities against his own people. For example, while participating in the Feast of Tabernacles at the temple in 90 B.C, Alexander Jannaeus broke an important religious custom involving sacrifices. The pious *Hasidim*, forerunners of the Pharisees, expressed their displeasure by pelting the king with citrus from branches carried during the celebration. He promptly had 6,000 of them executed. This act started a civil war which lasted from 90 to 85 B.C. and resulted in 50,000 more killed.

Even more than his predecessors, Alexander Jannaeus continued the practice of forcing circumcision and other Jewish religious rites on Gentiles in his kingdom. Those who resisted, such as all the citizens of Pella, Alexander utterly destroyed.[35]

Power seemed to have corrupted the formerly popular Hasmonean leadership. The same was true of the priestly aristocracy called "Sadducees." They controlled the temple at Jerusalem and therefore Israel's religious life. The Sadducees supported King-Priest Alexander Jannaeus. On the other hand, the *Hasidim* gained in popularity. The friction between these two parties long outlasted the Hasmonean Kingdom, up to the destruction of Jerusalem by the Romans in A.D. 70.

In 88 B.C. the *Hasidim* got help from the Syrians in overthrowing Alexander and expelling him to the mountains. But when the Syrians returned home, Alexander regained control of his kingdom. Seeking revenge, he had 800 Jews, mostly *Hasidim*, crucified together. He celebrated the event by conducting a banquet, carousing with his friends and concubines on the terrace of his palace in full view of the crucified. Before the victims expired, the king had their wives and children slain in their presence, an unheard-of cruelty.[36]

Surely today's pious Jews would agree with the early Pharisees, who refused to recognize the cruel and ungodly Alexander Jannaeus as an instrument in the hand of God for securing possession of Eretz Israel. Interestingly, W.D. Davies observes that early in the Maccabean revolt, "the absence of an appeal to the The Land is striking . . . Later on, territorial considerations did enter into the Maccabean movement,

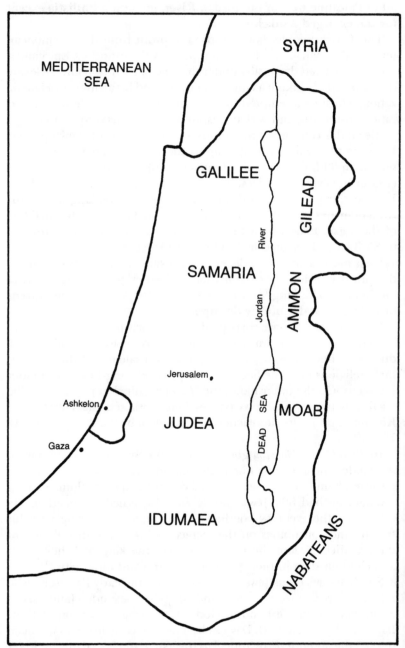

MAP 3: ALEXANDER JANNAEUS' HASMONEAN KINGDOM

but these were motivated more by political ambition than by religious concern with the promise."[37]

More than any other Jewish kingdom, Alexander Jannaeus' dominion is compared to that of David and Solomon. He possessed more of the Plain of Philistia than any of Israel's previous kings. His possession, from 96 to 76 B.C., probably exceeded all of Israel's previous combined years of occupation of any Philistine territory. **Throughout Israel's more than 1,100 year presence in Palestine, does Alexander Jannaeus' short twenty-year possession of most of the Plain of Philistia constitute sufficient evidence for the Jews' present claim to that land? Hardly!**

Afflicted with alcoholism, Alexander Jannaeus contracted malarial fever and died in 76 B.C. His widow, Salome Alexandra (reign: 76-67 B.C.), succeeded him. Queen Salome feared for her life and that of her children due to her husband's many enemies within his kingdom. In contrast to her husband, she ruled with a benevolent hand. Since her brother was a leading Pharisee, she extended kindness to them, granting Pharisees power in her realm. Nevertheless, civil war continued between the Pharisees and Sadducees. After her death, Salome's two sons fought over the kingdom its last four years.

Roman Empire

The Hasmonean Kingdom ended when the Roman general Pompey took Jerusalem and all of Palestine in 63 B.C. Pompey completely freed the coastal cities from Judean domination. He restored them, along with Jamnia, Ashdod and Gaza in the Philistine Plain, "to their own inhabitants."[38] They had been largely populated by non-Judeans,[39] which included a significant number of Greeks.

The Romans soon rebuilt many demolished cities in both Judea and the Plain of Philistia. These included the Philistine cities of Gaza, Anthedon, Raphia and Ashdod. Mark Antony completed the construction in 57 B.C., making them "securely inhabited" by the local population.[40] Julius Caesar later returned control of Joppa to the Jews.

Except for the district of Ashkelon, Pompey joined all of Palestine to Syria, then a Roman province. Ashkelon did not lose its independent status until it was made a Roman colony in the 4th century A.D.[41] Judea remained a Roman tributary, contained within its historical boundaries.

Rome always kept Judea and the Plain of Philistia separate. The Plain of Philistia was usually divided into three parts, with Rome awarding control of the parcels to various rulers.

Following the Hasmonean Kingdom, the Jews never possessed any of the Plain of Philistia again until the establishment of the modern State of Israel, in A.D. 1948—over 2,000 years later.

Conclusion

Three major points are to be gleaned from these first two chapters concerning the Israelites, the Philistines and their respective lands.

First, as He did with the Israelites, **God gave the Philistines their land**.

Second, **although the Promised Land includes the Plain of Philistia, God withheld it from the Israelites because of their disobedience**. Instead, He said He left the Philistines to test Israel (Jud 2.21-23; 3.3-4), a statement God has never given any indication of retracting.

Third, **throughout their entire ancient history, the Israelites possessed only a portion of the land of the Philistines and for only a very short period of time**.[42] Surely Israel's short-lived occupation of the Plain of Philistia does not justify its current claim to that land. On the other hand, throughout their long rivalry, the Philistines occupied more of the land of Judah, and for longer periods of time, than the Israelites ever occupied Philistine territory. What must be concluded from both history and the Hebrew Scriptures is this: **Modern Israel now occupies the Plain of Philistia apart from historical precedent and apart from the express will of God**.

Part II

THE
MODERN
PRESENT

Chapter 3

ZIONISM

*In the latter years you will come into the land that is restored from
the sword, whose inhabitants have been gathered from many nations to the
mountains of Israel which have been a continual waste* (Eze 38.8).

History of the Jews and the Land of Israel

The following summary highlights the history of the Jews and the
possession of their land before the establishment of the State of Israel:

2166 BC	Birth of Abraham
c.1446 or 1250	Exodus of Israel from Egypt
c.1406 or 1210	Entrance of Israel into the land of Canaan
1011 BC	David becomes King of Israel
971 BC	Solomon becomes King of Israel
931 BC	Israel split into two kingdoms
722 BC	Assyrian deportation of ten tribes of Israel
606 BC	First Babylonian invasion of Judah and deportation of Jews to Babylon
587 BC	Final Babylonian destruction of Judah
539 BC	Persian rule begins
537 BC	First return of Jews from Babylonian exile
330 BC	Greek rule begins under Alexander the Great
323-200 BC	Ptolemy (Egyptian) Dynasty predominant
200 BC	Seleucid (Syrian) Dynasty begins
167 BC	Antiochus Epiphanes IV forbids Jewish religion
164-63 BC	Maccabean/Hasmonean Kingdom Begins

63 BC	Pompey overtakes Judea and Jerusalem
63 BC-AD 395	Roman Empire rule
AD 63	First Jewish Revolt
AD 66-70	Roman siege and destruction of Jerusalem
AD 132-135	Second Jewish (Bar-Kokhba) Revolt
AD 395	Roman Empire divided
AD 395-616	Byzantine Empire rule
AD 616-630	Persian rule
AD 630-637	Byzantine rule
AD 619	Moslem Dome of the Rock built on temple grounds
AD 638-1085	Muslim Arabs rule
AD 1085-1099	Muslim Turks rule
AD 1099-1187	European Crusaders rule
AD 1187-1260	Muslim Ayyubids (Saladin in Egypt) rule
AD 1260-1517	Mamelukes (Turks in Egypt) rule
AD 1517-1917	Ottoman (Turkish) Empire rule
AD 1917-1948	British rule
AD 1922-1948	British Mandate
AD 1947	UN Partition Plan

Jewish Exile
It happened just as Moses said it would. Because of Israel's sin, God removed the nation from the good land He had given them.

In 722 B.C. Assyrian king Sargon II took the northern ten tribes (Israel) away to Assyria. Sargon boasted in his annals that he took 27,290 Jewish prisoners, fewer than commonly supposed. These so-called "ten lost tribes" were apparently assimilated into the Assyrian population.

Near the turn of the 7th century B.C., God sent Babylonian king Nebuchadnezzar to complete the Jewish exile from the rest of the Land. In 606 B.C. and again, twenty years later, Nebuchadnezzar attacked the two southern tribes (Judah). Following the 586 B.C. siege and massacre, the remaining influential citizens were deported to Babylonia to prevent any possible insurrection.

Neither the Assyrian nor the Babylonian exiles were total. Some Jews remained under foreign domination in both Israel and Judah. In the north, intermarriage between Gentiles and Jews produced the Samaritans, a mixed race later despised by the Judeans (Jews) in the south.

Just as Jeremiah had prophesied, 70 years later some of the Jews returned from Babylon to their homeland (Jer 25.11; cf. Dan 9.2).

For the next two centuries the restored Jewish community could do little more than settle and control Jerusalem and its environs.

Jewish Diaspora

In the late 4th century B.C., Alexander the Great (356-323 B.C.) befriended the Jews. Upon his premature death, his kingdom was divided. Cruel Ptolemy I of Egypt then subjugated the people of the region. Some Jews fled northward to Antioch, Syria. Ptolemy I took 120,000 Jews to Egypt as slaves. Many of these were resettled in Egypt's thriving metropolis of Alexandria. Jews regard this exodus as the beginning of their *Diaspora*, a Greek term meaning "Dispersion." In time the Diaspora extended over a wider area.

Egypt's next king, Ptolemy II Philadelphus, was the king under whose direction the Hebrew Scriptures were translated into Greek (Septuagint). He freed the Jewish slaves, most of whom chose to remain in Egypt.

The Seleucids of Syria gained control of Palestine from Egypt in the early 3rd century B.C. Their rulers included the infamous Antiochus Epiphanes, who desecrated the temple at Jerusalem in 167 B.C. The Maccabean Revolt returned power to the Jews for a century, until 63 B.C., when the Romans conquered them.

The Jewish Diaspora intensified with the Jews' First Revolt (A.D. 66-70). The Romans crushed it in A.D. 70 by destroying Jerusalem and its temple. When the Romans put down the Second (Bar-Kokhba) Revolt in A.D. 135, the Diaspora was almost complete. Moses had predicted this worldwide dispersion, "The LORD will scatter you among the peoples, and you shall be left few in numbers among the nations, where the LORD shall drive you" (Deut 4.27).

The Romans thereafter sought to expunge all traces of Jewish history from the land of Israel. All Jews were expelled from Judea and replaced by Syrians and Arabic-speaking colonists.[1] The whole land was renamed *Syria Palaestina*, shortened in the 5th century to *Palaestina*. Emperor Hadrian further humiliated the Jews by renaming Jerusalem *Aelia Capitolina*. Aelia was the name of the Emperor's mother; *Capitolina* was Rome's chief pagan temple, dedicated to the worship of their god Jupiter.

For the next three centuries it was unlawful for Jews to enter *Aelia Capitolina* on penalty of death. Emperor Constantine (reign: A.D. 306-337) continued this practice while making Jerusalem a Christian city. Anti-Christian Emperor Julian (reign: A.D. 361-363) tried to restore the city to the Jews and rebuild their temple, but he soon died. **Only a small minority of Jews lived periodically in Palestine after A.D. 363, until the late 19th century.**

Remembering Zion

Throughout the many centuries of their Diaspora, the Jews never forgot their forefathers' homeland. Living in Gentile lands and often oppressed, Jews' hearts often yearned to return to the Promised Land. The words of the homesick psalmist, mourning for Jerusalem while exiled in Babylon, applied to the Jews of the later Diaspora as well:

> By the rivers of Babylon,
> There we sat down and wept,
> When we remembered Zion.
> Upon the willows in the midst of it
> We hung our harps.
> For there our captors demanded of us songs,
> And our tormentors mirth, saying,
> "Sing us one of the songs of Zion."
>
> How can we sing the LORD's song
> In a foreign land?
> If I forget you, O Jerusalem,
> May my right hand forget her skill.
> May my tongue cleave to the roof of my mouth,
> If I do not remember you,
> If I do not exalt Jerusalem
> Above my chief joy (Ps 137.1-6).

Throughout their Diaspora the Jews preserved their religious heritage. It became a fixed tradition for Jews to say to one another at the close of each of their three primary feasts, "Next year in Jerusalem." This expressed the hope that they would someday return to live in their forefathers' homeland and celebrate the feasts of Yahweh at Zion.

Zion

The word "Zion" occurs 154 times in the Hebrew Bible. Its etymology is uncertain; its primary meaning may be "to protect." Originally, Zion identified the fortress on the hill southeast of Jebus, the former name of Jerusalem. King David captured this stronghold and developed it into "the city of David, which is Zion" (1 Kg 8.1; 2 Chron 5.2). Afterwards, the name Zion was applied in various ways. The word was used interchangeably for either Jerusalem or its temple. A scene often portrayed in Scripture depicts the Jews going up to Zion to worship Yahweh, the God of Israel. Zion is the seat of Yahweh.

Jewish Passivity

Zionism is the name given to the movement to restore the Jews to their former homeland. Incipient Zionism always existed in the hearts of many scattered Jewish people. It is found in early Jewish literature. The writer of 1 Maccabees states in the mid-2nd century B.C., "We have neither taken other men's land nor have we taken possession of that which belongeth to another but only of the inheritance of our fathers, howbeit it was held in the possession of our enemies wrongfully for a certain time" (1 Macc 15.33). This statement capsulizes the Jews' argument of historical precedent in the present Israeli-Palestinian conflict.

Due to the Spanish Inquisition, some European Jews began immigrating to Palestine in 1492. Most were Orthodox in faith. They believed that the Inquisition was the final persecution of Jews predicted in their scriptures, signaling the imminent coming of Messiah.[2] They regarded the Romans' expulsion of their forefathers from their homeland and their subsequent suffering in host Gentile countries as necessary prerequisites to, and hasteners of, the coming of their blessed Redeemer.

These pious, non-agrarian Jews lived in the few cities of Palestine as a distinct minority. Many were financially subsidized by distant relatives and friends. Within these cities they formed their own communities, later called "Old Yishuv." Until the late 19th century, Arabs outnumbered Jews throughout Palestine at a ratio of over 20 to 1.

The rabbis had taught that the restoration of the land of Israel would not be accomplished by the will and strength of the Jews themselves. Only after the coming of Messiah were Jews to be regathered to their homeland and the land fully restored.

Vivid evidence of this belief remains in Israel today. According to *halacha* (Jewish religious law), Jews are still not permitted to enter Jerusalem's temple mount. This rule was established in the 12th century by the distinguished Spanish rabbi, Maimonides. Many rabbis explained that only Messiah, or perhaps some great prophet, could lead the Jews into this area. Today, the reason given for this prohibition is that if Jews walked on the former area of the Holy of Holies, the location of which remains undetermined, this would be an irreverent act of the gravest sort. How strange it is to see Palestinian Arabs walk on the temple grounds to worship in their Muslim Dome of the Rock,

yet Jews are forbidden from the entire area except for the lower
western "wailing wall."

For many centuries, therefore, Jews were taught by their rabbis to
be passive, waiting in the lands of their dispersion for the coming of
Messiah to deliver them. It is alleged that passivity under persecution
pervaded the minds of many religious Jews who suffered under the
Nazi Holocaust in WWII.

Furthermore, the Jews of the Diaspora were divided on whether
to attempt to assimilate into the Gentile population or to establish
separate Jewish communities in order better to preserve their religious
and cultural heritage. Jews in Western Europe had become quite
integrated into the Gentile population. The non-assimilationists (later
Zionists) risked greater persecution for preserving their "Jewishness."
This was attested in Eastern Europe and Russia in the late 19th and
the 20th centuries, when the Jewish ghettos suffered organized attacks
called pogroms.

Modern Zionism

Two millennia of the Diaspora and passivity brought no Messiah, so
Jewish thinking began to change. **Irreligious Jews emerged who
would not wait until Messiah brought restoration of Israel, called
"the redemption of Israel." They would accomplish it themselves.**

Modern Zionism thus began as a secular movement. At first it was
opposed by Orthodox Jews. Gradually, the Orthodox became divided
between non-Zionists and anti-Zionists. This changed drastically after
the Nazi Holocaust and Israeli statehood. Today, some of the most
ardent Zionists are of the Orthodox Jewish faith.

The first Jewish agricultural colony to be established in Palestine
in recent times was in 1878, called "New Yishuv." These were not
religious communities, as were the Old Yishuv. Mass immigrations to
Palestine soon followed. These were brought on by the two worst
persecutions the Jews have suffered since the medieval Crusades: the
Russian pogroms of the late 19th century and Hitler's Holocaust in
the 20th century.

The most despicable Russian pogroms occurred in 1881. They effected a mass emigration of approximately 2.5 million Jews from
Russia. Most sailed to the U.S.; some went to Palestine. Thus, the first
wave of the modern Jewish migration to Palestine began in 1882. It
was aided by the weakening of the Ottoman Empire's hold on Palestine.

This first significant Jewish immigration to Palestine was the beginning of what Jews call "The Return." Called in Hebrew, *aliyah*, it
means "going up" due to the many references in Scripture to the

Jews' "going up" to Zion, or Jerusalem, to worship. The holy city is situated in hill country at 2500 feet in elevation. Travelers to Jerusalem literally "go up."

Jewish historians mark five stages of *aliyah*. The first occurred from 1882-1903 and consisted of about 25,000 Jews. The second transpired from 1904-1914 and totaled about 50,000 Jews. Interestingly, most, again, were Russian Jews.

In 1882 a Lithuanian Jew changed his name to Ben Yehuda, emigrated to Jerusalem and revived the Hebrew language. Today, Israeli Jews speak Hebrew as the official language, while Palestinians speak an Arabic dialect.

Also in 1982, Leo Pinsker (1821-1891) wrote a pamphlet entitled "The Self-Emancipation of the Jews." He claimed that the Jews of the Diaspora had largely been forced into finance and trade, which has indeed been their legacy and a cause of anti-Semitism. Pinsker urged Jews to return to their ancient land and reclaim their heritage as descendants of sheepherders and farmers. Ironically, following 1892, it was a French millionaire banker, Edmund de Rothschild, who remained for many years the movement's most generous contributor.

Theodor Herzl

Modern Zionism accelerated at the close of the 19th century. It was formulated by Theodor Herzl (1860-1904). Herzl was an Austro-Hungarian Jew with a background that well qualified him to inspire and lead the new Zionist movement. He was first a lawyer, then a playwright, then a Vienna journalist.

As a correspondent in Paris in 1894, Herzl became disturbed by his coverage of a military court martial. A Jewish French army officer, Captain Dreyfus, was found guilty of treason on the basis of perjured testimony. His conviction resulted in the public outcry, "Death to the Jews."

Emotionally stirred, Herzl published a booklet in 1896 entitled *The Jewish State*. He argued that host countries prevented the Jews' assimilation. Herzl agreed with Pinsker that Jews were forced into finance. He admitted that rich Jews tended to exploit the poor, thus contributing to anti-Semitism. Herzl therefore urged especially the poorer class Jews, who had nothing to lose, to emigrate to Palestine and become agrarian. He suggested that a fund be created to aid resettlement. That way wealthy Jews could soothe their consciences and avoid criticism for not emigrating by making financial contributions.

Surprisingly, at first Herzl had entertained the idea of establishing the Jewish home in Argentina. He later accepted an offer by the

British government to found it in Uganda, Africa. After considerable opposition from fellow Zionists, however, Herzl conceded that the Jewish home would succeed only in Palestine. That's where Jews were historically and emotionally connected.

First Zionist Congress (1897)
The idea of a Jewish state in Palestine caught fire in Jewish communities around the world. The next year, in 1897, Herzl called Jews together in Basel, Switzerland, for the First Zionist Congress. Elected its first president, Herzl devoted the last seventeen years of his life to the Zionist dream.

The World Zionist Organization was created at the First Zionist Congress. A resolution was passed stating the purpose and objectives of the movement:

> Zionism strives to create for the Jewish people a home in Palestine secured by public law. The Congress contemplates the following means to the attainment of this end:
> 1. The promotion on suitable lines of the colonisation of Palestine by Jewish agricultural and industrial workers.
> 2. The organisation and bringing together of the whole of Jewry by means of appropriate institutions, local and international, in accordance with the laws of each country.
> 3. The strengthening and fostering of Jewish national sentiment and consciousness.
> 4. Preparatory steps towards obtaining Government consent where necessary to the attainment of the aim of Zionism.

This first official statement on Zionism says nothing about the indigenous Arabs in Palestine. Early Zionists gave the impression that they ignored the local Arabs. Herzl's associate, Israel Zangwil, popularized his spurious slogan, "A land without people for a people without a land." Yet in 1897 Arabs outnumbered Jews in Palestine 20 to 1. In addition, 99% of the land was owned by Arabs.[3] Herzl hoped western nations would "admit our sovereignty over a neutral piece of land" and would support the Jews' alleged right to continue emigration.

Therefore, a fundamental error of early Zionism was that it failed to recognize adequately the native Arab population. Herzl thought the Jews' transformation of the country would considerably improve life for the native Arabs, for which they would be grateful. Furthermore, he naively fantasized a Jewish-Arab brotherhood, in which the

Arabs would be assimilated into the proposed utopian Jewish state.

The Zionist resolution also left God out, as well as Judaism. Herzl was an irreligious man; but he was not opposed to religion. At first, Zionism was strictly a secular movement: faith in land rather than faith in the God Who gives land. This characteristic appeared again in Israel's Proclamation of Independence (1948). It states that throughout the centuries of their dispersion, "the Jewish people kept faith with their Land."

Herzl died young, at the age of 44. The mantle of Zionist leadership fell to Chaim Weizmann. He enjoyed a long career, aiding Britain in WWI as a notable chemist and serving as Israel's first president in 1949.

In 1901 the important Jewish National Fund was established to receive finances to buy land in Palestine. A twofold discriminatory rule was attached: once acquired, such land would forever remain in possession of Jews, and only Jewish labor could be employed on it. This last point distinguishes Zionism from South African apartheid. Both movements have been criticized and compared as "racist" in conception.

Over the succeeding years, vast land holdings were purchased from absentee Arab landlords, many living in Beirut. Deals were always made against the wills of Arab tenant farmers.

McMahon-Hussein Letters

The Ottoman (Turkish) Empire ruled the Middle East, including Palestine, for nearly 400 years, until 1917. When WWI broke out, the Ottoman Empire joined Germany and the Central Powers against the Western Allies. At the beginning of the war, the British high commissioner in Cairo, Sir Henry McMahon, corresponded in a series of letters with Arab leader Hussein of Arabia. **In these McMahon-Hussein letters, McMahon promised independence to the Arabs of the Middle East and persuaded them through Hussein to sever relations with the Moslem Turks and join the Allies.**

WWI first arrived in Palestine in early 1917, when the British attacked the Turks' most formidable outpost—the fortress at Gaza. Three battles later, the British took Gaza, a victory which became the subject of an award-winning American movie, "Lawrence of Arabia." Native Palestinian Arabs helped the Allies rout the Turks from Palestine. Famed British General Allenby later described them as "invaluable."

When Allenby and his troops marched into Jerusalem, the Arabs were ecstatic. They expected this liberation of Palestine would lead to a revival of Greater Syria, which in antiquity had included Syria, Lebanon, Jordan and Palestine. In addition, as the armistice approached, U.S. President Woodrow Wilson publicly assured the Palestinian Arabs of "an undoubted security of life and an absolutely unmolested opportunity for autonomous development."[4]

Sykes-Picot Agreement
Soon after the Arabs joined the Allies, the British government badly mishandled the Palestine situation. Foreseeing victory, Britain and France secretly negotiated the future division of authority over the Middle East. Called the Sykes-Picot Agreement, it undermined Britain's earlier promise of independence to the Arabs.

This British duplicity arose due to a conflict of interest. Besides the support of Arab forces, Britain had sought and received considerable financial aid from the Jewish community for the war effort. British authorities later claimed that this aid helped tip the balance in favor of the Allied Powers. They wanted to return the favor. Winston Churchill later pointed out that the Arabs of Palestine were never specifically mentioned in the McMahon-Hussein correspondence.

Balfour Declaration
On November 2, 1917, with the approval of the British War Cabinet, Foreign Secretary Lord Balfour wrote to Lord Lionel Walter de Rothschild, a British Jew and financier of Zionism:

> His Majesty's Government view with favour the establishment in Palestine of a national home for the Jewish people, and will use their best endeavours to facilitate the achievement of this object, it being clearly understood that nothing shall be done which may prejudice the civil and religious rights of existing non-Jewish communities in Palestine or the rights and political status enjoyed by Jews in any other country.

For the next thirty years this single sentence, known as the Balfour Declaration, became the guide for British policy in Palestine. It clearly favored Jewish immigrants over the native Arabs. The British had consulted with Zionist leaders in America and Britain on the wording of the letter. Palestinians and others have correctly alleged that in 1917, Britain possessed no legal authority over Palestine. The development of international law, however, was in its infancy.

The purposely ambiguous Balfour Declaration raised many questions. What is a national home? Does it constitute an independent, sovereign Jewish state? In all, or part, of Palestine? If part, what part? Did the Jewish right to a national home in Palestine exceed that of the non-Jewish community there? If so, could the civil rights of non-Jews be safeguarded in a Jewish state? These were important questions which the brief Balfour letter either did not address, or concerning which it seemed to contain contradictions.

Lord Balfour later stated his personal sentiments quite clearly:

> For in Palestine we do not propose even to go through the form of consulting the wishes of the present inhabitants of the country. . . . The Four Great Powers are committed to Zionism and Zionism, be it right or wrong, good or bad, is rooted in age long tradition, in present needs, in future hopes of far profounder import than the desires and prejudices of the 700,000 Arabs who inhabit that ancient land.[5]

Balfour's refusal to ascertain the aspirations of the Palestinians represented a firm denial of their basic human rights. While it indirectly led to the creation of the Israeli state, the Balfour Declaration doomed British involvement to failure.

Palestinians: "Non-Jewish"
As did the Zionists, the British ignored the interests of the Palestinian Arabs. In 1917 there were approximately 600,000 Arabs living in Palestine west of the Jordan Depression and only 60,000 Jews, a ratio of 10 to 1.

The Balfour letter angered the Palestinian Arabs by designating them only as "non-Jewish." Yet the non-Jewish population of Palestine was difficult to define. It consisted of Arabs, Druze, Christians and others. Furthermore, it had been the custom of Europeans to identify populations in the Middle East by religion rather than race. The government of Israel still officially identifies the Palestinians as "non-Jews." Palestinians regard this as a denial of their identity.

Paris Peace Conference (1919)
The first peace conference following WWI was held at Versailles in France. The Treaty of Versailles established the League of Nations, the forerunner of the UN, to settle disputes between nations. It was decided that the League would administer a mandate system over former Ottoman territory in the Middle East.

At the 1919 Paris Peace Conference, Zionist leaders were invited to offer their plan for establishing the Jewish National Home. They

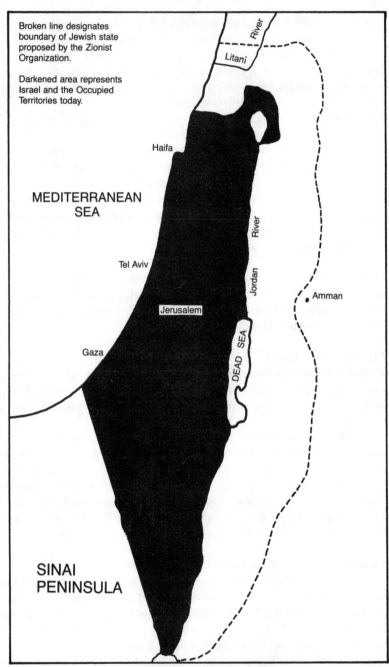

Broken line designates
boundary of Jewish state
proposed by the Zionist
Organization.

Darkened area represents
Israel and the Occupied
Territories today.

Litani River

Haifa

MEDITERRANEAN
SEA

Jordan River

Tel Aviv

Jerusalem

Amman

DEAD SEA

Gaza

SINAI
PENINSULA

MAP 4: ZIONIST PLAN (1919)

proposed a Jewish state in the present lands of Palestine, southern Lebanon and western Jordan. They argued that the extra land was needed for a larger-scale Jewish immigration than what later took place. For support they cited Israel's ancient history, when the monarchy and the Hasmonean Kingdom possessed these lands. When the Allies rejected the Zionists' proposal, Weizmann retorted like a Palestinian might today. "Where is the principle of justice for small nationalities, for which everybody is fighting?" he exclaimed. However, when U.S. Secretary of State Robert Lansing asked Weizmann if "Jewish National Home" meant an autonomous Jewish government, Weizmann answered in the negative. He explained that the Zionist Organization did not want an autonomous Jewish government until unrestricted Jewish immigration resulted in a substantial Jewish majority in Palestine's population. Then Jewish autonomy would reflect the aspirations of its citizenship.

King-Crane Commission (1919)
A special commission had been appointed by U.S. President Wilson to determine which nation the indigenous Arabs desired as the Mandatory over Palestine. The King-Crane Commission learned that the Palestinians rejected a mandate and wanted an independent country. If a mandate were to be unavoidable, they feared British colonialism and preferred the U.S. as the mandatory. The commission rejected a Jewish state, recommending limited Jewish immigration and the revival of a single state of Greater Syria, to include Palestine. European leaders ignored these recommendations.

The King-Crane Commission pointed out ambiguities in the Balfour Declaration and insightfully projected the future Israeli-Palestinian conflict. Two points from their report illustrate:

1. "It can hardly be doubted that the extreme Zionist Program must be greatly modified. **For 'a national home for the Jewish people' is not equivalent to making Palestine into a Jewish State; nor can the erection of such a Jewish State be accomplished without the gravest trespass upon the 'civil and religious rights of existing non-Jewish communities in Palestine.'** The fact came out repeatedly in the commission's conference with Jewish representatives that the Zionists looked forward to a practically complete dispossession of the present non-Jewish inhabitants of Palestine, by various forms of purchase" (emphasis added).

2. "The Peace Conference should not shut its eyes to the fact that the anti-Zionist feeling in Palestine and Syria is intense and not lightly to be flouted. No British officer, consulted by the Commissioners,

believed that the Zionist program could be carried out except by force of arms. . . . 50,000 soldiers would be required even to initiate the program. That of itself is evidence of a strong sense of the injustice of the Zionist program, on the part of the non-Jewish populations of Palestine and Syria. . . . For the initial claim, often submitted by Zionist representatives, that they have a 'right' to Palestine, based on an occupation of 2,000 years ago, can hardly be seriously considered."

Thus, for a long time the U.S. government was pro-Palestinian while the British government was pro-Jewish.

First White Paper (1922)
In 1922 the British issued its first of a series of five "White Papers" to clear up questions about the Balfour Declaration and its anticipated mandate over Palestine. It was presented by Secretary Winston Churchill, who was to become an ardent supporter of Zionism. Some points follow:

1. **"The terms of the [Balfour] Declaration referred to do not contemplate that Palestine as a whole should be converted into a Jewish National Home, but that such a Home should be founded *in Palestine*"** (emphasis added; italics in original). The Balfour letter contained the important phrase "in Palestine," which might allow for two separate and independent states. The League of Nations had earlier rejected the Zionist plea for a "reconstitution of Palestine as the National Home of the Jewish people."

2. "When it is asked what is meant by the development of the Jewish National Home in Palestine, it may be answered that it is not the imposition of a Jewish nationality upon the inhabitants of Palestine as a whole, but the further development of the existing Jewish community."

3. **"The existence of a Jewish National Home in Palestine should be internationally guaranteed, and . . . it should be formally recognized to rest upon ancient historic connection"** (emphasis added). Here, the British disagreed with America's King-Crane Commission, which dismissed the Zionists' claim to the land based on historical precedent.

British Mandate (1922-1948)
The U.S. seemed the logical choice for the mandatory over Palestine. Its population contained the largest concentration of Jews in the world—nearly half at the time. But the U.S. Senate took an isolationist stance following the war. It refused to join the League of Nations and accept a participatory role in the Middle East mandates. Without

Arab consent, the mandate for Palestine and Iraq went to Britain. The British could now keep their promise to Zionist Jews, but U.S. President Wilson could not fulfill his pledge to the Palestinians.

At the Paris Peace Conference of 1919, the name "Palestine" was officially revived from the Greek and Roman past. For a long time the designation "Palestine" had included present Jordan. It never included the Sinai Peninsula.

In 1922 the unofficial, larger Palestine was split into two separate administrations; the Jordan Depression became the dividing line. Palestine east of the Jordan River was renamed "Transjordan;" Palestine west of the river became "Mandate Palestine."

France was assigned mandates over Syria and Lebanon.

Article 22 of the Versailles Treaty had clarified the purpose of these mandates. It declared that the "well-being and development of such people" in these territories should be cared for by designated, advanced nations until they could "stand by themselves." France eventually withdrew from Syria and Lebanon. Britain withdrew its mandate and awarded statehood to Transjordan in 1946, renamed "Jordan" in 1949. **Thus, after WWI all Arabs, except for the Palestinians, eventually gained independence and statehood.**

The Balfour Declaration was accepted almost verbatim by the League of Nations as an integral part of the British Mandate. This made the provision of a Zionist homeland in Palestine an international law. Years later, Prime Minister Shimon Peres compared the Balfour Declaration to the decree of Persian King Cyrus when the king proclaimed the right of exiled Jews in his kingdom to return to their homeland (Ezra 1.2-4).[6] Many students of biblical prophecy regard the Balfour Declaration as an important element which fulfilled biblical prophecies concerning the reestablishment of present Israel.

The first British census of Mandate Palestine was taken in 1922 and the next in 1931:

Year	Total population	Muslim	Jewish	Christian
1922	757,182	78%	11%	9.6%
1931	1,035,154	73.4%	16.9%	8.6%.

Haganah

Early Jewish settlements in Palestine suffered from Bedouin raids. To meet this threat, they formed a security organization called *Hashomer*, meaning "the watchmen." Hashomer was later transformed into the more thoroughly trained *Haganah*, meaning "defense." Its members lived in the settlements as both permanent guards and farm laborers. Under the mandate, *Haganah* was illegal, even though British protection remained sorely inadequate. As an underground defense militia, *Haganah* smuggled arms into Palestine.

Plan for Settlement
Zionists appealed to world Jewry for funds to assist Jewish immigrants in settling and developing Palestine. These finances were later channeled through the Jewish Agency for Palestine. They far exceeded any that became available to the indigenous Arab Palestinians.

In 1935 David Ben-Gurion became chairman of the two foremost Jewish organizations in Mandate Palestine: the World Zionist Organization and the Jewish Agency for Palestine. Ben-Gurion remained the foremost Zionist leader for the next twenty-one years and became Israel's first Prime Minister.

The Zionist strategy was to avoid conflict with the Palestinian Arabs by settling areas where they did not live. This method was, in fact, recommended by the British Mandate. The Jews bought tracts in the Galilee, the Haifa District and throughout the coastal plain south of Mount Carmel. The Arabs had avoided these lowlands; some had marshes full of malaria-infected mosquitoes.

Careless Custodians?
When the Zionists first arrived in Palestine, they discovered a mostly barren land that had laid waste for centuries. Forests had been denuded; streams were clogged, forming mosquito-infested swamps which caused malaria. The Zionists set themselves to the laborious task of restoring the land to productivity, for which they are to be commended. Visitors to Israel are always impressed by what the Jews have achieved in reclaiming the land.

Many people have criticized the earlier Palestinians as careless custodians of the land. They argue that because the Jews have put the land to better use, they are more entitled to it than the Palestinians. Several factors nullify this assertion.

One important factor which brought the land of Palestine to ruin was its history under the Ottoman (Turkish) Empire's increasingly oppressive feudal system. The Turks imposed a heavy, 15% annual land tax. It was not based on assessed land values but the number of trees, in woodlands and orchards, and the number of fruitful vines. In order to pay their taxes, many land owners harvested trees in what was once rich forestland, resulting in severe erosion. Others were forced to destroy their orchards.

Such burdensome taxes, as well as the foolish method of levying them, led to less cultivation and, correspondingly, less settlement of the land. Furthermore, the *fellaheen* (Arab agrarians) continually suffered from the lack of Turkish protection from raiding Bedouin. Thus, the Ottoman Empire exacted outrageous taxes and gave little or nothing back to the residents.

Another major factor was that the Palestinian Arabs lacked the considerable financial resources later donated by world Jewry to the Zionists. Furthermore, as the Mandator, the British government created several public works projects, such as Israel's largest port, the Port of Haifa. Some British private capital was also invested in the country. Later, the Jews received much assistance from the U.S. government and its agencies, such as the U.S. Department of Agriculture.

Zionists were also aided by advances in science and technology. Marshland, which the Arabs had to avoid, the Zionists were able to drain using mechanized earth-moving equipment.

A Divinely Decreed Wasteland

The prophet Ezekiel predicted the modern return of Jews to their ancient homeland. He foresaw that they would settle a "land that is restored from the sword, whose inhabitants have been gathered from many nations to the mountains of Israel which had been a continual waste" (Eze 38.8).

According to Yahweh's covenant with His Chosen People, their land would reflect the extent of their obedience to His commandments. Like the Jews themselves, in either blessing or cursing, the land would serve as a testimony to the Gentiles of the truth and power of Almighty God. On the negative side, Moses predicted the Diaspora and added that

> the foreigner who comes from a distant land, when they see the plagues of the land and the diseases with which the LORD has afflicted it, will say, "All its land is brimstone and salt, a burning waste, unsown and unproductive, and no grass grows in it, like the overthrow of Sodom and Gomorrah, Admah and Zeboiim, which the LORD overthrew in His anger and in His wrath." And all the nations shall say, "Why has the LORD done thus to this land? Why this great outburst of anger?" Then men shall say, "Because they forsook the covenant of the LORD, . . . Therefore, the anger of the LORD burned against that land, to bring upon it every curse which is written in this book; and the LORD up-

rooted them from their land in anger and in fury and in great wrath, and cast them into another land, as it is this day" (Deut 29.22-28; cf. Lev 26.32).

How could Arabs or anyone else restore land so cursed by God?

Moses further explained that the Israelites' sins would defile the land, so that the land itself would vomit them out (Lv 18.25-28; 20.22). Jeremiah provided the perspective that, through their sin, the Jews themselves would "make their land a desolation" (Jer 18.16). And God appeared to King Solomon to warn:

> If you or your sons shall indeed turn away from following Me, . . . then I will cut off Israel from the land. . . . And this house [temple] will become a heap of ruins; everyone who passes by will be astonished and hiss and say, "Why has the LORD done thus to this land and to this house?" And they will say, "Because they forsook the LORD their God" (1 Kgs 9.6-9).

Therefore, the desolate condition in which the Zionists found Palestine should not be blamed on the Arabs. It was divinely decreed that the Holy Land should lie desolate while its people were in exile. **In this forsaken condition, God's special land should have been recognized as a testimony to His existence and to His mighty power, and to the inevitability of His judgment upon sin. If anyone is to blame for the centuries that the land of Palestine laid waste, it is the people who turned away from their God.**

Jews in the Coastal Plain

After land reclamation, the Zionists created territorial centers, mostly agricultural, called the "New Yishuv." When Israel's War of Independence ended in 1949, the Jewish population was clustered in these centers. The Arabs occupied primarily the hill country of Judea and Samaria. Later called the West Bank, this Arab territory constituted much of the historic land of Israel. Israeli professor Yehuda Elizur observes that

> the modern State of Israel has introduced a noteworthy innovation. . . . [During the first Commonwealth] the coastal strip was occupied by the Philistines in the south and by the Phoenicians in the north. During the second Jewish Commonwealth the Mediterranean coast was largely dotted with Greek cities, with the Jews occupying the mountain area. The reverse is the case

in our days, with the coast and fertile valleys being largely occupied by the Jews, whereas the hill country contains considerable elements of non-Jewish population.[7]

Indeed, 80% of the Jewish population in Palestine today is concentrated in the coastal plains.

Scholar Abba Eban served many years as Israel's first ambassador
to the UN and to the U.S., and later as Foreign Minister. He explains
how the Zionists' settlement pattern later affected his presentation of
Israel's request for UN membership.

> . . . Since the main concentrations of Arab population were
> in areas associated with the ancient Jewish kingdoms, it followed
> that modern Jewish settlement was destined to concentrate itself
> elsewhere, namely the land of the Philistines in the coastal plain,
> as well as in the valleys of Jezreel and Esdraelon, which Arab
> populations had avoided because of insalubrious conditions. . . .
>
> In the United Nations' discussions leading to Israel's member-
> ship of the UN, we relied on the general premise of a historic
> connection, but made no claim whatever for the inclusion of
> particular areas on our side of the Partition boundary on the
> grounds of ancient connection. Since Hebron was full of Arabs,
> we did not ask for it. Since Beersheba was virtually empty, we
> put in a successful claim.[8]

**Thus, when Israeli officials later sought membership in the UN,
they could not claim historic connection to specific areas of land
because much of Israel was located in the Plain of Philistia, where
their forefathers almost never lived.**

Arab Palestinian Revolt (1936-1939)
Jewish immigration to Palestine increased from 1933 to 1936. Most
came from Germany and Poland, driven by Hitler's ascendancy to
power. If that rate of Jewish immigration had continued, Jews would
have soon been a majority in Mandate Palestine.

Until 1936 the Zionists advocated a single Jewish-Arab state in
Palestine, sometimes called a binational state. The next ten years
convinced the Zionists that co-sovereignty was untenable.

More strife led to increased Jewish militarization. In 1925 Vladimir
Jabotinsky had led radical Zionist dissidents, who demanded that
Mandate Palestine include Transjordan, to form the Revisionist Party.
In 1935 the Revisionists broke from the World Zionist Organization

and founded the New Zionist Organization. Like the later Palestine Liberation Organization (PLO), its purpose was to "liberate" Mandate Palestine, as well as Transjordan, by armed force. The same year, former members of Haganah created *Irgun Zvai Leumi*, meaning "national military organization," and made Jabotinsky its head. Jabotinsky later became Menachem Begin's mentor.

The Arab Palestinians demanded a secular Palestinian state, disallowing further Jewish immigration. In 1935 the Palestinians requested that the British end the Jews' mass immigration (c. 61,000 that year) and land acquisition in Palestine. The British high commissioner of Palestine recommended to the British Parliament that a Legislative Council be established in Palestine, with 28 seats evenly divided between Jews and Arabs. Though Jewish representation was disproportionate to the population, the Palestinians assented. The next year the plan was defeated in the House of Commons due to pro-Zionist members.

Palestinians called a peaceful labor strike and boycott against Jewish businesses. It soon degenerated into a violent revolt, continuing sporadically for the next three years. Palestinian Arabs attacked both Jews and British administrators and military forces.

Peel Commission (1936-1937)
In 1936 Lord Peel headed the Royal Commission, appointed to investigate the Arab riots and make recommendations to His Majesty's Government. Three groups made appeals. The new Arab Higher Committee demanded that all Jewish immigration and acquisition of land cease and that an Arab Palestinian state be formed to replace the mandate. The Revisionists requested a Jewish state to extend on both sides of the Jordan River. The Jewish Agency offered a median proposal: a binational state with a legislative council having equal representation from both sides.

All three proposals were rejected. Considering coexistence impossible, **the Peel Commission recommended that Mandate Palestine be divided into two separate, sovereign states: a Jewish state and an Arab Palestinian state**. This so-called "Peel Plan" proposed that the Jewish state be established in the area where Jews were concentrated in the territorial centers: the coastal plain, extending from three miles south of Ashdod northward to Mount Carmel, the Haifa District and eastward to include all of the Galilee and the Plain of Jezreel. This Jewish territory would represent 20% of Mandate Palestine. The Arabs would get about 75%, consisting of all of the Negev and most of Samaria and Judea. It would be united with King Abdullah's Trans-

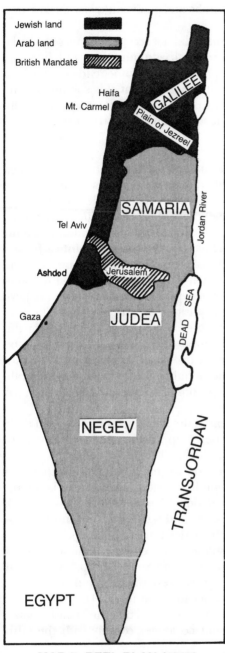

Jewish land

Arab land

British Mandate

Haifa

Mt. Carmel

GALILEE

Plain of Jezreel

SAMARIA

Jordan River

Tel Aviv

Ashdod

Jerusalem

DEAD SEA

Gaza

JUDEA

NEGEV

TRANSJORDAN

EGYPT

MAP 5: PEEL PLAN (1937)

jordan as the Arab Palestinian state. The remaining 5% would stay under a continuing British Mandate. This corridor would include the holy sites of Jerusalem, Bethlehem and perhaps Nazareth, and stretch to the Mediterranean Sea. Thus, **the Peel Plan granted most of the Plain of Philistia to the Palestinians, in close agreement with the proposal of this author and, to a lesser extent, with the later UN Partition Plan**.

The Peel Commission also recommended that the estimated 200,000 Arabs living in the Jews' allotted territory be transferred, forcibly if necessary, to their designated land.

The Jews accepted the Peel Plan, with minor objections regarding the division of land. Except for Transjordan, the surrounding Arab states and the Palestinians vehemently rejected it. Arab hostilities increased in Palestine.

Further Deliberations

In 1938 the British appointed a Partition Commission. Its proposed division of Palestine closely resembled that of the Peel Plan. These recommendations for two separate states reveal that after prolonged investigation, experts concluded that Arabs and Jews could not coexist in a single state in Palestine.

However, the British government did not accept these recommendations, concluding that, "The political, administrative and financial difficulties involved in the proposal to create independent Arab and Jewish States inside Palestine are so great that this solution of the problem is impracticable." This objection no longer applies today, since the PLO has created a viable national infrastructure.

Fifth White Paper (1939)

In mid-1939 the British government issued its fifth White Paper. British authorities finally admitted to the ambiguities of the Mandate and therefore of the Balfour Declaration. They rendered this uncertainty in British policy as the chief cause of Arab hostilities in Palestine. The paper explicitly stated that **"the framers of the Mandate . . .could not have intended that Palestine should be converted into a Jewish State against the will of the Arab population of the country."** The purpose of the Balfour Declaration—to provide for a Jewish homeland—was now deemed accomplished. It was explained that the Jews' unrestricted immigration and acquisition of land was becoming contrary to the intent of the League of Nations in issuing Britain the mandate over Palestine. It was proposed that Jewish immigration be restricted to 75,000 over the next five years, in order to maintain a two-thirds Arab majority of the population. An independent, Arab-dominated binational state was proposed, to be established within ten years.

The Fifth White Paper appeased the Arabs' wrath and ended their three-year revolt. They had suffered approximately 5,000 casualties, the Jews about 1,200 and the British, 500.

But the paper dealt a severe blow to Jewish aspirations. Incensed Zionists argued that it was a "repudiation of the Balfour Declaration," that it surrendered the Jewish National Home (which many mistook as synonymous with a Jewish state) and was "cruel and indefensible in its denial of sanctuary to Jews fleeing from Nazi persecution." They warned of increased hostilities. Sure enough, radical dissident members of Irgun soon left to form "the Stern Group." Also called "the Stern Gang," its terrorist targets were mostly the British.

Britain, however, soon turned its attention to WWII.

In early 1943 David Ben-Gurion announced that the Zionist Organization and Jewish Agency would no longer comply with the Fifth White Paper.

WWII and Palmach

With the outbreak of WWII, the Zionists had to decide whether to oppose Britain as the Mandatory or support its war effort against Hitler. Some 30,000 Palestinian Jews served, many more than did Palestinian Arabs. Jews understandably had stronger reasons for volunteering: compassion for their brethren caught in the Holocaust and the threat of Hitler invading Palestine. Their rationale was to "fight the war as if there were no White Paper and to fight the White Paper as if there were no war."[9]

To oppose an anticipated invasion by Hitler, Haganah forged *Palmach*, specially-trained and mobilized "shock troops." Haganah and Palmach developed unprecedented military tactics of mobility, surprise attacks, deception and night operations. These maneuvers became the legacy of Haganah and Palmach when they were converted into the Israel Defense Forces (IDF) at the outbreak of Israel's War of Independence (1948-1949).[10] Haganah and Palmach "made it possible for Israel to come into being."[11]

Anglo-American Commission (1945-1946)

At the end of WWII, the Anglo-American Committee of Inquiry was appointed to examine the conflict between the Arabs and Jews in Palestine. It recommended ending restrictions on Jewish immigration and land acquisition, allowing immediate immigration of 100,000 Jews and continuing the mandate under auspices of the new United Nations. (The League of Nations was dissolved in 1946.)

Several nations refused to recognize this commission; France was one, because it was not included. Both Jews and Arabs rejected most of the commission's recommendations.

The Jewish Agency responded by submitting a plan for two separate states, giving the Arab Palestinians central and eastern Samaria and central Judea. This plan provided the simplest division of the land offered up to that time.

Throughout the tenure of its mandate, the British government had spurned the advice of its investigators and would not budge from its goal of a single Israeli-Arab state. Now it abandoned hope.

Effect of the Jewish Holocaust

When the shocking facts of the Holocaust (*Shoah* in Hebrew) became known at the end of WWII, Europeans and Americans felt both remorse and overwhelming sympathy for surviving Jews. The ghastly figure of six million Jews who died in the Holocaust accounted for approximately one-third of world Jewry. During the war the U.S. had barred immigration of European Jews to its shores except for only a few thousand. Moved with compassion, President Truman opposed the Fifth White Paper and asked the British to relax restrictions on Jewish immigration to Palestine. They refused.

After WWII there followed a desperate and illegal wave of Jewish immigration to Palestine, mostly from war-torn Europe. The British refused to permit immigrant ships to dock and unload at harbors in Palestine. One example was a ship named Exodus. It carried 4,500 Jewish survivors of Hitler's concentration camps to Palestine. But British authorities repelled the Exodus and forced its return to Europe. This story was made into a successful Hollywood movie that awakened sympathy to the plight of the suffering Jews.

British Withdrawal

Following WWII, violence increased in Palestine. It will be recalled that in 1919, a U.S. delegation had determined that 50,000 soldiers were needed to implement the plan for a Jewish homeland. In 1946 that was the exact size of the British force, which now proved inadequate. The newly-formed Arab League (1945) declared that the Palestinians should take up arms against both the British and the Jews. Radical Jewish underground militias, such as Irgun and Stern, stepped up terrorism directed mostly against the British. Thus, after the British had established the Jewish National Home, these Zionist zealots turned their guerrilla warfare on their benefactors, attempting to force Britain's withdrawal and to create a Jewish state.

After thirty years of failure to resolve the conflict and weakened by the war effort, the British requested in April, 1947, that the UN take over the problem of Palestine. They had given up and wanted to withdraw, no matter what the outcome.

UNSCOP

In May, 1947, the UN Special Committee on Palestine (UNSCOP) was formed to study the problem and recommend a solution. UNSCOP recommended both termination of the British Mandate and the formation of two separate states—a partition plan similar to the Peel Plan. In case of its non-acceptance, UNSCOP added a minority plan for an independent federal state, combining an Arab state with a Jewish state.

As with the Peel Plan, a majority of Jews in Palestine were favorable to the Partition Plan, except for its specific division of the land.

On the other hand, Arab leaders displayed their intransigence by fiercely opposing both plans. They demanded that Palestine become an independent Arab state and requested that the question be decided by the World Court of Justice at The Hague. They argued that according to principles of international law (which was new but acquiring increased acceptance), the UN had no right to determine Palestine's future without consulting its population. Obviously, the Arab majority would have chosen independence and created an Arab rather than a Jewish state. However, two other factors needed to be considered: "the Jewish problem" (persecution of Jews during their Diaspora) and worldwide compassion aroused by the Holocaust. Palestinians have since argued that they should not have suffered for the misdeeds of the Third Reich.

UN Partition Plan (1947)

On November 29, 1947, after much deliberation, the UN General Assembly passed Resolution 7. **Called the UN Partition Plan, it proposed that two separate states be established in Palestine. But its proposed division of land was a drawback, being more of a patchwork than any previous plan.** The Jewish state would comprise the following: eastern Galilee, the Haifa District, the entire coastal plain south to Ashdod (similar to the Peel Plan) and most of the Negev. The Arab Palestinian state would have western Galilee, a slightly enlarged West Bank (again, comparable to the Peel Plan) and an L-shaped section, one leg including much of the Plain of Philistia and the other leg extending southeast into the Negev, reaching Kadesh Barnea. Joppa and its environs (present Tel Aviv) would be an Arab enclave. The UN would act as trustee over an enlarged Jerusalem. It would be an international district due to its religious significance for the world's three primary monotheistic faiths: Judaism, Christianity and Islam. The Partition Plan also provided for the 325,000 Arab Palestinians living in the Jewish-designated territory to be transferred to the Palestinian-designated area if they so chose.

The Arabs rejected this plan while the Zionist Jews accepted it. The Arabs refused to accept the Jews' right to have a national existence in Palestine. Today, the Jews refuse this same right to the Palestinians. The Arabs also objected to the Jews being granted 56% of the land since Jews constituted only 30% of the population and possessed only 8% of the land.

The major weakness of the UN Partition Plan was inherent in the UN itself: the Security Council possessed no authority to implement a resolution passed by the General Assembly. The British refused a UN request to assist in transferring Arabs to their designated territory.

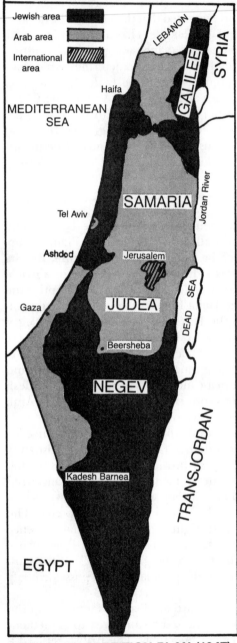

Jewish area
Arab area
International area

LEBANON

SYRIA

GALILEE

Haifa

MEDITERRANEAN SEA

SAMARIA

Jordan River

Tel Aviv

Ashdod

Jerusalem

DEAD SEA

Gaza

JUDEA

Beersheba

NEGEV

TRANSJORDAN

Kadesh Barnea

EGYPT

MAP 6: UN PARTITION PLAN (1947)

Their transfer, however, was not mandatory as under the Peel Plan.

Civil war broke out immediately after the Partition Plan passed. Thereafter, the U.S. maintained that the plan was impractical because it could not be implemented without military force, and no nation following WWII wanted to commit troops. The Soviets insisted that it be effected immediately. The U.S. opted for a delay, proposing before the UN in March, 1948, that it act as trustee over the entire region, a variation of the mandate policy. The Jews protested vehemently.

Assessment of Britain's Role

Both Jews and Arabs have severely criticized Britain for its role as the Mandatory of Palestine. In its efforts to win WWI, Britain indeed erred in making contradictory commitments to Arabs and Jews.

Many Arabs fault the British for not giving Palestine its independence before the State of Israel was founded. They cite all the other Arab countries, which were granted national sovereignty. But the continuing struggle between the Palestinian Arabs and Jews revealed that conditions in Palestine did not meet the criterion set in the mandates for independence: that the residents could "stand by themselves." There was no comparable turmoil in the other mandates.

Should Britain be faulted for its role as the Mandatory of Palestine? Humanly speaking, had it not been for the Balfour Declaration and Britain's support of Zionism, Israel might not be a nation today. Yet, over 40 years later, after constant UN attention, the problem remains unresolved and may be worse. Such a history reveals that the Palestinian-Israeli conflict is indeed a very complex and difficult problem.

Toward Statehood
The founding father of Zionism, Theodor Herzl, wrote a diary, published posthumously. During the First Zionist Congress, in 1897, he had written: "At Basel I founded the Jewish State. If I said this out loud today, I would be greeted with universal laughter. In five years perhaps, and certainly in fifty years, everyone will perceive it." Like an ancient Hebrew prophet, Herzl predicted what came true: 50 years later his dream of a Jewish state became a reality. But fulfillment of the Zionists' dream of a Jewish state was to result in a nightmare for the Palestinians. Instead of a dream, their legacy was a nightmare of dispossession, violence, terrorism and war that still afflicts the world community.

Chapter 4

THE STATE OF ISRAEL

History of the State of Israel

1948	Proclamation of Independence
1948-1949	War of Independence
1956	Sinai Campaign
1967	Six-Day War; Acquisition of Occupied Territories
1973	Yom Kippur War
1978	First Invasion of Lebanon; Camp David Accords
1979	Egypt-Israel Peace Treaty
1980	Annexation of East Jerusalem
1981	Annexation of the Golan Heights
1982	Relinquishment of the Sinai to Egypt
	Second Invasion of Lebanon
1987-	Intifada

Israel's War of Independence (1948-1949)

Jews had settled mostly in eastern Galilee and the Haifa District, with the largest concentration extending along the coastal plain to a few miles south of Tel Aviv. They did not settle south of the Nahal Sorek, the historic northern border of ancient Philistia, except for some isolated settlements just east of what later became known as the Gaza Strip. These areas, though slightly reduced, had been allocated to the Jews under the UN Partition Plan.

In February, 1948, Britain officially announced it would withdraw its mandate over Palestine and relinquish its authority to the new UN. The date was set for May 14, 1948. The UN Partition Plan was scheduled to go into effect two months later.

Hostilities intensified in Palestine in the succeeding months. Battles between Jews and Arabs broke out in various sectors of Palestine. For instance, Jewish guerrillas of Menanchem Begin's Irgun massacred 254 Palestinians in a small Arab village called Deir Yassin.

In spite of the unrest, the British began systematically to withdraw their administration and occupation forces on April 19, 1948, with completion planned for May 14th. Since it was undecided who would take up the reins of governmental administration, chaos ensued and war seemed inevitable.

When May 14th arrived, as president of the World Zionist Organization David Ben-Gurion proclaimed in Tel Aviv the founding of the State of Israel and announced its Proclamation of Independence. (See Appendix C.)

It was obvious that independently declaring statehood would lead to war. Moshe Sharett was then successor to Ben-Gurion. Ben-Gurion advocated the use of force; Sharett preferred diplomacy to achieve the same goals. His personal diary reveals that Ben-Gurion vetoed Sharett's negotiations with Arab and U.S. representatives.[1] Continuing these talks would have delayed Israel's Declaration of Independence by a few weeks.

The new State of israel immediately received important recognition. Only minutes after Israel's declaration of statehood, U.S. President Truman unexpectedly rejected the advice of his State Department and officially recognized the new State of Israel. Only the year before, he had aided passage of the UN Partition Plan. The USSR also endorsed Israeli statehood. Years later, the Soviets severed diplomatic relations with Israel and supported Palestinian guerrilla organizations having Marxist elements.

As was expected, war broke out the next day, May 15th, between the Jews and Arabs. The Arab Palestinians were still a negligible force. Armed forces from Egypt, Jordan, Syria, Lebanon and Iraq invaded Palestine and attacked the Jews. It was thought that the combined efforts of the Arab states, whose populations vastly outnumbered the Jews, would easily overcome and nullify the new state.

For years Jews had smuggled into Palestine whatever small arms they could obtain. Underground forces even fashioned some of their own. Yet when war broke out, Jewish fighting men were still woefully ill-equipped.

Nevertheless, the Jewish forces of Haganah, Irgun and Stern were far better trained and organized than the separate armed units of the Arab states. Years later, Jordan's crown prince, Hassan bin Talal, wrote, "The legend of a small armed force of Jews (David) fighting

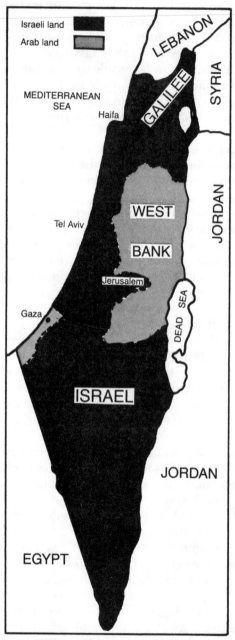

MAP 7: ISRAEL (1949-1967)

huge armed forces of some nine Arab States (Goliath) will not stand up to scrutiny. In fact, the total number of Arab armed forces which entered Palestine on and after 15 May 1948 amounted to 17,500."[2] Israel's total forces of 65,000 fighting men were officially united on May 31st and thereafter known as the Israel Defense Forces (IDF).

The Jews quickly gained the upper hand in their struggle for statehood. They secured possession of the more populated Jewish enclaves, including all of the Galilee. The British assisted the Arab Palestinians in holding their most populated territory. It became known as the West Bank because its eastern border is the west bank of the Jordan River. Most Israeli Jews refer to the West Bank by its biblical names of Samaria and Judea. This irregularly-shaped Arab West Bank is slightly smaller than the size proposed for the Palestinian state under the UN Partition Plan.

The Arabs also retained an enlarged Gaza Strip on the southern coast. Separated from the West Bank by about twenty miles, it too was to be allotted to the Palestinian state under the UN Partition Plan. It was to extend northward almost to Ashdod and southeastward to Kadesh Barnea. The Jews, however, held off the Arabs at Kibbutz Yod Mordecai, just north of the Gaza Strip.

At the start of the war, Jews owned less than 8% of the total land area of Palestine. Under the UN Partition Plan they were to receive 56% of Palestine. At the completion of the war, they possessed 77%. **Thus, the Jews gained over one-third more territory than was allotted to them under the UN Partition Plan.** Jerusalem became divided. Modern (western) Jerusalem was occupied by the Jews, while East Jerusalem, also called Old or Arab Jerusalem, remained in possession of the Arabs.

Israel's War of Independence lasted over eighteen months. Israel signed separate armistice agreements with its four Arab neighbors between February and July, 1949. They never led to the envisioned peace treaties.

The "Armistice Line" of demarcation defined the boundaries between these territories. It was also called the Green Line due to its green color on the official map. The West Bank was united with Jordan. No one really wanted the small, overcrowded Gaza Strip, populated mostly by impoverished Palestinians. Egypt, however, agreed to administer it.

The Jews now had their state. But it was surrounded by hostile neighbors who saw them as intruders in the Arab Middle East.

Palestinian Diaspora

During Israel's War of Independence, about 770,000 Arab Palestinians fled from their homes to Arab states; 160,000 remained to become permanent citizens of Israel. In accounting for this Palestinian exodus, various charges have been leveled by both sides. Israelis contend that the Palestinians were exhorted to leave by officials from Arab states, which they have flatly denied.[3] Many Palestinians no doubt expected that the Arab states would aid them in defeating the Jews, enabling them to return to their homes shortly. Probably most of them simply fled from the path of war in fear for their lives. Some were definitely terrified of the possibility of another massacre like the one at Deir Yassin.

Palestinians charge that some Jewish commanders threatened or exercised violence against them to force their exodus. Many Zionist Jews were zealous to achieve a victory which would result in a predominantly Jewish majority of the population in order to assure a future Jewish state. Instances have been documented in which Jewish troops pressured or forced Palestinian Arabs to leave their homes. Soldiers roamed city streets with loud-speakers, warning Palestinians to leave.[4] This was alleged by many Palestinians after the war, especially those who lived in the coveted rich agricultural region of eastern Galilee. However, it should be noted that David Ben-Gurion publicly tried to persuade Palestinians in the Haifa District to remain.

Jewish editor of the *Jewish Newsletter*, William Zukerman, wrote, "The flight of the Palestine Arabs, which created the refugee problem, was not a spontaneous act, nor due entirely to the propaganda call of the Arab leaders as the Zionists have claimed all along. It was a coldly calculated plan executed by Irgun but with the knowledge of the Haganah and the Jewish Agency."[5]

What became of abandoned Arab villages in Israel strongly attests to Jewish efforts to discourage the Palestinians' return. Almost 400 Arab villages existed on May 15, 1948, in what became the State of Israel; an estimated 385 were thereafter demolished with bulldozers.

The Palestinians' flight during Israel's War of Independence became the first stage of a Palestinian Diaspora. They call it *al-Nakba*, meaning "the Disaster." This Diaspora increased during later wars, especially the Six-Day War of 1967. UN refugee camps were established outside Israel for the displaced victims of war. About half of these dispossessed Palestinians resigned themselves to living in the refugee camps with their deplorable conditions of impoverishment, persistently waiting to return to their homeland. Just as Jews refer to Zionism as "the Return," the Palestinians hope for *al-Awada*, which means "the Return" in Arabic.

Aftermath of Israel's Independence

In 1950 the legislative branch of Israel's democratic government, the Knesset, passed the Law of Return. It proclaimed the right of any Jew to immigrate to Israel. This law sparked the question, "Who is a Jew?" A dispute arose which 40 years later, has not yet subsided. In Israel the only question that supersedes, "What is Eretz Israel?" is the question, "Who is a Jew?" It became legally established that a Jew is anyone born to a Jewish mother or anyone who adopts the Jews' religion, the latter of which can include a Gentile.

Also in 1950, Jordan annexed the West Bank, agreeing to equal representation of Palestinians and Jordanians in Jordan's parliament. Half of the combined population of Jordan and the West Bank was Palestinian.

By 1950 the U.S. position advocated by Secretary of State John

Foster Dulles was full compensation for economic losses to the up-rooted Palestinians. This view was eventually formulated into an important UN resolution.

Sinai Campaign (1956)
In 1956 Egyptian President Nasser asserted himself to unite the Arab world. The Suez Canal had been built by Britain 80 years earlier and operated by them ever since. Nasser first negotiated the removal of British troops from the Suez Canal, but then seized control and nationalized it. Nasser also broke international law by blocking Israeli navigation through the Canal and the Straits of Tiran at the southern end of the Gulf of Aqaba. He was clearly trying to force Israel into a military confrontation with Egypt and the Arab world. Nasser was confident that Egypt would easily emerge victorious.

Backed by Britain and France, Israel retaliated in late October, 1956, by assaulting Egypt's forces in the Sinai Desert. Israel succeeded in opening shipping lanes in the Straits of Tiran and returning control of the Suez Canal to Britain. The Israelis also temporarily took the Gaza Strip, from which they had suffered Palestinian guerrilla attacks.

The 1956 War lasted only one week. Britain and France quickly pressured Israel into a ceasefire. Israeli forces withdrew from the Sinai and Gaza Strip in May, 1957, after receiving international guarantees that shipping lanes would remain open. Perhaps the most significant outcome of the 1956 Sinai Campaign was that it resulted in the formation of the first UN peacekeeping force—the United Nations Emergency Force (UNEF). The UNEF then patrolled the borders of the Gaza Strip and the Sinai.

Six-Day War (June 1967)
Relations between Israel and Egypt were relatively quiet for the next ten years. But hostilities continued to build between Israel and its other neighbors.

Israel always publicly warned that any diversion of water from the Jordan River or the blocking of the Straits of Tiran would constitute an act of aggression against Israel and would require its retaliation. In 1964 Jordan began a project to divert Jordan River waters which would reduce Israel's water supply from the Jordan by two-thirds. Late that year an Israeli military operation halted Jordanian construction.

Syrian shelling and infiltration from Lebanon and Jordan into Israel increased in early 1967. Egypt's Nasser amassed 100,000 troops along the Sinai border and ordered the small UNEF out. It acceded to his demands. Nasser again declared shipping lanes through the Straits closed to Israel.

For several years, heads of Arab states had been hostile to each other. Assassinations had even been attempted. Yet on this occasion, these rulers quickly banded together to destroy Israel. War on Israel's three fronts seemed imminent and hopeless. Its allies offered no help, and diplomatic efforts in the UN failed.

The new Israeli defense minister, Moshe Dayan, recommended a preemptive air strike against Egypt as the only hope for Israel. On early June 5, 1967, the Israeli air force, flying at low altitude to avoid radar detection, destroyed nearly the entire unsuspecting Egyptian air force on the ground. Three hours later the Israelis began to wipe out Jordan's air fleet. Syria lost two-thirds of its aircraft as the Israelis completed their three-pronged aerial attack. Most planes were destroyed on the ground. In two days Israel had gained complete air superiority over its enemies. This enabled its air force to support its encroaching ground forces.

To boost morale, the commander of Egypt's armed forces at first issued false reports to Egyptians about the progress of the battle. This caused President Nasser's poor advice to Jordan's King Hussein to attack Israel. Israel had assured Hussein that if he stayed out of the war, Israel would not attack Jordan or the West Bank. Pressured from the Arab world and a recent alliance with Egypt, Jordan entered a war which proved very costly. In addition, Hussein mistakenly consented to placing his forces under the direction of Egypt's commander to coordinate efforts.

The Israelis pushed Jordanian forces out of the West Bank and back across the Jordan River. It was the first time in over 2,000 years that the Jews had possessed all of Jerusalem. They were ecstatic.

Syria, despite its alliance with the Soviets and its many threats, never fully committed itself to the war. Israel took the small but militarily-strategic Golan Heights from Syria and expelled its approximately 10,000 Syrian residents. About 7,000 Druze were permitted to remain in its extreme northwest. This elevated area lies on the east side of Lake Kinneret (Sea of Galilee). From these heights the Syrians had frequently bombarded Galilean settlements across Lake Kinneret.

This war lasted only six days and became known as The Six-Day War. It proved to be one of the most brilliant and decisive victories in military history. Several Israeli commanders had superior military training in the western world. One, Moshe Dayan, became an instant national hero. Dayan was distinguished in appearance by a patch over

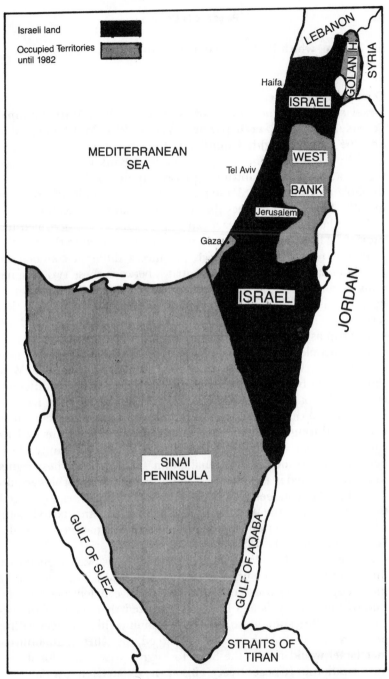

MAP 8: ISRAEL and the OCCUPIED TERRITORIES

his left eye, which he lost in combat during WWII as a member of *Palmach*.

Occupied Territories
Israel seized four new tracts of land in the 1967 War: the Sinai Peninsula and the Gaza strip from Egypt, the West Bank from Jordan and the Golan Heights from Syria. Its occupation of land almost quadrupled in size. The Sinai and the West Bank were large tracts; the Gaza Strip and the Golan Heights were quite small. Israel annexed the Golan Heights in 1981 and returned the Sinai Peninsula to Egypt in 1982. Israel still occupies the West Bank and the Gaza Strip.

These lands taken by Israel came to be called "the occupied territories." The Israeli government has usually referred to them as the "administered territories," which provides a different connotation. International law, however, differentiates between these two designations. A conqueror that administers new, non-annexed territory belligerently is designated an "occupier" and that land as "occupied territory." This is why the UN always refers to the West Bank and the Gaza Strip as "occupied territories."

Some people assert, "Israel ought to annex the territories because they won the war. That is what other conquerors have done. Why should Israel be any different?" The fact is that Israel **is** different, even if it is not judged more rigorously (by its moral codes, i.e., the law of Moses) than are other nations. The young country came into existence through mandate, and U.S. military aid has ensured its survival. There is also in our times a sense of world community which demands observance of individual and national rights. These rights were not observed in earlier times. So international law forbids acquisition of land by conquest. Nearly all Israeli leaders have acknowledged that annexation of the West Bank would be most detrimental to Israel's future because of the anticipated reaction from the nations, especially Israel's only ally—the U.S.

Before the Six-Day War, Israeli authorities had always argued that their country was too narrow to defend adequately. The addition of the occupied territories enabled Israel to have defensible borders. Nevertheless, many Israeli leaders strategized that some of the occupied territories might be used as bargaining chips in negotiating peace treaties with Arab neighbors. Indeed, the Knesset announced that Israel would return the Sinai to Egypt in exchange for its demilitarization and a peace treaty. This was negotiated ten years later.

The 1967 War did not result in any peace treaties. Instead, it exacer-

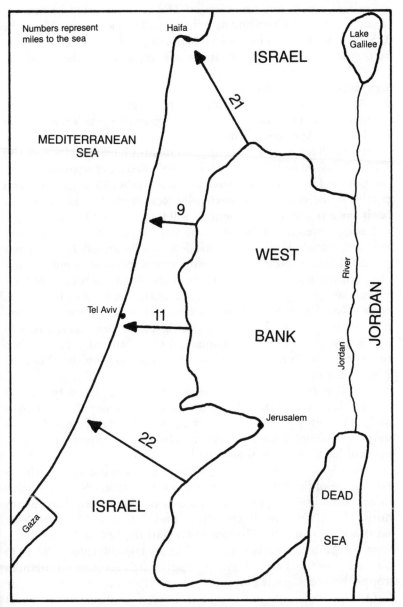

Numbers represent miles to the sea

Haifa

ISRAEL

Lake Galilee

21

MEDITERRANEAN SEA

9

WEST

Jordan River

JORDAN

Tel Aviv

11

BANK

Jerusalem

22

ISRAEL

DEAD

Gaza

SEA

MAP 9: STRATEGIC DEPTH OF ISRAEL

bated the Cold War between the superpowers. The Soviet Union severed diplomatic relations with Israel and began to arm the Arab states and supply military advisers. The U.S. deepened its commitment to Israel by increasing its military and economic aid. Thus, the U.S. enabled Israel to fortify its defenses against its hostile neighbors so that today it is the fourth largest military power in the world.

Egyptian Preparations for War

An Arab Summit was held three months after the '67 War. It was decided not to negotiate with Israel or recognize it as a state. There would be no Arab peace with Israel.

Despite these Arab statements, two months later **the UN Security Council passed Resolution 242. It established a negotiation process for the conflict between Israel and the Arabs. Most analysts and parties to the conflict still recognize Resolution 242 as the proper basis for a peaceful settlement.** It will be examined in Chapter 9.

Nasser, however, soon began preparing Egyptian forces for another war with Israel. This time the Soviets heavily armed Egypt. Their powerful Sam-2 missiles would add a new dimension to military history. During the next few years, both the Arab states and the new Palestinian guerrilla organizations instigated hundreds of hostile acts against Israel, in constant violation of ceasefire agreements. The least number of casualties inflicted by the Egyptians alone on the Israelis for one month was six, in January, 1970.[6] Naturally, Israel often retaliated. The Israelis call the period from 1967 through 1970 the War of Attrition.

In mid-1970 another ceasefire was reached between Israel and Egypt. Two months later, Egyptian president Nasser died unexpectedly. The new Egyptian president, Anwar el Sadat, expelled Soviet military advisors from Egypt in mid-1972. Yet Egypt continued to prepare for another showdown with Israel.

Egypt, however, did not prove to be Israel's worst enemy; with the emergence of the Palestine Liberation Organization (PLO), the Palestinians would be. Displaced Palestinians had fled from their homes during Israel's War of Independence and settled mostly in the West Bank and Jordan. King Hussein offered for the PLO to be headquartered in Amman, Jordan. It was. But shortly thereafter, the PLO accused Hussein of violating their unpublished agreement. Jordanian troops then massacred groups of *fedayeen* (Palestinian soldiers). The PLO responded with an unsuccessful assassination attempt against Hussein. Then they threatened his overthrow. Syrian forces invaded Jordan to assist the PLO. But they pulled back when Israel and the

U.S. threatened to intervene on Jordan's behalf. Hussein then drove the PLO out of Jordan in 1971.

The PLO promptly and uninvitedly established itself in southern Lebanon. Many Palestinian refugees had retreated there as well. The PLO entry into Lebanon would cause that country much upheaval.

Yom Kippur War (October 1973)

In 1973 Egyptian president Sadat convinced Syrian president Assad to join in an assault on Israel. Both nations were heavily equipped by the Soviets, with missiles lining their borders with Israel. The Egyptians had a massive army of over 800,000 troops.

The Egyptians and Syrians deceived Israeli authorities into thinking that their military training exercises conducted along shared borders were not a prelude to war. Israeli prime minister Golda Meir and defense minister Moshe Dayan were later criticized for not taking these military buildups seriously. Indeed, on the eve of October 6th, 1973, unlike in the Six-Day War, the Arab states struck first.

Egyptians refer to this action as the "October War;" the Jews call it the "Yom Kippur War." October 6th, 1973, was a Sabbath for religious Jews, a day of rest. Throughout Israel's ancient history, its enemies had often attacked on a Sabbath. But this day was also Yom Kippur, Israel's holiest day of the year, when Jews must also fast. The Arabs chose this day for two reasons: the Israelis would be most vulnerable on Yom Kippur, and the Gulf of Suez would be at its lowest tide in a year.

Egyptian forces crossed the Suez Canal by quickly placing pontoon bridges. They achieved early successes against the undermanned Israeli forces and advanced into the Sinai Desert. President Sadat largely directed Egypt's military offensive. Just the opposite of Nasser in the previous war, Sadat overruled the advice of his commander-in-chief and conducted a massive tank war in the Sinai. It proved a fatal mistake. Fighting between Israel and Egypt was fierce. After Israeli reserves arrived, the Jews won a decisive tank battle.

Another tank battle raged between Israel and Syria in the Golan Heights. Expelling Iraqi reinforcements, the Israelis emerged victorious and advanced farther northward into Syrian territory. They took Mount Hermon and were within striking distance of Syria's capital, Damascus, when the first ceasefire was effected, with Syria. Israel later returned a small section of the Golan Heights to Syria. Later, the first Jewish settlements in the occupied territories were located in the Golan Heights.

Israel's air force finally knocked out Egypt's Sam-2 missiles, enabling its ground forces to make a daring advance across the Suez Canal. The Israelis eventually encircled most of the Egyptian army. They could have completely destroyed it and threatened Egypt's capital, Cairo, but the U.S. and others pressured Israel to halt.

The Americans and Soviets intervened to achieve a second ceasefire, with Egypt, which ended the war. The 1967 War had lasted only six days; this one went eighteen days. Israel had achieved another victory over its aggressive neighbors. But it was not as decisive as before, Israel having suffered much heavier losses.

After losing, Sadat decided war was not the answer. He discontinued his belligerent tactics toward Israel and adopted a policy of diplomacy. Sadat turned statesman, first courting the favor of the U.S. in seeking to bring pressure on Israel to achieve a peace treaty. An Egypt-Israel Peace Treaty was eventually signed in 1979.

Oil Embargo
Some other Arab states decided they would try a little pressure of their own against Israel. They had no idea of what was to unfold.

During the Yom Kippur War, on October 17th, the Arab oil-producing states of the Organization of Petroleum Exporting Countries (OPEC) agreed to curtail exports to oil-importing nations that supported Israel. This 1973 oil embargo caused automobile gasoline prices in the U.S. to skyrocket and created long waiting lines at the gas pump. Americans forget that the Arabs did this solely in an attempt to cause the industrial nations to pressure Israel to relinquish the occupied territories and return to pre-1967 borders. An unexpected bonanza resulted for OPEC members, especially the Persian Gulf states. Demand so sharply outweighed supply that the price of a barrel of crude oil quadrupled in the next six months. This single act led to the largest transfer of wealth between nations in history. A small portion of these profits was passed on to the PLO.

First Invasion of Lebanon (1978)
After settling in southern Lebanon in 1971, the PLO began full-scale base camp operations. Sometimes the PLO located their bases within, or near, Palestinian refugee camps in hopes of avoiding retaliatory bombing raids by Israel. From these armed bases near the Lebanon-Israel border, Palestinian guerrillas launched missiles into the Galilee.

After a few years in southern Lebanon, the Palestinians had developed a thorough governmental infrastructure, resulting in a distinct national entity. They established schools, hospitals, trade unions, a military and a parliament. Former U.S. president Jimmy Carter called it a "state within a state."[7] Yet Israeli leaders have continually denied that the Palestinians have ever achieved anything resembling a national entity.

Due to its militant posture, the PLO was never welcomed in Lebanon. Without foreign military aid, the Lebanese government remained impotent to expel the PLO from southern Lebanon. The Lebanese suffered much misery due to the presence of the PLO and the Israeli retaliatory strikes against the PLO.

The modern history of Lebanon is indeed a tragic story. Lebanon has a government fractured by various religious factions, mainly Druze, Sunni and Shiite Moslems and Greek Orthodox, Catholic and Marionite Christians. For over 100 years Lebanon has been ruled by a governor (by agreement, a member of the Christian Marionite party) and a fifteen-man council (formerly twelve). Members of the council represent the various Lebanese religious parties.

Lebanon's mountainous terrain isolates its communities, making them difficult to administer. Lebanon's governor has always lacked an adequate military force with which to control the country. Lebanon's religious groups therefore have developed their own militias for protection.

The PLO presence in southern Lebanon further aggravated the constant friction between the ruling Christian Marionites and various Moslem groups. Civil war broke out in Lebanon in 1975 and continues to the present. The first eighteen months alone, 60,000 people were killed.[8] The war's fifteen-year death toll is believed to exceed 150,000.

At first there was internal warring among the PLO guerrilla organizations. Later, the PLO fought many battles against militias representing Shiite residents in southern Lebanon. These battles, as well as skirmishes with the government's South Lebanese Army (SLA), continued to inflict far more damage and casualties to the PLO than did any Israeli assaults.

During Israel's wars with its Arab neighbors, Lebanon had remained on the sidelines. In 1978 the Marionite Christians requested Israel's help in routing the PLO from Lebanon. Israeli forces invaded southern Lebanon, driving fifteen miles to the Litani River.

The U.S. had sold armaments to Israel under agreement that they be used only for defensive purposes. U.S. President Carter now threatened to condemn publicly Israel's presence in Lebanon and cut off U.S. military aid to Israel.

Israeli forces quickly withdrew and were replaced by the smaller UN Interim Forces in Lebanon (UNIFIL). This peacekeeping force of 5,500 troops was stationed in a "security zone" in southern Lebanon.

Annexations and Cession

Although international law forbids annexation of territory by a conqueror, on July 30, 1980, the Knesset annexed East Jerusalem. The whole city was declared "the eternal and indivisible" capital of the State of Israel. Israeli governmental departments were moved from Tel Aviv to Jerusalem. Most nations still show their disapproval of this action by continuing to keep their diplomatic offices and embassies in Tel Aviv.

The next year Israel annexed the Syrian Golan Heights. About 13,000 Druze and 5,000 Jewish settlers were living there in 1988.

In April, 1982, in accordance with the time schedule of the Camp David Accords, Israel relinquished the Sinai Peninsula to Egypt after removing its military forces and dismantling its Jewish settlements. At peace with Egypt, Israel turned its attention again to its most troubled frontier—the border with Lebanon.

Second Invasion of Lebanon (1982)

In June, 1982, Israel invaded Lebanon a second time, this time with a massive force. Israeli leaders originally announced their purpose for the invasion was to punish the PLO for shooting its ambassador in London. Did a single assassination warrant a full-scale invasion? The PLO had denied responsibility. The British apprehended two suspects and Prime Minister Margaret Thatcher announced that the PLO had nothing to do with the assassination. Later, a non-Palestinian terrorist group admitted to the shooting.

To satisfy a restriction agreed upon with U.S. President Reagan, Israel announced that it would remove Palestinian guerrillas from a twenty-five mile strip in south Lebanon in order to prevent future attacks. Their overt purpose was to destroy the PLO base camps from which rockets were sometimes launched into nearby Galilee. To further justify its invasion, the Israeli military code-named it "Operation Peace for Galilee." Yet a cease-fire arrangement had been in effect, and no rockets had been fired into Galilee for ten months.

Israeli leaders clearly had at least three reasons for their 1982 invasion of Lebanon: (1) to put a complete end to the PLO by destroying its highly developed infrastructure in southern Lebanon, (2) to force the Syrian military out of Lebanon and (3) to obtain a peace treaty with the Lebanese government. Prime Minister Begin had said on several prior occasions that this was the time to "get rid of the

PLO once and for all."[9] Sure enough, a thorough destruction of PLO buildings, including those in refugee camps, was carried out with the use of bulldozers.

Most of the Palestinian commandos fled northward to Beirut, the capital of Lebanon. Against President Reagan's restriction, the Israelis moved farther north, 60 miles inside Lebanon, and encircled West Beirut. There, the PLO *fedayeen* had taken up sanctuary. The Israelis kept up a steady bombardment of PLO positions with heavy artillery and aerial bombing. The Lebanese government's Phalangist forces controlled East Beirut.

This war in Lebanon lasted almost three months. West Beirut was under siege for two months. Its half a million people suffered miserably, being cut off from water, food and electricity. Estimates of Palestinian and Lebanese casualties went as high as 40,000 to 100,000.[10]

Evacuation of the PLO

Israel had the PLO trapped, and its annihilation appeared inevitable. But Yasser Arafat and his PLO are like cats with nine lives. The UN arranged a ceasefire, which provided for the evacuation of the PLO guerrillas upon their agreement that they would not reestablish in Lebanon. Right away, Israel broke the agreement, firing upon the PLO as they evacuated.

When the PLO forces evacuated Beirut, Israel deemed its second invasion a success. Meanwhile, Arafat and his approximately 11,000 soldiers were transported by ship to Greece, where they were hailed as heroes by the populace and dignitaries. From there they sailed south through Egypt's Suez Canal. For security reasons, they scattered into various Arab states, particularly Sudan and Yemen.

Arafat soon accepted an invitation by the Tunisian government to locate the PLO in Tunis, on the central Mediterranean coast in North Africa.

The next year Arafat tried to establish a PLO base in the northern Lebanese port city of Tripoli. This was an infraction of the earlier ceasefire agreement. After waging a six-week battle with Syrian-backed PLO dissident forces, Arafat and his 4,000 *fedayeen* were ousted.

Massacres at Sabra and Shatila

Two weeks after the PLO evacuation in 1982, Lebanon's president-elect Bashir Gemayel was assassinated. Israeli forces entered West Beirut to quell a possible uprising. The Israelis claimed that two Palestinian refugee camps there—Sabra and Shatila—still harbored an estimated 2,000-3,000 Palestinian guerrillas. Israel's right-wing minister of defense, Ariel Sharon,[11] permitted Lebanese Phalangist troops to enter these camps to clear out suspects. The Phalangist troops, however, had been Gemayel's personal militia. Entering the camps only two days after their leader's assassination, they clearly sought revenge against the Palestinians, whom they held responsible. **For the next 42 hours, the Phalangists were allowed a free hand to massacre hundreds of men, women and children. An Israeli investigation estimated 700-800 killed.** The Lebanese government buried 762 bodies. Both they and the Red Cross estimated another 1,200 were buried privately by relatives.

The whole world, including most of Israel, was outraged. Under popular pressure, Prime Minister Begin allowed a blue ribbon national board to be selected to investigate the matter. After 12,000 pages of investigation and testimony, **the Kahan Commission of Inquiry determined that Israeli forces had complete control of the camps from outside, that they approved of the Phalangists' entry and provided them with "vital assistance and logistical support."**[12] Defense Minister Sharon had ignored deputy Prime Minister David Levy's warning against allowing the Phalangists to enter the camps. The Commission therefore charged Sharon with "neglect of duty" and recommended his resignation or dismissal. He was forced to resign. Since Begin knew of the operation about fourteen hours after it began but did nothing to stop it, he was held indirectly responsible and charged with "indifference." Prime Minister Begin resigned later that year, supposedly for health reasons.

Withdrawal from Lebanon

Israel partially withdrew from Lebanon in three stages. In September, 1983, Israeli forces drew back from around West Beirut to southern Lebanon. This time Israel wanted to maintain a large buffer zone between itself and Lebanon. But in early 1985, Israel succumbed to U.S. insistence and moved its troops farther south. Since then, Israel has controlled a 6-10-mile self-declared buffer zone just inside Lebanon.

Syria, on the other hand, maintained its military presence in northern Lebanon. Under agreement with the Arab League, approximately 25,000 Syrian troops have remained in Lebanon as a peacekeeping force.

Since 1982 the Israelis have carried out scores of bombing raids against Palestinians still ensconced in southern Lebanon. Hundreds of Palestinian guerrillas have been killed, far outnumbering those Jews killed by the Palestinians, as is always the case.

The Palestinians are not wanted in the politically-fragmented and war-torn country of Lebanon. While a contributing factor, they have not been the main cause of Lebanon's turmoil.

Israel's 1982 invasion of Lebanon brought about some significant changes in the Palestinian-Israeli conflict:

1. For the first time, an Israeli military incursion into a foreign country was opposed by a majority of Israeli Jews.

2. It spurred the growth of Jewish peace organizations which support human rights for the Palestinians, including their demand for sovereign statehood in Palestine.

3. It was the first war Israel fought against the Palestinians alone, not involving any Arab states. This gave further worldwide recognition to the PLO.

4. It proved most hurtful to Israel's cause by increasing worldwide sympathy for the Palestinians.

Intifada

Back on Israel's homefront, on December 8, 1987, the worst Palestinian uprising in Israel's twenty-year occupation erupted in the Gaza Strip and the West Bank. Called *intifada* in Arabic, it means "the shaking off." *Intifada* has been a grass roots resistance movement consisting mostly of unarmed Palestinian youths throwing rocks and bottle bombs at Israeli police and soldiers, setting up road blocks and burning piles of tires to hinder Israeli vehicles from entering Arab villages. Israeli authorities do not permit Arabs living in either Israel or the occupied territories to own guns. In contrast, Jewish settlers in the West Bank are usually well armed.

The Israelis have imposed curfews in various cities and refugee camps in the territories, sometimes throughout the entire Gaza Strip. Police and soldiers usually use tear gas and plastic or rubber bullets on agitators. Official policy has been to inflict injury, including breaking bones with bats, rather than shooting to kill. Thousands of Palestinians have been severely beaten and jailed; their homes are often bulldozed. Thousands more have been imprisoned without formal charges. Some have been deported.

At the end of 1989, almost 25 months after *intifada* began, 640 Palestinians had been killed, along with 43 Israelis.

Israel's Survival Worries

Israeli authorities have always worried about Palestinian Arab birth rates. Palestinian women in Israel and the occupied territories have over twice as many children as Israeli Jewish women. In the past, many experts have predicted that at the present rate of birth, Palestinians will outnumber Jews in Israel within twenty years.

Before recent changes in the USSR, Israeli officials were also concerned over an exodus of Jews from Israel. For the first time, Jewish emigration exceeded immigration in 1989. Several factors contributed to this: high inflation, rising taxes and a rising cost of living. Inflation sometimes exceeds 100% annually. Then there is the constant tension of military preparedness, which requires all males to serve three years in the military. Now, the anticipated Russian Jewish emigres are expected to provide a considerable net increase in Jewish population for Israel over the next five years.

One factor that could inhibit Jewish immigration would be if the religious parties in Israel succeeded in getting the Law of Return changed. They want to redefine "Who is a Jew." Non-Orthodox Jews, who comprise the large majority of religious Jews outside Israel, could no longer emigrate to Israel without first being converted by an Orthodox rabbi. Such a change would not affect so many potential immigrants to Israel, but the psychological effect on world Jewry could be devastating, causing a wide split.

Furthermore, continued Israeli intransigence towards the Palestinians threatens to split the Jewish community. Non-Israeli Jews generally take a more conciliatory stance regarding the Palestinian problem. Many fear that Israel's hard-line tactics toward Palestinians could ignite a renewed anti-Semitism throughout the world.

In spite of the need to maintain a Jewish majority, right-wing Israelis want to annex at least the West Bank. Annexation of the West Bank could result in mass expulsion of Palestinians. This is the position advocated by Gush Emunim, a Jewish fundamentalist group very active in settling Jews in the West Bank. Israeli moderates fear this could prove the demise of the State of Israel. Prime Minister Shamir has disavowed annexation of the West Bank.

The Israelis remain divided on what to do with the occupied territories. There has even been talk in the Knesset of the possibility of civil war between the government and Jewish West Bank settlers. Besides wanting annexation, they demand that the government exercise stronger measures to put down the *Intifada*. On the other hand, the Orthodox Hasidic Jews now call for two separate states in Palestine.

In early 1990 Shamir announced that most of the anticipated half a million Russian Jewish emigres would be settled in the West Bank and East Jerusalem. The PLO declared that this would be an "act of war" and threatened to withdraw its disavowal of terrorism. Dispute

over this question caused the dissolution of Shamir's coalition government in March, 1990.

Israel as Goliath?
**During the '80s, world opinion shifted significantly to favor the
Palestinians over the Israelis. This was mostly due to Israel's 1982
invasion of Lebanon, the massacres at the two refugee camps and
Israel's handling of the Palestinian uprising in the occupied territories.** For the first time in Israel's modern history, most of the
world views the Jewish state as the Goliath in the ongoing Israeli-Palestinian struggle.

Mathematical genius Albert Einstein remarked nearly a generation
ago, "Peace in Palestine cannot be achieved by force but only through
understanding." In 1988, eleven of Israel's senior generals, constitut-
ing a considerable portion of its military establishment, conceded that
no solution will be achieved by police or military means.[13] Many
religious leaders, Jewish, Christian and Muslim, agree, adding that
peace can only be achieved through dialogue and the building of trust.

Without question, the two greatest problems facing Israel, and growing every day, are what to do with the Palestinians and the occupied
territories.

Chapter 5

THE PALESTINIANS

*"However you want people to treat you, so treat them,
for this is the Law and the Prophets"* (Mt 7.12).

Who Are the Palestinians?

When the Zionists came to Palestine in the late 19th century, they found Arabs. (See Appendix B: Who Are the Arabs?) Many farmed the agriculturally-rich Galilee. Most of these were *fellaheen*, Arab tenant farmers who leased their farmland from wealthy Arab land owners living in Lebanon. However, most Arabs throughout Palestine were poor, transient nomads called Bedouins.

Ironically, the Hebrew patriarchs themselves had been transient semi-nomads. Abraham, Isaac and Jacob were sheepherders living in tents, constantly moving throughout the land of Canaan and the Negev to provide their livestock with forage and water.

Early Zionists generally ignored Arabs living in Palestine or, because of their manner of life, dismissed them as uncivilized. Not until the Tenth Zionist Congress in 1911 did the Zionists officially address the Arab Palestinian problem.[1] As late as WWI, Arabs still outnumbered Jews 10 to 1 in Mandate Palestine. It will be recalled that the Balfour Declaration (1917) identified the indigenous population of Palestine only as "non-Jews," a description later adopted by the Israeli government, which embittered the Palestinians.

The Palestinian National Charter (1964) defines Palestinians as "those Arab nationals who, until 1947, normally resided in Palestine, regardless of whether they were evicted from it or have stayed there. Anyone born, after that date, of a Palestinian father—whether inside Palestine or outside it—is also a Palestinian." (The term "Arab national" was used to identify with the Arab dream for a single, united

Arab Nation and thereby further win Arab support to regain the land of Palestine.) Interestingly, the Palestinians define their people as those born of a Palestinian *father*, whereas religious Israeli Jews define a Jew as anyone born of a Jewish *mother*. As defined by both the Palestinian National Charter and the United Nations' Relief and Works Agency (UNRWA), **the designation "Palestinian" is strictly a geographic, not an ethnic, term. It was the same with the ancient Philistines**, from whom the Palestinians derive their name.

Palestinian Ancestry
The principal disagreement between Palestinians and Jews is over the right to ownership of the land of Palestine. Some Palestinian families had owned land in Palestinian for many generations, even centuries. But most Palestinians lost their land when they fled from the path of war in 1947-48 and 1967 and were not allowed back. Both the Israeli government and individual Jews confiscated these Palestinian lands and houses.

On the other hand, Israeli Jews claim a prior right to the land, to which they think they have a weightier claim. Their forefathers first possessed the land nearly 3,500 years ago, occupying it for 1,500 years until expelled by the Romans in A.D. 135. Responding to this Jewish historical argument would require the Palestinians to establish an ancestral link with those who lived in Palestine before the arrival of the Jews.

Palestinian ancestry is generally regarded as an irrelevant issue, since the Arabs' invasion of Palestine dates back only to the 7th century A.D. In contrast, the Jews first possessed Palestine about 2,000 years earlier. But does Palestinian ancestry only trace back to the Arab invasion?

Two things have confused the issue of Palestinian ancestry. First, the word "Arab" is not properly an ethnic term but a cultural and linguistic one. Second, the popular notion that Ishmael is the father of the Arabs is without historical foundation. (See Appendix B: Who are the Arabs?)

The Palestinians did not descend only from the Arabians (original inhabitants of the Arabian Peninsula.) Instead, they are an amalgamation of many groups. It is true that the Arabian conquest of Palestine later resulted in the intermarriage of the ruling class with the indigenous population. But the ruling class became subsumed by the larger indigenous population, rather than the reverse. Arabian stock likely constituted only a small portion of Palestinian ancestry, as it did of all the Arab countries outside the Arabian Peninsula.

Also to be considered in the population mix of the Palestinians are the Ottoman Turks. They ruled Palestine for 400 years, from A.D. 1517 to 1917. Though most were Muslims, Turks never spoke Arabic nor regarded themselves as Arabs, a distinction still observed today.

Going back in time, the Romans possessed Palestine for a long time before the Muslim conquest. Following the last wave of the Jewish Diaspora—brought on by the Second Jewish Revolt of A.D. 132-135—the Romans colonized Palestine with Romans, Syrians and some Arabians. Already living in the area were Samaritans, Idumaeans (former Edomites) of the Negev, Aramaic-speaking Nabataeans of present southern Jordan, remnants of both the Phoenicians and Philistines, and Greeks, as well as some Egyptians.

Continuing farther back in history, during the Hellenistic period, Greeks settled along the coastland of Phoenicia and Palestine. Some inevitably intermarried with the local population.

Farther back in antiquity, the Egyptians often controlled the coastal plain of Philistia. Because of the close proximity of today's Gaza Strip to Egypt, many Palestinians presently living in the Gaza Strip are of Egyptian descent.

Finally, it will be recalled that some Canaanites survived the Israelites' conquest to remain their slaves. They contributed somewhat to the population mix in Palestine.

Therefore, **the early ancestors of some of today's Palestinians are no doubt the Canaanites, Philistines, Phoenicians, Egyptians, Idumaeans, Nabataeans and Samaritans.** In later periods, their intermarriage with conquering peoples, such as Greeks, Romans, Arabians and Turks, merely added to the genetic mix in Palestine.

It must be concluded that at least **some** Palestinian ancestors lived in Palestine before the Israelites possessed that land. This ancestry provides some justifiable basis for a Palestinian claim to an earlier historical connection to the land of Palestine than that of the Jews. Economist Richard Ward observes that some "Arabs of Palestine claim, therefore, and with some historical justification, that they are the descendants of the original inhabitants of Palestine."[2] PLO representative Abdallah Frangi concurs, specifically citing the Philistines and Canaanites as the original ancestors of the Palestinians.[3] Does such a historical connection strengthen the Palestinians' right to land in Palestine?

Palestinians' Rejection of the UN Partition Plan
Many Israeli Jews have argued that the Palestinians are not entitled to a sovereign state in Palestine because they forfeited that opportu-

nity given them in 1948 by their rejection of the UN Partition Plan.
However, in effect, the Zionists rejected it as well. Not content to wait
for the plan's implementation two months later, the Jews proclaimed
Israel's statehood, which they knew would inevitably result in war.

The Arab Palestinians had some good reasons for rejecting the UN
Partition Plan.

The plan provided that 56% of the land of Palestine would go to
the Jews. Yet Jews comprised only 30% of the population and possessed less than 8% of the land. However, this latter figure was due
partially to British restrictions on the Jews' land acquisitions.

In addition, Arabs were convinced that the Jews would eventually
become discontent at being confined to their territory designated
under the UN Partition Plan. They feared the Jews would seize more
land in order to realize the Zionist proposal offered in 1919, which
included southern Lebanon and western Jordan.

Arabs also feared the favor Western powers bestowed upon the Jews.
There were several reasons for this. Even though Arabs far outnumbered Jews in global population, more Jews lived in western nations,
especially in the U.S., than did Arabs. Arab culture was very different
from that of westerners. Jews had a religious connection to the so-
called "Christian" nations that Arabs, who were mostly Muslim, did
not have.

Finally, the Jews' worldwide economic and political resources
dwarfed those of the Palestinians, causing them to fear being engulfed.

First Dispossession (1948)
The Arab Palestinians were first expelled from their land during
Israel's War of Independence in 1948-1949. Israel insists that the
dispossessed Palestinians were invited and permitted to return to
their homes. However, with only a few exceptions, this privilege ended
when the last armistice agreement was signed on July 20, 1949.

In 1950 Israel's parliament, the Knesset, passed the "Law of Return." It encouraged foreign-born Jewish citizens of other countries
to immigrate to Israel and obtain citizenship there. In contrast, the
dispossessed Palestinian Arabs, most of whom were born in Palestine,
were thereafter denied the same right of return.

Palestinians who had refused to return in 1949 had their reasons.
Many were bitter over the Jews' victory and were unwilling to live
under their domination. Others feared that if they returned, as the
minority they would not receive their full rights and would be mis-
treated by both the Jewish government and the populace. A large
number had nothing left to return to. At the outbreak of Israel's War

of Independence, there were about 475 Palestinian cities, towns and villages in the territory which Israel soon seized. We have already seen that afterwards, approximately 385 of these had disappeared, razed by bulldozers.

Jews still live in vacated Palestinian homes or on property confiscated by the Israeli government. Economist Don Peretz alleges that the refugees' abandonment of their property "was one of the greatest contributions toward making Israel a viable state." He reports that, of the 370 new Jewish settlements established by 1953, "350 were absentee property, and nearly a third of the new immigrants (250,000) settled in urban areas abandoned by the Arabs."[4] Most were cleared and rebuilt.

UN Resolution 194

On December 11, 1948, the UN General Assembly passed Resolution 194 concerning the dispossessed Palestinians:

> Refugees wishing to return to their homes and live in peace with their neighbors should be permitted to do so at the earliest practicable date, and that compensation should be paid for the property of those choosing not to return and for loss or damage to property which, under principles of international law or equity, should be made good by the government or authorities responsible.

Over 40 years later, Israel still refuses to abide by Resolution 194. The dispossessed Palestinians have not been compensated for their financial losses. The world has deplored this failure of Israel, yet nothing has been done about it. The Israelis have maintained that they will compensate the dispossessed Palestinians when one condition is met: when the approximately 600,000 Jews, who fled from Arab countries to Israel between 1948 and 1972, are compensated as well. These Jews claimed they were persecuted in their Arab home countries and driven out. Many no doubt were ill-treated on account of Israeli statehood and its accompanying dispossession of the Palestinians; for others, persecution was not a significant factor. They simply preferred the good life in Israel, where the standard of living was steadily improving. Whatever the Jews' reasons, the Palestinians are not responsible for actions of Arab states.

If the Palestinian-Israeli conflict is ever resolved, it seems that UN Resolution 194 will have to be implemented. A tribunal might be established, before which the Palestinians would present and prove their claims. There has been little, or no, attempt to estimate the extent of the loss of property by the dispossessed Palestinians. To their credit, however, the Israelis have kept thorough records of their confiscation of Arab property.

Demographics in Palestine

Just prior to Israel's War of Independence in 1948, approximately 930,000 Palestinians lived in what was to become Israeli territory. Palestinian demographics expert Janet Abu-Lughod estimates that during the 1948 war period, from April to December, 770,000-780,000 Palestinians fled from their homes to other Arab territory.[5] This left 160,000 Palestinians living in Israel.[6]

Jews did not live in the occupied territories until they seized them in 1967. From then until 1982, 120 Jewish settlements were established in the West Bank, the Gaza Strip and the Golan Heights. These now contain approximately 82,000 Jewish settlers. Nearly all are in the West Bank. Due to pressure from the U.S. government, no new Jewish settlements have been built in the occupied territories since 1982. However, at the close of 1988 the Israeli government defied the U.S. administration by announcing plans to construct eight new settlements in the territories, plans they have not yet implemented.

It will be seen from the figures below that a very small percentage of the population in the Gaza Strip is Jewish—0.5%. Population-wise, it makes no sense for Israel to keep the overcrowded Gaza Strip. On the other hand, Jews now comprise 8.5% of West Bank residents.

Worldwide Distribution of Palestinians in 1980[7]

Country	Palestinians	Percentage
(Mandate) Palestine	1,774,000	43%
Lebanon	330,000	8%
Jordan	1,035,000	25%
Syria	207,000	5%
Other Arab states	650,000	15%
Rest of world	144,000	4%
Total	4,140,000	100%

Approximate Population Inside Mandate Palestine and Outside

Location	Palestinians	Jews
In Palestine	2,300,000	3,800,000
Outside Palestine	2,650,000	14,200,000
Total	4,950,000	18,000,000

Occupied Territories		
West Bank	850,000	65,000 (8.5%)
Gaza Strip	650,000	2,700 (0.5%)
Golan Heights		5,000
Total	1,500,000	73,700
In Israel	800,000	3,726,300
Outside Israel		14,273,700
Total	4,950,000	18,000,000

Birth Rates per Mother in 1981[8]

Jews	2.7
Christians	2.4
Moslems	5.6
Druze and others	5.6

Demographic statistics worry most Israeli leaders, who are desperate to preserve Israel's Jewish majority. This is because Palestinians who are citizens of Israel (not the occupied territories) can vote, a right they have not exercised much so far. Three factors could cause the predicted decline of the Jewish majority: (1) Israel annexing the remaining occupied territories, (2) Jewish emigration exceeding immigration and (3) Arab birth rates continuing to exceed those of the Jews by 2 to 1. Israeli Jews worry about the wide difference in birth rates. The acclaimed West Bank Data Project forecast in 1985 that the number of Jews and Palestinians living in Israel and the occupied territories would be the same by the year 2010. However, if present reforms continue in the Soviet Union, an estimated half a million Russian Jews are expected to immigrate to Israel over the next five years, which would considerably delay the projected parity of the two populations.

Hard-line Israeli authorities would like to annex the West Bank. To do so would bring the population of Israel much closer to an Arab majority. That is why some advocate severe oppression of the Palestinians to compel them to emigrate.

For the first time in modern Israel's history, Jewish emigration slightly exceeded immigration during the 1980's. Israeli officials constantly attempt to attract Jews from around the world to immigrate to Israel.

Some Israeli military experts are concerned about the demographics problem too. Yehoshafat Harkabi was a former Israeli general who headed Israel's military intelligence and is now a professor at

Hebrew University. Supposing that Israel must some day relinquish the occupied territories, Harkabi observes, "With difficulty a state can defend poor borders, of the kind we will have after withdrawing from the West Bank and Gaza, but it cannot defend itself if half its population is loyal to the enemy."[9]

Refugees

Many of those Arabs who fled from their homes in Israel became refugees and remain so today. The United Nations Relief and Works Agency (UNRWA) was formed in late 1949 solely in response to the Palestinian refugee problem. At first viewed as a temporary agency, its purpose was to assume responsibility for assisting the Palestinian refugees. Refugee camps were set up in neighboring Arab states, usually near the border with Israel. The camps were administered by UNRWA to supply shelter, food, education and medical assistance.

Eventually, refugees had to be registered with UNRWA and issued identification cards in order to receive UNRWA assistance. UNRWA defined a Palestinian refugee as "a person whose normal residence was Palestine for a minimum of two years immediately preceding the outbreak of the conflict in 1948, and who, as a result of this conflict, has lost both his home and means of livelihood." Children born later to refugees were also recognized as such.

The second Palestinian expulsion came in 1967 during the Six-Day War. About 650,000 additional Palestinians fled from their homes in Israel and the occupied territories. Many of them remain in the refugee camps.

There are 60 Palestinian refugee camps scattered throughout the West Bank (20), Gaza Strip (8), Lebanon (12), Jordan (10) and Syria (10). Some are severely overcrowded, such as *Aim al-Hilweh* in Lebanon, with 80,000 refugees.

Population of Palestinian Refugee Camps in 1987[10]

Refugees in UNRWA camps	766,973
Refugees resettled outside camps	1,434,150
Total	2,201,123

Some critics accuse the Palestinian refugees of slothfulness for not leaving the camps and rising above their impoverished conditions. A closer look reveals other Palestinian motivations.

In the early years, refugees stayed in the camps because they thought their situation would soon be resolved. Anticipating a quick return to Palestine, they would not even allow UNRWA officials to improve their dwellings to more permanent, weather-proof shelters. To acquiesce to improvements was viewed as abandoning hope of returning home.[11] Many also feared that in case of a future settlement, such an act would be interpreted as tantamount to relinquishing their claim to compensation for loss of property.

In addition, Palestinian leaders have exhorted the refugees to remain in the camps to arouse international sympathy and help develop the Palestinian nation-in-exile. Consequently, the refugees have largely retained their separateness, without much contact with the outside world or intermarriage outside the camps.

Objections to Palestinian Assimilation in Arab States

Many people have criticized the Arab states for refusing to settle the Palestinians permanently in their countries. However, such criticism ignores fundamental objections by both Palestinians and Arab heads of states.

Arab leaders strongly disagreed with leaders of western nations, especially Britain and the U.S., who believed the Jews had a right to return to their ancestors' homeland. Instead, Arabs perceived the Jews' immigration to Palestine, their acquisition of land and especially Israeli statehood as seizure of the Palestinians' land. They insisted that the land be returned to the Palestinians and that Jewish emigres return to their former countries. Both Arab heads of states and the Palestinians themselves have objected to their being assimilated in Arab countries for the following reasons:

1. **Assimilating Palestinians into Arab states would signal their tacit approval of the Jewish takeover of Palestine and extinguish any hope for the Palestinians' return to their former homeland.**

2. Assimilating Palestinians into Arab states would result in the demise of the refugee camps, the PLO and the development of the Palestinian national identity, without which Palestine will never be liberated.

3. With the exception of Lebanon, Arab countries bordering Israel are economically incapable of sustaining the influx of a Palestinian population because it would significantly increase unemployment. Lebanon is unsuited due to its political instability.

4. Palestinians are often resented in their host countries because they obtain better jobs due to their superior education and skills.

5. Out of self interest, some Arab leaders view the Palestinians as an obstacle impeding Israeli expansion into their own countries. If the Palestinian resistance movement ceased, they reason Israel would likely annex the occupied territories, then pursue further expansion.

Indeed, right-wing Israeli leaders, such as Ariel Sharon, have urged a military invasion and takeover of both Lebanon and Jordan.

Education

The English word "Philistine" connotes "uncultured, unenlightened." The word "Palestinian" derives from "Philistine," but Arab Palestinians are not uncultured and uneducated.

Among the approximately 165 million Arabs in the world today, the Palestinians are the best-educated, most literate, industrious and worker-skilled.[12] A greater percentage of Palestinians attend schools of higher education than do their counterparts in any Arab country, including the very literate Lebanon, or even in most European nations.[13] Palestinian parents are obsessed with educating their children. Forced from their simple agrarian lifestyle, Palestinians discovered that education was the key to their employment in Arab countries. Both UNRWA and the PLO have emphasized the building of a good educational system in the refugee camps and have provided substantial amounts of financial aid for advanced education to Palestinian students.

Before 1967 the West Bank had no colleges or universities. Bir-Zeit College, located eight miles north of Jerusalem, was the first. Three West Bank universities, Bir-Zeit, Bethlehem and Al-Najah, have played a crucial role in the development of the Palestinian national identity. Demonstrations against the Camp David Accords began in 1979 at Bir-Zeit University and swept the West Bank. Palestinian West Bank mayors met there to denounce the Accords. Consequently, Israeli authorities began temporary closings of Bir-Zeit and other schools. Bir-Zeit's president, Hanna Nasser, was charged in 1974 with subversive activity and deported to Jordan.

Israeli officials have permitted the importing of funds for the Palestinians. The PLO was allowed to channel funds to the West Bank university system, but Ariel Sharon convinced Israeli leaders to stop this policy.[14]

Palestinian Right to Self-Determination

Besides a dispute over land, the Palestinian-Israeli conflict concerns autonomy versus self-determination. The Camp David Accords (1978) provided only for Palestinian autonomy, in an association with Jordan. The Palestinians were not consulted in the drafting of these accords. They vehemently reject autonomy and demand self-determination.

Autonomy and self-determination have both been clearly defined and distinguished in international law. Autonomy signifies limited self-government under the auspices of, or in conjunction with, another state. Self-determination means the sovereign right of a people to determine their own future.[15] The 1970 UN Declaration on Principles of International Law states:

> All peoples have the right to determine, without external interference, their political status . . . The establishment of a sovereign and independent State, the free association or integration with an independent State or emergence into any other political status freely determined by a people constitute modes of implementing the right of self-determination by that people.[16]

This concept is gaining worldwide acceptance, as attested by recent events in Eastern Europe and the Soviet Union.

Under international law the Palestinians are just as entitled to self-determination in the land of Palestine as are the Jews. This is the position of former U.S. senator and 1972 Democratic candidate for president, George McGovern. McGovern wrote in 1987 that the U.S. has

> supplied Israel with military and economic subsidies on a scale that dwarfs what we are doing for any other country in the world. As a U.S. senator I supported this program.
>
> But I have also come to believe in self-determination, including an independent homeland for the Palestinians. Their claim is every bit as strong on moral, legal and historic grounds as the Israeli claim. . . . We are damaging our influence and respect in the international community and especially in Arab and Palestinian eyes when we not only side so heavily with Israel, but also close our eyes, ears and hearts to the Palestinian cause.[17]

Indeed, the U.S. has for many years furnished Israel with $3 billion per year in aid. The U.S. also gives $2 billion a year to Egypt. Together, that's half of America's total aid to foreign countries.

Struggle for Palestinian National Identity

Westerners do not comprehend the intense spirit of nationalism that pervades throughout the Middle East. At the turn of the 20th century, statehood did not exist there, anywhere. This nationalistic passion was fostered by centuries of suppression by the Ottoman Empire and many decades of western colonialism. The British restricted many Arabs from controlling their own affairs. Scholar Samuel

F. Welds, Jr. surmised concerning the Middle East, "You really have a situation where the ability to control the destiny of one's country is among the highest goals to be achieved."[18] In 1982 a poll was taken in the occupied territories. The question was asked, "Are you in favor of an independent Palestinian state?" Among Palestinians, 98.2% answered "Yes."[19]

U.S. citizens need only reflect on the history of the American colonies to understand the Palestinians' struggle. The colonists opposed British subjugation and fought the American Revolution to gain freedom and self-determination.

Dispossessed Palestinians have been struggling from outside Palestine to establish a national identity. They have sought to achieve enough international recognition that Israel would be pressured into relinquishing a portion of Palestine wherein to establish the Palestinian state. So far, every Israeli prime minister, with the exception of Shimon Peres of the moderate Labor Party, has denied the existence of a Palestinian national identity. Israeli prime minister Golda Meir asserted in 1969, "It is not as though there was a people in Palestine considering itself as a Palestinian people, and we came and threw them out and took their country away from them. They do not exist." This bold denial shocked many observers and further embittered the Palestinians.

Some Jews argue that there was no Palestinian nationalism prior to Israel's War of Independence. But neither was there Israeli nationalism *per se*. Other Israelis contend that when the Palestinians rejected the UN Partition Plan of 1947, they relinquished their right to achieve a national identity and homeland in Palestine. What if the Palestinians were to say that they now accept the UN Partition Plan? "A people without a land do not constitute a nation," some argue. Prior to May 14, 1948, the Jews themselves had not constituted a national entity for over 1,800 years.

Before Israel became a state, guerrilla leader Menachem Begin asserted a Zionist national entity by declaring on behalf of fighting Jews in Palestine, "We fight, therefore we are."[20] Yasser Arafat could certainly say the same thing. Regardless of whether or not there was a Palestinian national identity years ago, the nations unanimously agree that there is one now. Actually, **even without residing in Palestine, the PLO now has a far more highly developed governmental infrastructure than the Zionists had prior to Israeli statehood.**

Interestingly, Israeli Jews regard all Jews in the world as one with them. Yet most Jews born in Gentile lands have citizenship there and speak a Gentile language. In contrast, Israeli Jews refuse to recognize

the Arab Palestinians as one people with a national identity, despite
the facts that all Palestinians (except children born later to dispossessed Palestinians) were born in the same country (Palestine) and speak
the same language (Arabic)!

Wilbur Eveland reminds the Jews, "More than any other people in
the world, the Jews should know that even centuries of oppression
and dispersion cannot destroy the determination of the Palestinians
to acquire a homeland and a national identity."[21]

Palestinian and Zionist Similarities

Many analysts have pointed out how Palestinian nationalism has much
in common with Zionism. A look at Israel's Proclamation of Independence (Appendix C) makes an unbiased observer ask, "Why do the
rights claimed by Israeli Jews not apply to the Palestinians as well?"
The language of the document lends itself almost equally to the
Palestinian cause:

Both peoples claim a right to possession of Palestine based on a
historical connection of their ancestors to that land.

Both peoples have suffered rejection in the host countries of their
diaspora, evidencing their need to return to their homeland.

Both peoples assert the same inalienable rights, including self-determination and its ancillary, sovereign statehood, in Palestine.

Both peoples developed a viable national existence despite dispossession and an ensuing diaspora from their homelands.

Both peoples appeal to UN resolutions which recognize their existence as legitimate and support their right to statehood.

In addition to applying equally specifics in Israel's Proclamation
of Independence, both peoples formed armed resistance movements
and resorted to terrorism in an effort to regain Palestine.

**About the only differences in the alleged rights and cir-
cumstances of the two parties is Israel's important support from
the U.S. and the Jewish claim to the land by divine promise.**

Palestinian Grievances

In administering the occupied territories since 1967, Israel has consistently denied the Palestinians many human rights guaranteed by
international law, as contained in the UN General Assembly's Universal Declaration of Human Rights (1980). At the UN Second Seminar
on the Exercise of the Inalienable Rights of the Palestinian People,
evidence was presented to show that "no less than fifteen of the thirty
articles of the declaration refer to rights that at present are denied
to Palestinians living in the West Bank and Gaza Strip."[22]

The UN has not been the only international organization that has repeatedly condemned Israel for its denial of Palestinian rights. So has the respected International Red Cross, as well as Amnesty International and the World Conference of Christians for Palestine. In the wake of Nazi German atrocities during WWII, the Fourth Geneva Convention was formed in 1949 to guarantee human rights. The International Red Cross was to oversee its compliance. One blatant violation by Israel has been its disregard for Article 47 of the Geneva Convention, which forbids the occupier to settle any of its own citizens in the occupied territories.

In 1984 former U.S. president Jimmy Carter, as a private citizen, visited the occupied territories on a fact-finding tour. After interviewing many Palestinians, Carter summarized grievances of Palestinians in the occupied territories:

> The Palestinian leaders emphasized that for a generation their people had been deprived of basic human rights. They could not vote, assemble peacefully, choose their own leaders, travel without restrictions, or own property without fear of its being confiscated by a multitude of inexplicable legal ruses. As a people, they were branded by Israeli officials as terrorists, and even minor demonstrations of their displeasure brought the most severe punishment from the military authorities. They claimed that they were arrested and held without trial for extended periods of time, that some of their people were tortured in attempts to force confessions, that their trials were often held with their accusers acting as judges, that their own lawyers were not permitted to defend them in the Israeli courts, and that any appeals were costly, long delayed, and fruitless.
>
> Their schools and universities were frequently closed down, educators were arrested, bookstores padlocked, library books censored, . . . [23]

Many grievances could be added to this list, such as long detentions, sometimes *incommunicado*, with no formal charges being brought or trial held before release or deportation. Israeli officials enter homes without warrants for arrest and demolish homes with bulldozers as punishment of suspected agitators, even though the homes are often owned by the suspects' parents, who themselves are not suspected as perpetrators. In July, 1989, Israel's Supreme Court finally ruled, in the Palestinians' favor, that it was unlawful for the Israeli government to demolish Palestinian homes before legal appeals were completed.

Deportation of Palestinians

Since 1967, the Israelis have deported over 2,000 Palestinians by releasing them just across the borders with Jordan or Lebanon. Deportation has always been against the will of these states and contrary to international law. These Palestinians were accused of being agitators in the administered territories, though not formally charged or given a court hearing.

A few Israeli politicians and political parties, e.g., former Knesset member, Rabbi Meir Kahane, and the Moledet party, which presently has two seats in the Knesset, have publicly advocated deporting all Palestinians to either Jordan or Lebanon. In the past, Jordan was suggested because, before 1967, the West Bank was part of Jordan. This idea is rejected outright by Jordan's King Hussein for the reasons previously given as Arab objections to Palestinian assimilation. In addition, Hussein now supports only what is advocated by the PLO.

World Support

For over a generation, the UN has devoted more attention to the Palestinian problem than to any other problem in the world. During the '80s the Palestinian-Israeli conflict gained much attention in the world news media. This was partly due to earlier PLO terrorism and Israel's 1982 invasion of Lebanon. Recently, Palestinian turmoil within the occupied territories has heightened world interest.

How have individual nations around the world perceived the Palestinian-Israeli conflict? Europe has been somewhat divided in its response. Britain and France favored the Israelis until the 1967 War. Germany has understandably remained pro-Israel, assuaging its guilt for the Jewish Holocaust. Of all the Europeans, Scandinavians have been the most pro-Israel. Under the influence of the Vatican, Catholic Spain and Italy have remained staunch supporters of the Palestinians. Many individual Europeans, some no doubt motivated by self-interest, sided with the Palestinians following the oil embargo in 1973.

China was the first non-Arab nation to grant the PLO full diplomatic status. The Chinese press has consistently endorsed Palestinian terrorism to regain Palestine and condemned the U.S. for refusing to recognize the PLO.

India has been influenced by its large Muslim population. India and Palestine shared similar status under British control. India has a long history of support for the Palestinians and their cause, dating back to Mahatma Gandhi.

The many UN Resolutions favoring the Palestinians reveal that world support is heavily inclined toward them and their goal of an independent state in Palestine. Former U.S. ambassador to the UN, Andrew Young, once stated at a Security Council debate about Israel and the Palestinians: "I think that no group can consistently defy the universal consensus of the nations of the world and survive, whether it be a nation or a liberation movement."[24]

The U.S. government has sought to avoid the risk of severing relations with Israel. This is an emotionally charged issue in the U.S. As the only democratic nation in the Middle East, Israel has been viewed as a stabilizing influence in the region and a deterrent to Soviet intrusion.

A 1988 Gallup Poll reported that just over one-third of U.S. citizens favored the establishment of an independent Palestinian state within the occupied territories, just under one-third were opposed, and one-third were undecided. Asked whether the Israeli-Palestinian conflict would ever be resolved: 55% thought so, 37% were negative and 8% undecided. Only 18% of Americans foresaw a peaceful resolution within the next five years.[25]

Jimmy Carter believes that the U.S. administration should apply diplomatic pressure on Israel to resolve the Palestinian conflict, even if the U.S. must threaten to reduce financial aid.[26] Indeed, **on March 4, 1990, President Bush announced that the U.S. would reduce its financial aid to Israel if its government resumed settlements in the occupied territories.** This new development in U.S. policy contributed to the collapse of Israel's coalition government two weeks later.

Jews for Palestinians

Some Israeli Jews are genuinely concerned for the Palestinians. Others worry that their government's intransigence threatens the survival of the State of Israel. Jewish peace organizations have emerged in Israel to defend the rights of the Palestinians. The Peace Now organization is presently the most prominent. It condemns Israel's policy of expansionism through Jewish settlements in the occupied territories, yet it rejects the concept of a sovereign Palestinian state in Palestine. These views are similar to the New Zionism Movement and *Os We Shalom*. There are some Jewish peace groups in Israel that do advocate two sovereign states in Palestine, such as Shelli, as well as the *New Outlook* newspaper. The Democratic Front for Peace and Equality goes farther, accepting the PLO as the Palestinians' legitimate representative.

Intifada

As mentioned in Chapter 4, the Palestinian uprising called *intifada* has been going on in the occupied territories for over two years. It

was started by mostly Palestinian youth. Since 1967, over 60% of all
Palestinians living in the occupied territories have been born there.
These young people are even more determined than their parents
to overthrow their occupiers.

The PLO clearly did not start *intifada;* Arafat disclaims control of
it.[27] Israeli authorities nevertheless accuse the PLO of infiltrating the
occupied territories to bolster the uprising. Actually, a clandestine
organization was quickly formed, called the United National Leadership for the Uprising (UNLU), to continue the uprising and link it
with the PLO. UNLU represented the Palestinians' first organized
resistance within the territories.

Pressure has often been exerted among Palestinians themselves to
prolong *intifada.* For example, Palestinian businessmen in the occupied territories called for a shutdown of Arab businesses and a
strike by the Palestinian residents who commuted to work in Israel.
The majority complied at first. Any who refused to cooperate risked
incurring violence from their militant brethren. Of course, those who
did lost income.

At the end of 1989 the respected Tel Aviv University Jaffee Center
for Strategic Studies published its study on *intifada.* It was based on
army figures and conducted by a retired army general and former
military governor of the West Bank in 1976-1978. The study reveals
that after two years of *intifada* the army had demolished 244 Palestinian houses and sealed 116 as punishment. The report disputes army
claims that such reprisals are a deterrent, asserting rather that they
inflame the uprising.[28]

Intifada caused a worldwide public outcry to arise against Israel's
police brutality. At the close of 1989, after nearly twenty-five months
of *intifada,* 640 Palestinians had been killed. An additional 155 Palestinians, suspected as collaborators with Israeli police, were killed by
Palestinians themselves. Palestinians also killed 43 Jews. Over 7,000
Palestinians, many of them teen-age boys, were wounded, some being
maimed for life. In mid-1989 Israeli authorities had over 10,000 Palestinians corralled in barbed wire detention centers under deplorable
conditions.

Summary

Early Zionist leaders in Palestine largely ignored the rights of the
indigenous Arabs. Later, about half of these Palestinians fled from
their homes in 1948 and 1967 to escape the path of war. The State
of Israel refused to allow their return, confiscated their lands and
destroyed most of their homes and villages. Israel has never compen-

sated them for their losses despite UN demands to do so. Many have lived in intolerable conditions in refugee camps. In the occupied territories, Palestinians have suffered many injustices under Israel's military rule. Israel's belligerent administration of the occupied territories has tarnished its image in the world.

Today, the Palestinians are no longer ignored. They have gained much world sympathy for their cause. Assimilation of the Palestinians into Arab states is no longer an alternative. Most world leaders think the Palestinians ought to have the same right of self-determination in their homeland as do other peoples in the world.

The dispossessed Palestinians have created a national identity in exile, determinedly preparing for their expected return to Palestine. To this hope we now turn.

Chapter 6

PALESTINE LIBERATION ORGANIZATION

Palestinian Resistance Movement

The beginning of the Palestinian resistance movement is usually traced to the mid-1930s. Hitler's rise to power in Germany caused a wave of Jewish emigration from Europe to Palestine. This influx eventually sparked the Arab (Palestinian) Revolt in 1936-1939. Just before it broke out in late 1935, one of the first underground Palestinian guerrilla groups was formed by Sharkh Izz al-Din al-Qasim, the recognized founder of the Palestinian resistance movement.

The Arab Higher Committee was created in 1936, with local committees throughout Palestine. Principles of India's Gandhi were adopted in forming a non-violent resistance movement of strikes and boycotts. But friction soon exploded the movement into a full-blown, violent Arab uprising against both the British and the Zionists. Several Palestinian guerrilla groups were then created. When Britain issued its fifth White Paper in 1939, Arab Palestinian violence subsided, and their resistance movement waned until after WWII. Israeli statehood in 1948 injected renewed vigor into the Palestinian resistance movement.

At first, the Palestinians placed their hopes for the "liberation" of Palestine in the UN and in the Arab states. It was believed that the only barrier to liberating Palestine was Arab disunity. The Arab League, formed in 1945 to unify the Arab states, eventually began to nurture the Palestinian resistance movement.

Following the Arabs' loss to Israel in the 1956 War, more Palestinians grew disillusioned with their dependence on the Arab states to liberate

Palestine from the Zionists. Interests of the Arab states sometimes conflicted with those of the Palestinians. In particular, Palestinian youth began to realize that neither the weak Arab states nor the UN would be able to liberate Palestine. They themselves were going to have to do it by further developing the resistance movement, hopefully to be aided by the Arab states. In the mid-'50s, new Palestinian organizations began to emerge for the purpose of regaining Palestine. Still, the resistance movement remained virtually non-violent until the mid-'60s.

Palestine National Council (PNC)

In the 1960s the Palestinian problem was becoming more serious for Arab states bordering Israel because of the Palestinian refugee camps. "The 'Palestine problem' became the major preoccupation of Arab thinkers and politicians."[1]

Consequently, in January, 1964, Egyptian president Nasser convened a special summit of Arab heads of state in Cairo, Egypt. The twofold purpose of this summit was to "embody Palestinian existence" and to plan strategy to prevent Israel's recently-announced plan to divert water from the Jordan River to irrigate western Israel. As it turned out, Israel never diverted the Jordan waters.

Nasser appointed the inflammatory Arab politician, Ahmad Shukairy, to organize a Palestinian assembly. Shukairy invited 422 elitist Palestinians, mostly professionals: politicians, businessmen, doctors and bankers, but no members of the guerrilla organizations. It was Shukairy, not Nasser, who first threatened that the Arabs would "drive Israel into the sea." Both Nasser and Arafat denied ever saying it.

At the first meeting, in 1964, the Palestine National Council (PNC) was formed for the purpose of developing a Palestinian national identity. The PNC continues to serve as a parliament-in-exile by establishing policy for the Palestinians. The Central and Executive Committees of the PNC oversee the economic welfare, education and health of the refugees. These work closely with UNRWA, which helped establish and continues to administer the refugee camps.

The number of members in the PNC has varied from about 100 to 450. Most members live in exile in Arab countries. At least two are U.S. citizens living in the U.S., both professors at prominent universities. Since 1968, about half of the seats of the PNC have been filled by members of the Palestinian guerrilla organizations. A token 50 empty seats symbolize recognition of Palestinians living in the occupied territories. Because its many members are dispersed geographically, the PNC usually meets for only a few days every two or three years. A Central Council of the PNC, consisting of about 80 members, meets more often and acts as an intermediary between the entire PNC membership and the PLO.

Through the years the PNC has achieved a well-balanced membership. It is made up of representatives from trade unions, as well as professional associations of teachers, doctors, engineers, lawyers, artists, writers, journalists, etc. The largest association represented is the Palestinian Teachers' Association. Its 80,000 members (1982) are evidence of the well-known Palestinian commitment to education.

Palestine Liberation Organization (PLO)

In June, 1964, at the first PNC meeting, held in Arab East Jerusalem, the Palestine Liberation Organization (PLO) was formed. Its two primary purposes have been to unite the various Palestinian resistance organizations under one umbrella and to execute policy resolutions passed by the PNC. The PLO is the more visible organ of the Palestinian resistance movement. The PLO conducts day-to-day operations and is responsible to the PNC.

A 15-man executive committee was established for the PLO, over which a chairman has always presided. Nasser appointed Shukairy as the first chairman of the PLO. Some Palestinians objected that Shukairy was not elected and forced his resignation. In 1969 Yasser Arafat was elected president of the PLO executive committee and chosen as its chairman, positions he still holds today.

Though known mostly for its military, the PLO consists of many other departments. Each member of the PLO executive committee is the head of some PLO department. The PLO has established hospitals, medical clinics, orphanages, a martyrs' relief fund, schools, banks, courts, and many other necessary elements of social and governmental infrastructure.

The PNC and PLO claim to operate according to the democratic principles stated in their documents. An experienced American correspondent for the Near East, David Lamb, attended the 16th congress of the PNC, held in 1984 in Algiers. "What struck me about the council," Lamb observed, "was that it was indeed far more democratic than any government in the Arab world." He reported that 400 journalists attended, and that sessions and votes were open to their questioning.[2] Arafat, however, is sometimes accused from within the PLO of unilateral decision-making which reflects the interests of his own organization, al-Fatah, which he continues to lead.[3]

PLO Organizations

The PLO is an umbrella organization consisting of eight Palestinian resistance organizations. All eight have been represented in the PNC, but some have vacated their seats to demonstrate their opposition to Arafat's moderate leadership. PLO organizations are as follows:

1. Al-Fatah (by far the largest)
2. Arab Liberation Front (ALF)
3. Popular Front for the Liberation of Palestine (PFLP)
4. Popular Front for the Liberation of Palestine-General Command (PFLP-GC)
5. Democratic Front for the Liberation of Palestine (DFLP)
6. Al-Saiqa
7. Palestinian Liberation Front (PLF)
8. Popular Palestinian Struggle Front (PPSF)

Some leaders of PLO organizations have been Marxist. For years the Soviets armed a few PLO organizations, but this subsided in the '80s.

Palestinian National Covenant

The Palestinian National Covenant (Charter) was adopted by the PNC in 1966 and amended in 1968. It enumerates Palestinian aspirations and goals. **If the PLO and Israel ever negotiate a two-state settlement, some of these Charter articles will no doubt have to be deleted or altered.** In recent years, Arafat has publicly admitted that some are obsolete. The following Covenant articles are most relevant to the conflict:

Article 2: Mandate Palestine is "an indivisible territorial unit."

Article 3: "The Palestinian Arab people possess the legal right to their homeland and have the right to determine their destiny after achieving the liberation of their country."

Article 6: Jews who immigrated after an undetermined date must return to their former countries. Palestinians have not agreed on the cut-off date. Years suggested have been 1882, 1917 and 1947.

Article 9: "Armed struggle is the only way to liberate Palestine." PLO leaders have since explained repeatedly that this conclusion was only reached after many years of exhausting all peaceful attempts at mediation.

Article 19: "The [UN] partition of Palestine in 1947 and the establishment of the state of Israel are entirely illegal, regardless of the passage of time, because they were contrary to the will of the Palestinian people and to their natural right in their homeland." Some international lawyers maintain that the UN Partition Plan is still applicable.

Article 20: "Claims of historical ties of Jews with Palestine are incompatible with the facts of history and the true conception of what constitutes statehood . . . . Nor do Jews constitute a single nation with an identity of its own; they are citizens of the states to which they belong."

Article 21: "The Arab Palestinian people, . . . reject all solutions which are substitutes for the total liberation of Palestine."

Article 23: "All states [ought] to consider Zionism an illegitimate movement, to outlaw its existence, and to ban its operations."

Article 26: The PLO is the sole representative of the Palestinian revolutionary forces and has responsibility for retrieving the Palestinian homeland.

Article 31: This establishes a national flag, an oath of allegiance and a national anthem. (Israeli law bans the Palestinian flag in both Israel and the occupied territories.)

Financing the Resistance Movement

The Palestinian resistance movement is financed in two chief ways. A 5% income tax from Palestinian residents living in Arab states goes to the National Fund of the PLO. The other means of finance is from oil-rich Arab states contributing large sums to the Arab League's fund for the PLO. Arafat has proved himself an effective politician by successfully soliciting Arab heads of state. For instance, Saudi Arabia contributed about $300 million in just over two decades.

In June, 1988, the Arab League established another fund, this one to assist the Palestinians living in the occupied territories to continue and escalate *intifada*. It has been reported that the wealthy oil states were expected to contribute the bulk of between $350 and $400 million dollars annually to this fund.[4]

Al-Fatah

Yasser Arafat heads the most prominent Palestinian resistance organization. Called *al-fatah*, it means "conquest by *jihad*" (holy war). Formed in 1964 by Arafat and some friends, al-Fatah was first located in Damascus and backed by the Syrian government. Later, Arafat and Syrian President Assad parted company.

At first, al-Fatah and other PLO organizations disagreed on how to liberate Palestine. PLO members have since judged al-Fatah's strategy superior because it insisted on (1) establishing a Palestinian national identity while in exile, (2) maintaining some unity among the various Palestinian organizations and (3) developing an armed resistance movement against Israel.[5]

In the beginning, the Arab world strongly opposed al-Fatah and its policy of armed resistance. Al-Fatah carried out 200 guerrilla operations from 1965 to 1967.[6] Arab states generally condemned these violent acts.

Arab opposition to al-Fatah changed drastically after the 1967 War, when Israel militarily humiliated the surrounding Arab states, seized the occupied territories and further dispossessed the Palestinians. **Arafat remarked, "We have waited twenty years for world conscience to awaken, but it was at the cost of more dispersion."**[7] To the Arab world, al-Fatah's terrorist strategy for liberating Palestine seemed to have been proven correct. Al-Fatah had already established military training camps in some Arab states; recruits now swelled their ranks.

Al-Fatah became the first guerrilla organization to develop its own base camp. It was located in the small Jordanian border town of Karameh, near the Allenby bridge over the Jordan River. Many of the refugees of the Six-Day War fled to nearby Karameh, which became a major refugee camp. Thereafter, Palestinian guerrilla organizations usually established their base of operations within, or near, refugee camps just outside Palestine. The drawback was that whenever Israel later attacked these guerrilla bases, the refugees often suffered casualties as well.

Al-Fatah not only conducted guerrilla operations, but it developed politically as well. It was the first resistance organization to organize the refugees and give them hope. Committees were formed. Medical services, tribunals and schools were soon established. Newspapers and magazines were created to make known the Palestinians' cause.

With Arafat at the helms of both, al-Fatah and the PLO became aligned in 1969. Today, al-Fatah remains numerically the strongest Palestinian organization within the PLO.

Yasser Arafat
Since his 1969 election as PLO chairman, Yasser Arafat has remained the most prominent Palestinian. He has become one of the most famous people in the world.

The PLO claims Arafat was born in 1929 in Jerusalem; most analysts cite Cairo. One of seven children, Arafat and his family lived mostly in Gaza, and for a short time in Cairo. Arafat's father was a wealthy merchant, and his mother was a member of the politically powerful Husseini clan. His older brother joined the Palestinian resistance movement in its infancy, during the 1936 Arab uprising.

While an engineering student at the University of Cairo, Arafat co-founded the non-violent Union of Palestinian Students (1952-1956) and became its first president. It was a forum for Palestinian students to discuss their aspirations for a Palestinian national identity. After graduation, Arafat served in the Egyptian Army during the 1956 Suez War with Israel. He later worked as a civil engineer for the Kuwaiti government. There he formed his own construction company, employing only Palestinians. His purpose was to amass a small fortune with which to help fund a Palestinian resistance movement. At thirty-six years of age, he dissolved his successful company, went to Syria and founded al-Fatah.

Arafat's picture appears frequently in newspapers around the world. The former terrorist chieftain presents no imposing figure. He stands only five foot four, is slightly built and prematurely bald. He sports a scruffy beard. Arafat usually dresses in army fatigues and boots, wears a black-and-white checkered Arabian headdress and carries a pistol in a holster strapped to his side.

In the '80s the PLO chairman spent almost all of his time travelling by private jet on diplomatic missions in the Arab world. He has a fantastic memory, conducts a huge amount of correspondence and requires little sleep, often gotten when flying.

Arafat's personal life is the subject of much speculation. He was active in the underground Muslim Brotherhood movement as a Sunni Muslim but is admittedly not devout. He does, however, renounce worldly pleasures and is very health-conscious. For example, Arafat has never owned a house or many material goods. A lifelong bachelor, he does not drink or smoke, and he rarely sees women socially. He contends, "I am married to the Palestinians."[8] A dedicated soldier and politician, Yasser Arafat is a hero to most Palestinians.

PLO Recognition and a Policy Shift

After the 1973 War, an Arab summit was held in Algiers. Arab heads of states declared their unequivocal support of the PLO as the representative of the Palestinians and demanded Israel's withdrawal from the occupied territories. Arafat was accepted as an equal head of state, signifying recognition of the PNC/PLO as a state-in-exile.

In March, 1974, member nations of the Non-Aligned Movement (third world nations not aligned with either of the two superpowers) met and declared their "full recognition of the Palestine Liberation Organization as the sole representative of the Palestinian people and its struggle." The language "sole representative" thereafter became fixed in describing PLO status.

Under the influence of al-Fatah, the PNC met in June, 1974, and made an important policy change. The Palestinian National Charter had demanded the return of all of Palestine to the Palestinians and rejected the concept of two independent states therein. Without changing the Charter, the PNC adopted a more moderate position. Called the Phased Plan, or "step-by-step" approach, it meant that the PLO would "consider any step toward liberation which is accomplished as a stage in the pursuit of its strategy for the establishment of a democratic Palestinian state." Other changes were that UNSC Resolutions 242 (Appendix D) and 338 (Appendix E) were rejected, and negotiation was approved as a means of liberating Palestine.

In October, 1974, the Arab League met at Rabat, Morocco, to align itself with the recent PNC change. The League issued a statement, that it "affirms the right of the Palestinian people to set up an independent national authority under the leadership of the PLO, in its capacity as the sole legitimate representative of the Palestinian people, on any liberated Palestinian land."

In late 1977 the PLO reaffirmed its right to "an independent Palestinian national state, on any part of Palestinian land, . . . as an interim aim of the Palestinian Revolution."

Since 1974, Arafat has stated publicly many times that the PLO would accept any part of Palestine in which to establish the Palestinian state. However, many of Arafat's statements revealed that such a transfer of land would not end PLO efforts to regain all of Palestine.

In mid-1989 Arafat announced for the first time that the PNC Charter was obsolete.[9] However, it is unlikely that the Israelis will accept such a disavowal until the Charter is revised.

The Israelis have contended that it is unproven that the PLO is the favored representative of the Palestinians. Yet, in both 1972 and 1976, Israeli authorities permitted free elections for mayors and city councilmen in major cities of the West Bank. They were stunned when pro-PLO Palestinians were elected in the three largest West Bank cities: Nablus, Hebron and Ramallah. Ironically, the PLO had at first opposed such open elections. In 1982 the Israelis discontinued the elections and deported the mayors.

No other Palestinian group has ever emerged to contest the PLO's leadership. To achieve undisputed representation, "the Palestinian organizations waged a bitter and relentless struggle against any attempt at independent political organization in the territories."[10]

Sometimes Palestinians who collaborated with Israeli officials were assassinated. Yet in all polls taken, both outside Palestine and inside the occupied territories, **a large majority of Palestinians—often exceeding 95% of those outside Palestine—claimed the PLO as "the sole legitimate representative" of the Palestinian people.**

It is very remote that a political alternative to the PLO could ever emerge within the occupied territories. Palestinians everywhere believe that the PLO has been looking out for their interests. If a Palestinian organization did arise within the occupied territories to usurp PLO leadership, displaced Palestinians would feel betrayed by their brethren. Such an organization would no doubt face violent retaliation from the PLO.

Arafat's UN Speech (1974)

In October, 1974, the UN General Assembly voted unanimously to invite Yasser Arafat to attend a future assembly to discuss the Palestinian problem. This privilege had never been granted to any non-member other than the Pope. The next month Arafat made a historic address before the UN General Assembly in New York City. Dressed in his usual attire of army fatigues and checkered headdress, he pled for Palestinian rights, including an independent Palestinian state in Palestine. In such a state, he claimed, Muslims, Christians and Jews could live together in peace.

Arafat denied that the PLO commits terrorist acts: "The difference between the revolutionary and the terrorist lies in the reason for which each fights. For whoever stands by a just cause and fights for the freedom and liberation of his land from the invaders, the settlers and the colonialists, cannot possibly be called terrorists."[11] Westerners understand "terrorism" as violence directed against innocent civilians. But Arafat argues that Israeli Jews are not innocent, charging that they have stolen the Palestinians' land.

In his speech Arafat also maintained that the resistance movement at first exhausted all political possibilities before turning to armed resistance as a last resort. He further asserted that the growing Palestinian identity was indestructible.

> When the majority of the Palestinian people was uprooted from its homeland in 1948, the Palestinian struggle for self-determination continued under the most difficult conditions. We tried every possible means to continue our political struggle to attain our national rights, but to no avail.

... Neither the Palestinian's allegiance to Palestine nor his determination to return waned; nothing could persuade him to relinquish his Palestinian identity or to forsake his homeland. The passage of time did not make him forget as some hoped he would. When our people lost faith in the international community which persisted in ignoring its rights and when it became obvious that the Palestinians would not recuperate one inch of Palestine through exclusively political means, our people had no choice but to resort to armed struggle.[12]

Arafat reiterated the Palestinians' "undisputed right to return to our homeland" and asserted that "the Palestine Liberation Organization has earned its legitimacy because of the sacrifice inherent in its pioneering role." He concluded with an emotionally stirring plea:

I announce here that we do not wish one drop of either Arab or Jewish blood to be shed; neither do we delight in the continuation of killing, which would end once a just peace, based on our people's rights, hopes and aspirations had been finally established. . . . Today I have come bearing an olive branch and a freedom fighter's gun. Do not let the olive branch fall from my hand. I repeat: do not let the olive branch fall from my hand.

War flares up in Palestine, and yet it is in Palestine that peace will be born.[13]

Delegates of 140 nations gave the PLO chairman a resounding standing ovation.

One wonders what Arafat meant by peace being born in Palestine. In the closing chapters of this book, we will see how peace will indeed be born in Palestine, to affect the entire world.

UN Acceptance of the PLO

UN General Assembly Resolution 3236 was soon passed. It affirmed "the inalienable rights of the Palestinian people," including their "right to national independence and sovereignty" in Palestine. The UN Committee for the Enforcement of the Inalienable Rights of the Palestine Nation was created. The PLO thereafter referred to this and other General Assembly resolutions as affirming Palestinian rights.

Moreover, the UN recognized the PLO as the legitimate representative of the Palestinian people by granting it non-voting observer

status. PLO officials could attend all General Assembly sessions and other UN meetings. This was the first and only time the UN granted such status to a revolutionary organization.

PLO Worldwide Offices

Many nations quickly demonstrated their individual recognition of the PLO by allowing PLO diplomatic offices in their countries. The PLO now maintains offices, which serve as foreign embassies, in over 100 countries throughout the world, at an approximate cost of $50 million annually.[14]

In 1987 the U.S. Congress passed the Anti-Terrorism Act. The Reagan administration first invoked it by having PLO offices closed in the nation's capital. The same thing was tried against the PLO's UN offices in New York City. The UN reacted by threatening to withdraw a substantial portion of its offices from the U.S. A federal judge overruled this attempt to close the PLO's UN offices because of its UN observer status. The U.S.–UN Headquarters Agreement (1947) clearly supersedes any laws passed by Congress. This agreement provides that the host country for the UN, which is the U.S., cannot prevent attendance to UN sessions by its members, observers or invited guests. Thus, the Reagan administration was barred from evicting the PLO from U.S. soil.

PLO Unity?

Following the PLO's 1982 ouster from Lebanon, the PNC met at Algiers in early 1983. Attendance was expected to be 1,000. Heightened world interest was most evident when 6,000 showed up, including 600 journalists.

Many thought that the PLO, weakened from the war in Lebanon and hampered by infighting, would disintegrate. Hard-liners George Habash (head of the PFLP) and Nayif Hawatmeh (head of the DFLP), had condemned Arafat's recent negotiations with King Hussein of Jordan. Surprisingly, they laid aside their differences, and the PLO achieved temporary solidarity. A resolution was passed approving the concept of a confederation between Jordan and the occupied territories.

In early 1985 Hussein and Arafat announced an agreement calling for an international conference. It was to include the PLO's participation, based on its recognition of Israel and acceptance of UN Resolution 242. Due to PLO disunity, however, within a year Arafat reneged concerning recognition of Israel.

At the 18th PNC congress in April, 1987, Habash and Hawatmeh reunited with Arafat. Arafat agreed to renounce his more than two-year-old agreement with Hussein for a confederation. He was unable, however, to achieve reconciliation with Abu Nidal, head of Fatah-Revolutionary Council. Nidal and his organization have remained outside the PLO since 1973. Nidal walked out of the 1987 conference, charging that Arafat held too much authority in determining PLO policy.

A moderate in the '80s, Arafat has walked a tightrope in order to preserve PLO unity and maintain his chairmanship.

Jordan's Administrative Withdrawal
In mid-1988 Jordan's King Hussein announced a major policy shift away from the Camp David Accords. Seeking to distance himself from responsibility for the Palestinians and to demonstrate his support of PLO leadership, Hussein withdrew Jordan's long-time administrative assistance in the West Bank. He fired 21,000 Palestinians who, under an administrative agreement with Israel, worked as medical and agricultural personnel, teachers, etc., in the West Bank yet resided in Jordan. The king renounced Jordan's claim to the West Bank and proclaimed that an independent Palestinian state should be established in the occupied territories under PLO auspices. "Jordan is not Palestine," said King Hussein to Israeli right-wingers, who still insisted that Jordan was the Palestinian state.

Declaration of the State of Palestine
Meeting in Algiers on November 15, 1988, and though in exile, **the PNC officially declared the existence of the State of Palestine.** This was a political and psychological move to fill the vacuum that had been left by Jordan's administrative withdrawal from the West Bank. Although the declaration did not explicitly claim any particular land, it seemed to anticipate the occupied territories as the location of the Palestinian state. An undivided Jerusalem was declared as the capital of the new state. Of course, Israel's government condemned this move.

The declaration included an attempt to meet certain U.S. demands and thereby open dialogue between the U.S. and the PLO. For the first time in twenty-one years, the PNC/PLO accepted UN Security Council Resolution 242 and 338. These resolutions had always been rejected by the PNC/PLO because they did not specify the Palestinians' right to a state in Palestine. Most significant was the declaration's reaffirmation of Arafat's 1985 disavowal of all terrorism except for that directed against Israeli military targets.

Debate ensued as to whether the PNC acceptance of Resolution 242 signaled implicit recognition of Israel.

Arafat Refused U.S. Visa

A special UN General Assembly meeting was scheduled in late 1988 to discuss the Palestine question and hear from Arafat for only the second time in fifteen years. The Reagan administration refused Arafat's request for a visa. It argued that Arafat had ties with known Palestinian terrorists and that his entrance to the U.S. would violate the new Anti-Terrorism Act.

Rejection of Arafat's visa was once again a clear violation of the U.S. agreement as the host country of the UN. The General Assembly made an unprecedented move, postponed the session and held it two weeks later in Geneva, Switzerland. The U.S. suffered a loss of world prestige when all UN members except the U.S., Israel and Britain passed a resolution condemning the refusal of Arafat's visa. Britain abstained only because it assessed the resolution's language as too severe.

U.S. Dialogue with the PLO

On December 13th, 1988, Arafat delivered his long-awaited speech to the UN General Assembly in Geneva. He called for an international peace conference under UN auspices, to include the PLO and to be held at Geneva with a goal of a comprehensive settlement involving all parties, and Israeli troop withdrawal from the occupied territories during the interim, to be replaced by a UN international peacekeeping force. The PLO chairman's most significant affirmations came a few days later, when **in late 1988 Arafat clarified ambiguities by declaring explicit PLO recognition of Israel and denouncing all forms of terrorism.**

The next day President Reagan announced that the PLO had met all his demands. Reagan assuaged Israeli fears and anger by warning that if the PLO did not back up its words with deeds, the U.S. would discontinue contact with the PLO. The U.S. immediately entered into "substantive dialogue" with the PLO in Tunis.

Reagan's announcement dealt a severe blow to Israel's shocked government officials. Prime Minister Shamir predicted future U.S. dialogue with the PLO would not advance the cause of peace in the region. Even Foreign Minister Peres, a moderate, said the U.S. move constituted a "sad day for all of us [Israeli Jews]."

Despite Arafat's assurances to the contrary, in the Arab press, PLO and PNC leaders continued to espouse a step-by-step plan to liberate all of Palestine. In late December, 1988, Arafat's chief deputy, Abu Iyad, explained, "At first a small state, and with Allah's help it will be made large and expand to the east, west, north and south—I am interested in the liberation of Palestine step by step."[15] At the same time, the chairman of the PNC, Sheikh Abd al-Hamid El-Sayekh, stated, "If the PLO succeeds in establishing a state in the West Bank and Gaza, it would not prevent the continuation of the struggle until the liberation of all of Palestine is achieved—we are working to achieve what is possible in the present phase and afterwards we will demand more."[16] Thus, both of these Palestinian leaders reaffirmed the Phased Plan of 1974. Here is evidence that either Arafat is not fully forthcoming or that there remains dissension among these leaders regarding goals for the Palestinian state.

Nevertheless, with the PLO recognition of Israel and its disavowal of all terrorism, most analysts consider that the ball is now in Israel's court. It is up to Israeli politicians to end their intransigence, affirm Palestinian rights and recognize the PLO as the Palestinians' representative.

Conclusion

Most Palestinians feel a strong sense of loyalty to the PLO. The Palestinian people are convinced that it is only the PLO that has been looking out for their best interests. Its members have continuously risked their lives on behalf of all Palestinians.

It can no longer be denied that the PNC and PLO have created a Palestinian national identity. **Without a land, they have developed a governmental infrastructure that is more effective than some national governments around the world.**

It seems only a matter of time until the Palestinians, like the Zionists, will obtain a national home in Palestine. Much to Israel's chagrin, it appears that this will be accomplished through the determined leadership of the PLO and its parliament, the PNC.

The PLO is now recognized not only by the UN, but by every nation in the world, except Israel, as the Palestinians' sole legitimate representative.

Chapter 7

TERRORISM:
PALESTINIAN AND JEWISH

Terrorism has been a frightful phenomenon in the late twentieth century. Until recently, the Palestine Liberation Organization (PLO) has been at the top of the list of those responsible for such reprehensible acts. When most westerners hear of the PLO, they immediately envision masked terrorists committing incomprehensible, detestable killings. Indeed, many PLO victims have been innocent Jewish civilians, even women and children; some have included non-Jewish citizens of countries far from Israel. There are, however, many other Middle East terrorist groups whose deeds should not be confused with the PLO.

Without justifying political terrorism, it may be readily seen that there exists some similarity between it and war. Just as established nations with militaries go to war for what they perceive to be just causes, political terrorists rely on violence to achieve their goals. Whereas "civilized" nations drop bombs on civilians in time of war, terrorists commit violent acts against civilians. Terror is the tactic of the powerless, the disfranchised, the dispossessed. As pygmies among giants, they conclude that it is their only way to wage war.

As mentioned before, terrorism was not always the policy of the Palestinians. After Israel became a nation, dispossessed Palestinian leaders waited fifteen years for the world to do something about getting back their land. After nothing happened through peaceful resistance, some began to turn to violence as the only way to obtain their perceived rights.

When the PLO was formed in 1964, Arafat's al-Fatah began to

pursue terrorism. Still, the PLO, leaders of Arab states and most Palestinians condemned terrorism. But when Israel initiated the 1967 War and seized the occupied territories, this proved to be the last straw. Disillusioned by the humiliating Arab defeat, leaders of all other Palestinian resistance organizations in the PLO decided that diplomacy was fruitless and joined al-Fatah in terrorism.

PLO Terrorism

Most PLO terrorist acts have been associated with border clashes. There have been hundreds of incidents in which Palestinian guerrillas have shot mortars, or the like, from just across the Lebanon-Israel border into Jewish setlements, indiscriminately killing men, women and children. In mid-1970, guerrillas near the Lebanese border fired on an Israeli school bus, killing 12 people, 8 of them children, and wounding 20 others. Israel immediately responded by shelling a nearby Lebanese village, killing 20 and wounding 40.

Leaders of PLO groups became further embittered following their 1970 ouster from Jordan. Thereafter, they escalated terrorism in order to draw world attention to their plight. Atrocities were directed not only against Israeli civilians, but against westerners as well, especially those whose governments supported Israel.

One of the more notable types of terrorist acts that some PLO groups turned to was aerial hijackings of commercial airliners servicing Israel. Many of these air piracies were perpetrated against Israel's El Al Airlines, but they included other major world airlines as well.

Dr. George Habash and his Popular Front for the Liberation of Palestine have been responsible for most Palestinian airplane hijackings. In 1969 Habash publicly declared war against travellers to Israel, asserting that travel to Israel was a form of supporting the Zionist state. The next year his group simultaneously hijacked three commercial aircraft bound from Europe to New York and diverted them to the desert in Jordan. The 310 passengers were held hostage and later released. The planes were blown up. Israel responded with a commando operation in Beirut. Passengers were corraled into the air terminal as fourteen jets belonging to Arab nations were blown up on the airstrip outside. Their estimated value was $100 million.

Other airline passengers were not so fortunate. In early 1970, Ahmed Jibril's Popular Front for the Liberation of Palestine-General Command planted a bomb in a Swiss plane bound for Tel Aviv that exploded in midair, killing all 47 aboard, 16 of them Israelis. The world adamantly condemned such atrocities. It was obvious that this kind of publicity was detrimental to the Palestinians' cause.

During this time Arafat disapproved of terrorist acts directed against non-Israeli citizens outside Israel. But it was not until 1975 that, as chairman of the PLO, he established a penal code against hijackings of any kind. It even included the death penalty for those responsible for killing passengers. Hijackings afterward subsided.

Habash's group and others also planted explosives in many public places in Israel, like travel terminals, cinemas and supermarkets, killing or wounding numerous innocent people. Habash defended these atrocities by alleging that nearly every Israeli citizen serves in the military reserves, so they are not innocent civilians.

Khalil al-Wazir was commander of the PLO military and second in line to Arafat. Al-Wazir was called Abu Jihad, meaning Father of Holy War. He planned several terrorist attacks which resulted in many Israeli Jews being killed, like the 1975 raid on a Tel Aviv hotel, where 21 Israelis died, or the 1978 attack on an Israeli bus that killed 35 Jews. In retaliation, seven Israeli masked commandos secretly entered Tunisia in 1988 and riddled al-Wazir's body with 170 bullets in his home. Also killed were his two body guards and his gardener.

Many Palestinian terrorist acts have been committed by non-PLO groups. Perhaps the most famous incident of this kind was Black Friday. Eleven Israeli Jewish athletes were massacred on a Friday during the 1972 Olympic Games in Munich, Germany. It was later determined that this dark evil was the work of Black September, a Palestinian group never associated with the PLO. Another of their infamous crimes occurred in 1973 when members of Black September took three diplomats as hostages at Khartoum, Sudan, and executed them.

Since 1973, the world's leading Palestinian terrorist has not been Al-Wazir, Arafat or anybody in the PLO. Without a doubt, it has been Abu Nidal, head of Fatah-Revolutionary Council. Nidal's terrorism, however, should not be attributed to the PLO, since he withdrew his membership in 1973. Western authorities believe that dissident Nidal has orchestrated over 100 terrorist attacks in 20 countries, resulting in over 900 casualties.[1] In late 1989 Nidal was believed to be responsible for most of the estimated eighteen western hostages in Lebanon. His organization, however, was in disarray; in early 1990 he was reported to have ordered dozens of his lieutenants killed.[2]

Israeli Retaliation

Most people don't realize that Israel's punishment of Palestinian terrorist acts always exceeds the crime. In fact, many analysts regard Israel's military reaction against Palestinian terrorism as terrorism itself. For example, in 1985 Palestinians assassinated three Israelis aboard a ship at Cyprus. In retaliation, the Israeli Air Force invaded Tunisian airspace and bombed PLO headquarters in Tunis, killing 52 Palestinians, 73 people in all. Of course, this particular act might be viewed as retaliation for a culmination of terrorist acts. But when you add up the number of Jews killed by Palestinian terrorism, it falls far short of the number of Palestinians killed in retaliation by the Israeli military.

Over the past generation, Israel's air force has responded to PLO atrocities by conducting hundreds of bombing raids over PLO bases and refugee camps, often killing women and children.[3] Former senior UPI Middle East correspondent, Wesley G. Pippert, reports: "This Israeli pattern of reacting with vengeance is all too common. There probably have been *more* Arab victims of Jewish terrorism than Jewish victims of Arab terrorism. . . . Almost always the Israeli air raids were bloodier than the Arab terrorist attacks that provoked the raids."[4]

Dispute Over Terrorism

Most nations have overwhelmingly condemned terrorism, but Communists have regarded it as necessary for revolutionary movements. In 1969, *Time* magazine didn't seem to persuade many Americans when it portrayed Yasser Arafat on its front cover, calling him a "freedom fighter." Nearly all Americans continued to strongly support their presidents in denouncing the PLO as terrorists. U.S. President Ronald Reagan once called the PLO a "gang of thugs."

Nevertheless, many analysts concede that, despite its despicability, the prolonged history of PLO terrorism achieved its purpose in gaining world recognition for the Palestinians' cause, without which they would have continued to be ignored. On the other hand, many observers also contend that Palestinian terrorism, especially that directed against civilians, has proved counter-productive in its effect on world opinion. Former president Jimmy Carter alleges that PLO violence has only hindered the Palestinians' cause.[5]

Palestinians resent being known in the west as terrorists. Instead, they condemn the Israelis as terrorists, asserting that the Jews took their land, destroyed most of their homes, continue to deny their return and refuse to compensate them for their loss.

Palestinians generally view the PLO as the military arm of their national existence. They maintain that the PLO is conducting a war of liberation against Zionist Israel to regain their homeland. Palestinians refer to the *fedayeen* (guerrillas) as "freedom fighters" rather than terrorists. What we call "terrorism" in the west, Palestinians see as war, the only kind of war the PLO is capable of waging. It was no different for the Jews before they attained their state.

Jewish Terrorism

An objective assessment of Palestinian terrorism requires consideration of Jewish terrorism as well. Palestinian terrorism has been well documented in the news media in the '70s and '80s. Many westerners condemn the PLO and view the Jews as guiltless, unaware of the terrorism perpetrated by Jews in the '30s and '40s, prior to Israeli statehood.

We saw in Chapter 3 that, prior to Israel's War of Independence, Jewish members of militant organizations committed many detestable terrorist acts which are little known today. These organizations had strong similarities to the PLO. For a long time Haganah, although illegal under the Mandate, acted as the military arm of the Zionists, just as the PLO does for the Palestinians today.

As already mentioned, in the 1930s, radical members of Haganah split to form underground terrorist organizations called Irgun and the Stern Group. Britain's 1946 White Paper claimed that Irgun then had 3,000-5,000 members and the Stern Group, 200-300. Former Israeli prime minister Menachem Begin headed Irgun from 1942 to 1948. Irgun committed terrorist acts against both the Palestinian Arabs and the British. Stern directed its hostilities exclusively against the British. Assassinations were carried out to force the British to relinquish their mandate over Palestine. This was attested by British prime minister Attlee before the House of Commons.[6]

Officially, the Jewish Agency and Haganah claimed no power over these "uncontrollable" guerrilla organizations. However, the British revealed in their 1946 White Paper that they had intercepted telegrams which clearly implicated Haganah and members of the Jewish Agency in co-planning terrorist acts with Irgun and Stern. More evidence for these British allegations surfaced when several weapons and ammunition caches belonging to all three military organizations were uncovered, revealing the same supplier.[7]

Abdallah Frangi comments on pre-1948 Jewish terrorism:

> From 1942, the incidence of Stern gang and Irgun attacks on British commissioners and police increased. By 1947, about 200 British officials had been killed in bomb attacks and other armed attacks. In 1946, Irgun took several British officials and judges hostage in an effort to force the release of imprisoned members of their organizations. Two of the hostages were hanged, two

others were attached to mines and blown to pieces. On top of this came maltreatment of hostages and prisoners and letter and parcel bombs which killed dozens of people.

Palestinian administrative centres were also attacked. Palestinian and British banks were favoured targets for attacks and robberies. Irgun and the Stern gang always claimed responsibility.

Attacks on public transport were a favourite Jewish terrorist tactic. Menachem Begin has described how he and the terrorists he led would allow the 'reconnaissance' locomotive to pass over mines but, as soon as the train followed, the mines were detonated. In 1946 and 1947, more than 100 people were killed in attacks on railways, trains, railway stations and vehicles.[8]

In 1947, in Tel Aviv alone, Irgun committed seventeen terrorist attacks against the British.[9] Palestinian historian Sami Hadawi documents over 100 specific Jewish terrorist acts from 1939 to May 14, 1948. Directed mostly against the British, they include hundreds of killings.[10] After the UN Partition Plan was announced in November, 1947, Jewish terrorists turned most of their assaults against the Palestinian Arabs.

Lord Moyne and Count Bernadotte Assassinations
British Minister of State Lord Moyne supported his government's White Paper of 1939 by publicly opposing further Jewish immigration. He argued that Jews were not demonstrably the true descendants of the ancient Hebrews and therefore without legitimate claim to the Holy Land. He meant that Jews were hardly a pure race, being a much more heterogeneous group than popularly conceived. For this, he was assassinated by the Stern Group on November 6, 1944. Eleven days later, pro-Zionist British Prime Minister Winston Churchill announced in the House of Commons:

> If our dreams for Zionism are to end in the smoke of assassins' pistols and our labours for its future are to produce a new set of gangsters worthy of Nazi Germany, many like myself will have to reconsider the position we have maintained . . . these wicked activities must cease and those responsible for them must be destroyed root and branch. . . . we must wait to see that not only the leaders but every man, woman and child of the Jewish community does his or her best to bring this terrorism to a speedy end.[11]

It was not uncommon in post-WWII days to compare the atrocities by Jewish terrorists in Palestine to the Nazi Holocaust. Eminent British historian, Arnold Toynbee, has been frequently quoted on his assessment: "In A.D. 1948, the Jews knew, from personal experience, what they were doing; and it was their supreme tragedy that the lesson learned by them from their encounter with the Nazi Gentiles should have been not to eschew but to imitate some of the evil deeds that the Nazis had committed against the Jews."[12]

The most heinous Zionist assassination of a public official occurred on September 17, 1948. Sweden's Count Bernadotte was then the UN Special Representative to Palestine. Both he and his assistant, Col. Andre P. Serot of the French air force, were assassinated in a UN demilitarized zone in Jerusalem by members of the Stern Group.[13] The three assailants escaped and were never apprehended. Although Zionist officials had sometimes publicly denounced terrorism, they had consistently failed to bring terrorists to justice. Within 24 hours of the Count Bernadotte assassination, however, Israeli Prime Minister David Ben-Gurion ordered such groups as Stern and Irgun to disband and surrender their arms. Begin's Irgun submitted only after a battle at sea.

Terrorist Menachem Begin

As Israel's Prime Minister, Menachem Begin called the PLO an "organization of assassins" and refused to recognize or negotiate with them.[14] Do Begin's pre-Israel activities reveal the hypocrisy of a self-righteous stance?

Begin was on the British wanted list of terrorists. Former U.S. President Jimmy Carter wrote that Begin "fought with every weapon available against the British, who characterized him as the preeminent terrorist in the region. . . . a man who would readily resort to violence to achieve goals in which he believed."[15]

Chaim Herzog was Israel's first director of Military Intelligence and first governor of the West Bank. He has been Israel's president since 1983. President Herzog remarks on Begin's terrorist activities: "The 2,000-4,000 members of Irgun, under the command of Menachem Begin, continued with militant anti-British activity even when the official Jewish policy was not to engage in such activity. Pursuing a policy of constant attack on British posts, government and army installations, it was trained primarily to carry out small-unit, commando-type raids."[16]

Several terrorist acts by Begin's Irgun deserve mention.

On June 22, 1946, Irgun blew up a wing of the King David Hotel in Jerusalem. The hotel had served as headquarters for the British in exercising their mandate. Ninety-one people were killed, including Arabs, British and even some Jews.

That same year Irgun publicly admitted hanging two British sergeants. One body was booby trapped. A note attached to the head read, "This is the sentence of Irgun's High Tribunal."

On April 9-10, 1947, five weeks prior to the declaration of Israeli statehood, Irgun attacked the Arab village of Deir Yassin near Jerusalem. Most of the men of the village were not present. Of approximately 700 inhabitants, 254 women, children and old men were massacred. Many of their bodies were stuffed down a well in the center of the village. Irgun called a press conference, claimed responsibility and warned that this massacre was the beginning of the Zionists' conquest of Palestine and Transjordan.[17]

Years later, Begin wrote unashamedly of the deplorable crime at Deir Yassin, "The massacre was not only justified, but there would not have been a state of Israel without the 'victory' at Deir Yassin. . . . All the Jewish forces proceeded to advance through Haifa like a knife through butter; the Arabs began to flee in panic shouting 'Deir Yassin.' "[18]

The massacre at Deir Yassin was not an isolated incident. More than 60 Palestinians were soon killed in their houses at Balad Esh-Sheikh. About 60 were massacred at the village of Sa'sa.[19] When war broke out, the fear of a repetition of such massacres caused many Palestinians to flee from their homes.

Irgun's last confrontation was with the Israeli government itself. A ship, loaded with arms, ammunition and 900 volunteer fighters for Irgun, sailed from Europe and ran aground off Tel Aviv. Ben-Gurion ordered Irgun to surrender arms to Israel's new army, later named the Israel Defense Forces (IDF). Begin refused, and fighting broke out between the two forces at sea. Fifteen men were killed and the ship was sunk. Irgun forces then submitted, swore allegiance to the State of Israel and were received into the IDF.[20]

Thus, for several years prior to Israel's War of Independence, Menachem Begin commanded a large terrorist force that launched guerrilla attacks similar to those of Arafat's PLO. These were directed not only against the Arabs but against the British as well. This was despite the fact that, humanly speaking, if it had not been for Great Britain, there would never have been a modern State of Israel.

Begin and others like him saw no difference between their pre-1948 terrorist activites and the war which followed Israel's Declaration of

Independence. This should be considered when judging PLO terrorism.

Former CIA operative in the Middle East, Wilbur Eveland, chides Israelis like Menachem Begin for accusing the PLO of being a bunch of terrorists:

> For those Israelis who once engaged in terrorism (and who continue it today behind the mask of preemptive military operations that kill hundreds of innocent people) now to condemn the Palestinians who have in desperation resorted to terrorist acts for an identical objective—the obtaining of a homeland in Palestine—is sheer hypocrisy.[21]

Terrorist Yitzhak Shamir

Like Begin, Israel's current Prime Minister, Yitzhak Shamir, was also a terrorist. In pre-Israel days, he was a commander of the anti-British Stern Group. In 1943 Shamir wrote, "Terrorism is for us a part of the political battle being conducted under the present circumstances, and it has a great part to play: speaking in a clear voice to the whole world, as well as to our wretched brethren outside this land, it proclaims our war against the occupier."[22] Both Begin and Shamir considered themselves in a war of liberation against the occupier: Britain. Fifty years later, Arafat and other PLO members feel likewise, that they are in a war against the occupier: Israel.

Shamir contended that the Zionists had a divine mandate for their terrorism: "Neither Jewish ethics nor Jewish tradition can disqualify terrorism as a means of combat. . . . We have before us the command of the Torah, whose morality surpasses that of any other body of laws in the world: 'Ye shall blot them out to the last man.' "[23]

Does Shamir mean to compare either the British or the Palestinians to the Canaanites? In Chapter 1 it was shown that God gave the Israelites their mandate to drive out or destroy the Canaanites because of their gross wickedness. In contrast, despite its faults, Britain was one of the great Christian nations of the world, a friend of the Jews that helped reestablish their nation Israel. As for the Palestinians, many are professing Christians and most are Muslims. Like Judaism, both Christianity and Islam are monotheistic; their adherents respect the Hebrew Bible and espouse its morality.

Sacred Terrorism?

Moshe Sharett held several political positions in Israel, including prime minister in 1954-1955. Israeli authorities succeeded in blocking publication of Sharett's 2,400-page diary for many years following his death, until 1980. It provides a shocking expose of Israel's early leaders. For instance, Ben-Gurion and Dayan established policies deliberately to provoke Arab hostilities in order to create pretexts for Israel's armed retaliation and territorial expansion. Sharett generally opposed such maneuvers and sarcastically called it "sacred terrorism." He wrote, "In the thirties we restrained the emotions of revenge. . . . Now, on the contrary, we justify the system of reprisal . . . we have eliminated the mental and moral brake on this instinct and made it possible . . . to uphold revenge as a moral value . . . a sacred principle."[24]

Arafat's Disavowal of Terrorism

So what has been the recent history of Palestinian terrorism? After years of prolonged terrorism, in the '80s Arafat began to shift from a radical to a moderate position, advocating diplomacy rather than terrorism. This change caused his leadership to be seriously challenged in the mid-'80s. It has endangered his life with hardline Palestinians.

Arafat must constantly take precautions to avoid being assassinated himself. He changes sleeping quarters almost every night. Throughout the '80s, Arafat has been accompanied at almost all times by his body guards. For security purposes, no one in his entourage ever knows where they are going or when.

In 1985 Arafat publicly denounced past PLO atrocities inflicted against civilians and vowed that, in the future, the PLO would attack only Israeli military targets. At the same time, Egyptian President Hosni Mubarak condemned U.S. President Reagan's refusal to recognize and negotiate with the PLO. "Yasser Arafat is a very moderate man," claimed Mubarak. "He is not a terrorist as some people think."[25]

In late 1988 Arafat renounced all forms of terrorism. Thanks to this PLO moderation, world terrorism was waning as we embarked on the '90s. In 1989 there were 25% fewer deaths caused by terrorism than the previous year. These lower statistics were attributed partly to the PLO's keeping Arafat's 1988 pledge to refrain from terrorism.[26]

At the present, the U.S., Egypt and Israel are trying to work out disagreements in order to proceed with Palestinian elections in the occupied territories. These elected Palestinians would negotiate the future of the occupied territories and of the proposed Palestinian state. U.S. and Egyptian leaders know that PLO approval of the election process is essential to its success. Mubarak predicted in 1985 that without PLO participation in negotiations, "peace will never be achieved."

It is unlikely that Palestinians in the occupied territories will ever agree to an election process not approved by the PLO. Indeed, if the PLO does not assent to an election process which is carried out, the PLO will likely retract its disavowal of terrorism. Such a situation could become worse than ever, for the PLO would no doubt attack the elected Palestinian officials in the occupied territories as well as Israeli Jews.

As mentioned previously, in early 1990 the PLO threatened to resume terrorism if Jewish Russian emigres are settled in the West Bank or East Jerusalem.

Conclusion

Terrorism, as reprehensible as it is, is a means of waging war. Dispossessed Palestinians have used it to grasp for their perceived rights, in particular, a state of their own in Palestine. In this they are not much different from those Jews, two of whom later became prime ministers, who conducted many terrorist acts against the Arabs and British in order to attain Israeli statehood. **It is hypocritical for Israel to refuse to negotiate with Arafat and the PLO on the grounds that they are terrorists.**

Chapter 8

THE CHURCH
AND CHRISTIAN ZIONISM

"You shall love your neighbor as yourself" (Lev 19.18)

Christians have always had a significant effect, either for good or for evil, on the lives of the Jews. On the negative side, it was so-called "Christian" nations who were responsible for the Inquisition, the Crusades and the Holocaust. On the positive side, Jews are indebted to the so-called "Christian nations" of Great Britain and the U.S. for the creation and survival of the State of Israel. The U.S. regularly provides $3 billion per year in foreign aid and armaments to Israel. **The views of Christians, especially those in the U.S., regarding the Palestinian-Israeli conflict are important because they affect American policy toward Israel.**

For many Christians, familiarity with the Palestinian-Israeli problem creates a tension. They experience both a theological identification with the Jewish people and a social concern for the suffering Palestinians. Most Christians probably see themselves as both pro-Israeli and pro-Palestinian, as does this author. Others have chosen one side or the other.

Palestinian Christians
Like other Arabs, most Palestinians are Muslim. Some, however, are professing Christians. Among the nearly 2 million Palestinians living in Israel and the occupied territories in 1980, about 100,000-120,000 were professing Christians.[1] Most are members of the Greek Orthodox Church.

The Greek Orthodox Church has championed Palestinian rights. They have many churches in the Middle East and have been involved

137

in relief work for the Palestinian refugees. **Christians in the Middle East, especially those among the Palestinians, generally feel that western Christians are no longer interested in them.**[2] This is despite the fact that some in the Mideast trace their churches' origins to the first century.

The Roman Catholic Church

The Roman Catholic Church has neither condemned nor promoted Zionism,[3] the movement to reestablish Jews in their ancient homeland. In 1904 Theodor Herzl requested Catholic Church approval for a Jewish national home in Palestine. Pope Pius X answered:

> We are unable to favor this movement. We cannot prevent the Jews from going to Jerusalem but we could never sanction it. As head of the Church I cannot answer you otherwise. The Jews have not recognized our Lord. Therefore we cannot recognize the Jewish people, and so, if you come to Palestine and settle your people there, we will be ready with churches and priests to baptize all of you.

The Catholic Church still refuses to have full diplomatic relations with the State of Israel. Israel earnestly desires these relations. The Vatican argues that its refusal does not reflect anti-Semitism, since over the years it has received several Israeli prime ministers and other leaders for talks. (The Pope also received Arafat twice, in 1982 and 1988.) Instead, the Church does not recognize Israel because of Israel's refusal to recognize Palestinian human rights, together with its declared sovereignty over Jerusalem without guaranteeing freedom of worship and international access to holy sites.

Pope John Paul II has stated the Catholic Church's position on the Palestinian-Israeli problem many times. During his historic visit to the U.S. in 1987, he met with the Jewish community in Miami and affirmed the Jews' right to a homeland. **The Catholic pontiff added that "the right to a homeland also applies to the Palestinian people."**[4] Note that he did not specify where the Palestinian state should be located, something he never does. Vatican policy is for the pope to speak out only on moral issues and allow disputants to negotiate specific solutions.

The Catholic Church has a history of anti-Semitism, but it has never officially admitted this. Since the Second Vatican Council (Vatican II: 1962), the Church has made strides in breaking with its anti-Semitic past. In 1965, Vatican II issued *Nostra Aetate*, No. 4, a conciliatory statement on other religions which expressly condemns anti-Semitism. **However, the Catholic Church's anti-Semitic history, and its continuing failure to deal adequately with this problem, has caused it and some other churches to lose their right to speak a prophetic word to modern Israel regarding its denial of Palestinian rights.**

U.S. Protestant Churches

Not only have the Greek Orthodox and Roman Catholic Churches been sympathetic to the Palestinians, so have most mainline Protestant denominations. While all have for many years recognized the existence of the State of Israel, they have also criticized Israel's intransigence in resolving the dispute. Most recognize UN Resolution 242 as a viable basis for effecting a settlement. Over the past two decades or more, many churches have issued resolutions or statements addressing the Israeli-Palestinian conflict.

The **National Council of Churches of Christ in the U.S.A.** (NCC) has devoted much attention to the dispute. Way back in 1969 the NCC issued a thorough policy statement on the conflict. It (1) backed UN Resolution 242, calling for Israel's military withdrawal and the return of the occupied territories to the respective Arab countries, (2) affirmed Israel's existence and right to defensible borders, (3) affirmed the Palestinians' right to self-determination by means of a sovereign state in Palestine and (4) requested the U.S. administration to open dialogue with the PLO. In 1983 the **World Council of Churches** issued a similar statement. Since then, the NCC has further suggested that the U.S. propose a UN Security Council resolution which would unequivocally support Palestinian self-determination.

In 1974 the **United Presbyterian Church of the U.S.A.** affirmed the right of existence of the State of Israel as well as "self determination by political expression" for the Palestinian people, with the PLO as their representative. In 1983 the same church issued a statement urging the U.S. government to threaten withholding military aid in order to pressure Israel into negotiations which would include PLO participation.

A 1975 resolution by the **American Baptist Churches** somewhat ambiguously affirmed "the attachment and claim of the Palestinian Arabs to the land as their homeland . . . [which] must not be allowed to destroy both the hope of Israel and the heritage of the Palestinians."

In 1976 the **United Methodist Church** issued a similar statement. It affirmed both Israel's right to exist and "the fulfillment of Palestinian national aspirations through a state of their own," with the PLO as the Palestinians' representative. It also condemned Israel's settlements in the occupied territories as detrimental to a resolution.

In 1976 the **Antiochian Orthodox Church of North America**, whose parent body is in the Middle East, called specifically for "the establishment of an independent Palestinian State on the West Bank and Gaza as a fulfillment of the right of the Palestinians to a state of their own."

In 1977 the **Reformed Church of America** stated succinctly that it "affirms the rights of both Israelis and Palestinian Arabs for nationhood." In 1987 the church (1) denounced U.S. administration efforts to close PLO offices in the U.S., (2) exhorted the U.S. to support full Palestinian rights of self-determination instead of autonomy, and (3) reaffirmed its call for Palestinian statehood.

One observer writes that "the mainline churches, especially in their more recent statements, have shown an amazing similarity of approach."[5] Another says these same churches have consistently shown concern for both Jews and Palestinians, and "refused to back an all-or-nothing solution for one side or the other."[6] Several churches also condemn the U.S. arms build-up in the region.

It is surprising that Catholic and Protestant churches in the U.S. have for many years supported equal rights for both Israeli Jews and Palestinians, including statehood, while most Americans have supported Israel and ignored the Palestinians until recently. Many factors have contributed to this disparity, including (1) the continuing sympathy for Jews due to the Nazi Holocaust, (2) the influence of 6 million U.S. Jews and their powerful lobbying force in Washington, (3) a democratic Israel being vital to U.S. interests in the Middle East and (4) PLO atrocities. However, during the past decade, perhaps nothing has convinced Americans to be pro-Israel more than the growth of the Religious Right in America and the proliferation of their beliefs on Bible prophecy.

Religious Right in America

Most U.S. mainline church denominations have lost members in recent decades. On the other hand, the following have experienced phenomenal growth: (1) Evangelicals, who stress evangelism, (2) Fundamentalists, who champion biblical inerrancy and other "fundamentals," and (3) Charismatics, who stress speaking in tongues and other "sign" gifts. These groups overlap. Many of these believers worship in non-denominational churches. Perhaps the main difference between these and other professing Christians is their emphasis on personal faith and experience over sacramental religion. They are often called the

Religious Right because they tend to be politically conservative.

The growing Religious Right in the U.S. has largely favored the Israelis and ignored the plight of the Palestinians. This dissimilarity with mainline churches can be traced back to the Modernist-Fundamentalist debate of the last generation. Modernists (liberals), found mostly in denominational churches, have emphasized a "social gospel" which addresses social needs. Their care for poor and suffering peoples has led them to sympathize with the Palestinians. Evangelicals and Fundamentalists, on the other hand, have in the past stressed the saving of the soul. Fundamentalists and Charismatics have also been strongly influenced by their interest in the prophetic scriptures. Much of this material describes the future of the Jewish people. **Believing that God will redeem the Jews and deliver them from their enemies in the endtime, the Religious Right has identified strongly with the Israeli cause and ignored the rights of the Palestinian people.**

Premillennialism Revived

Orthodox Jews of the Diaspora have always believed that the Jews would someday return to their fathers' homeland to reestablish a viable Jewish community. They have based this hope on a literal interpretation of their biblical prophets. They have held that, in contrast to Messiah ben Joseph, Messiah ben David would emerge to deliver Jews from their enemies, regather them from throughout the world, reign at Jerusalem and make Israel the head of the nations.[7]

Most Christians of the first four centuries agreed essentially with all these points.[8] Of course, the fundamental difference between Jews and Christians remained: Jews rejected Jesus as *Messiah* (Hebrew), or *Christ* (Greek). These early Christians also interpreted from the prophetic scriptures that a significant number of Jews would return to Palestine before the return of Jesus Christ.[9] From their NT scriptures they added that Christ would then reign for 1,000 years (Rev 20; 1 Cor 15.24). This view later became known by the Latin term, premillennialism. It signifies Jesus' return *before* the thousand years of His reign on earth.

Augustine and Jerome are credited with changing the church's eschatology (study of future things), beginning in the early 5th century. Augustine interpreted biblical prophecies allegorically. He understood the future, revived Israel in the scriptures to be a metaphor for the Gentile church.

Augustine was influenced in the formation of his eschatological beliefs by the tremendous success of the Catholic Church. As did

many others, he reckoned the church to be already in the blessed
millennial age, that Christ now reigned through the Catholic Church.
Augustine taught that when the literal 1,000 years were completed,
Jesus Christ would return to the earth. This "postmillennialism" became the predominant Catholic belief; premillennialism was afterwards regarded as heresy.

When Jesus did not return in A.D. 1000, Catholic scholars were
forced to alter their eschatology. They reinterpreted the 1,000-year
reign of Christ as non-literal, regarding it as a period of indetermin-
able length. This view was called "amillennialism" (Latin for "no
thousand"). Nevertheless, they left intact their teaching that the future
Israel of the prophetic scriptures was symbolic of the Gentile church.
Thus, there would be no future, literal Israel.

When the Protestant Reformation emerged, its leaders generally
held, as Augustine had, to a postmillennial belief. However, beginning
in the 16th century, there developed small pockets of premillennial
believers who, like the early Christians, expected a future restoration
of Jews to Palestine.[10]

In the early 19th century, a significant premillennialist movement
sprang up in the British Isles. Called the Plymouth Brethren, they
interpreted from Scripture that many **Jews would someday return
to Palestine, reestablish their nation and rebuild the temple in
Jerusalem, all before the return of Jesus Christ.**

Ernest Sandeen is an authority on Christian Fundamentalism, a
term he equates with premillennialism. He claims, "There can be no
question that the millenarian movement played a significant role in
preparing the British for political Zionism."[11] Both Lord Balfour of
Britain and U.S. President Woodrow Wilson were Bible readers influenced by premillennialism.[12] It will be recalled that the Balfour Declaration (1917) guided British policy for thirty years and led to the
reestablishment of Israel.

Two world wars in the 20th century awakened many postmillennialists to the reality that their times could not be identified as the
blessed promised millennium. Thus, there came a significant shift in
Christian eschatology, from post- and amillennialism to premillennialism, i.e., a return to the belief of the early Christians.

Dispensationalism
One of the early prominent Plymouth Brethren teachers was J.N.
Darby. He formulated a theological system which included premillen-
nialism. Called "dispensationalism," it is a thorough world view in

which the past, present and future are divided into several ages, during each of which man fails a divine test.

The most prominent feature of dispensationalism is that OT prophetic scriptures which depict future Israel are distinguished from those which deal with the predominantly Gentile church in the NT.

Darby's brand of premillennialism has become widespread among American Christians in this century. In recent times its popularity can be attributed mostly to the huge success of *The Scofield Reference Bible* and Hal Lindsey's *The Late Great Planet Earth* (1970). Lindsey's book, which has sold over 30 million copies to date, was named by *Time* magazine as the "Book of the '70s."

After Israel became a state in 1948, premillennialism gained even more adherents. When the Jews seized East Jerusalem and its temple mount in 1967, premillennialists became ecstatic. Today, most Christian Fundamentalists and many Evangelicals are premillennialists.

Christian Zionism

A new religious term came into vogue in the 80's. **"Christian Zionism" identifies those Christians who give uncritical support to the State of Israel and who ignore the plight of the Palestinians.** Thus, Christian Zionists, who consist mostly of some dispensationalists and some Charismatics, deny Palestinians an equal right to a state in Palestine. Furthermore, they usually approve of Israeli armed expansionism to acquire the remaining Promised Land.

Like other premillennialists, Christian Zionists are convinced that modern Israel is a fulfillment of biblical prophecies written thousands of years ago. Such fulfillments of prophecy increase one's faith in the God of the Bible. But related particulars of their eschatology cause Christian Zionists to be insensitive to the Palestinians. Their views are bringing disrepute on the literal interpretation of biblical prophecy and of Christ's second coming, but more importantly, on the very gospel of Jesus Christ. Noted American analyst of the Palestinian-Israeli conflict, Cheryl Rubenberg, perceives that premillennialism

> has led to a conviction on the part of many Fundamentalists that Israel is absolved from any criticism. Indeed, since they believe God is working his divine will through the modern state of Israel, such Fundamentalists believe it is exempted from contemporary international norms and laws and from proper and just state behaviour. In this context Palestinians are seen as merely an impediment to the fulfillment of biblical prophecy.[13]

Christian Zionists claim that God will not bless America if the U.S. fails to support the State of Israel. They want not only support, but uncritical, *carte blanche* support of Israel. However, even close friends offer loving, constructive criticism of one another. "Faithful are the wounds of a friend" (Pr 27.6), wrote wise King Solomon.

Venerable Kenneth Taylor is an Evangelical and author of the immensely successful, *The Living Bible*. In 1957 Taylor was ahead of his time when he rebuked his own pro-Israel Christian community, "To our way of thinking, everything the state of Israel does is right, making her political enemies both God's enemies and ours."[14]

Christian Zionists cite Gen 12.3 as their primary scriptural basis for advocating uncritical support of Israel. Therein, God promised Abraham and his descendants, "I will bless those who bless you, and the one who curses you I will curse. And in you all the families of the earth shall be blessed" (cf. Gen 27.29). But is this to be applied to the present political State of Israel? Is the state equivalent to the people of Abraham? Most biblical scholars would argue to the contrary. Many go so far as to interpret Gen 12.3 to refer exclusively to the *spiritual* seed of Abraham, i.e., the true people of God, whether Jew or Gentile (cf. Rom 2.28-29). **Regardless of one's interpretation of Gen 12.3, criticizing Israel is not the same as cursing Israel.**

A most elementary understanding of the Hebrew Bible is that God Himself did not give uncritical support to Israel. He sent many prophets to correct the nation, rebuke its kings and people and turn them back to Him. For Christians to approve Israel's maltreatment of the Palestinians, and for this situation to continue or worsen, will inevitably lead to renewed anti-Semitism. In addition, anti-Christianism now pervades the Middle East, partly because of western Christians' uncritical pro-Israeli stance.

Christian Zionists hold disconcerting views on the outcome of the Israeli-Palestinian conflict. In *The Late Great Planet Earth* (1970), Hal Lindsey asserts that the Israeli-Palestinian conflict is "an unsolvable problem," and that the Palestinian effort to regain their homeland is merely "a matter of racial honor and sacred religious duty."[15] Yet the Palestinian National Charter (1968) expressly guarantees religious freedom. In contrast, in 1978 the Knesset passed Israel's "anti-missionary law" which forbids Christian proselytizing of Jews. Israeli police have been known to look the other way when bands of Orthodox Jews disrupt meetings and destroy property of some of the 29 Messianic *Yeshua* (Hebrew for "Jesus") congregations presently meeting in Israel.

Furthermore, both Hal Lindsey and John Walvoord, former longtime president of Dallas Theological Seminary, claim that it is only the Antichrist who will settle the Israeli-Palestinian controversy.[16] This very speculative interpretation no doubt leads some Christians to conclude, "Whatever the Antichrist is going to do, I sure wouldn't want to support *that*!" Such interpretations discourage efforts toward conflict resolution and encourage Jewish intransigence.

American Televangelists

Christian Zionism thrives in the U.S. In the U.S. alone, an estimated 40 million Christian Zionists far outnumber the 18 million Jews worldwide.[17] According to Douglas Kreiger, a prominent American Christian Zionist, there are approximately 250 pro-Israel evangelical organizations in the U.S. now.[18]

Nowhere is the message of Christian Zionism spread more powerfully than on America's television airwaves. One phenomenon of the '80s was the rise of U.S. televangelists. The most prominent were Christian Zionists. By satellite they reached millions of U.S. households, plus multitudes around the world. **Televangelists have had a strong influence on U.S. politics and on the growth of Christian Zionism.** Nielson TV ratings provided the following statistics on how many U.S. households listened to the leading televangelists in 1985:[19]

Pat Robertson (Charismatic Baptist); 16 million households; 19% of viewers.

Jimmy Swaggart (Assembly of God); 4.5 million households, 10.9% of Sunday viewers.

Jim Bakker (Assembly of God); 6 million households, 6.8% of viewers.

Jerry Falwell (Independent Baptist); 5.6 million households, 6.6% of viewers.

Kenneth Copeland (Pentecostal); 4.9 million households, 5.8% of viewers.

Richard DeHaan (Independent); 4 million households, 4.8% of viewers.

Rex Humbard (Pentecostal); 3.7 million households, 4.4% of viewers.

Pat Robertson was the most popular televangelist in the 1980's. As founder and president of Christian Broadcasting Network (CBN), he became a pioneer in Christian television broadcasting. Robertson is also very political. He campaigned for the 1988 Republican nomination for President and placed third. The Charismatic Baptist was including himself when he said in 1985, "There is regard and concern among Fundamentalists for the Arabs, but it pales into insignificance compared to feelings toward Jews."[20]

Jerry Falwell and Tours of the Holy Land

Despite Robertson's bid for President, televangelist and church minister Jerry Falwell exercised the most influence on U.S. politics and Christian Zionism in the '80s. His Moral Majority organization, disbanded in 1989, wielded enormous political clout.

Falwell has boasted that he is Israel's best Gentile friend. Indeed, Israel's Prime Minister Begin awarded Jerry Falwell the Jabotinsky medal, the only time it has ever been presented to a Gentile.

The Lynchburg, Virginia, minister has been a devoted servant of Jesus and preacher of the gospel. He has taken a strong and courageous stand against the current breakdown of morality in American society. But Jerry Falwell has worn blinders when it comes to the immorality of Israel's oppression of the Palestinians.

Jerry Falwell takes large groups of Christian tourists to the "Holy Land." Journalist and author Grace Halsell attended two of the Falwell tours in the mid-'80s. She claimed Falwell had no contact with Palestinian Christians and that in his speeches and discussions, he completely ignored the Palestinians and their trouble with Israel. Halsell claimed Falwell's custom on these trips was to contact top officials in Israel's government or military, give them his unequivocal support and frequently have them speak to his tour group.[21] Halsell recounts:

> On each tour, I attempted to count the hours we spent at Christian sites and hearing about Christ, and the time we spent learning the political and military achievements of the Zionist state. I came up with a ratio of about one to 30. That is, for every hour for Christ's teachings, we spent about 30 hours on the political-military aspects of Israeli life. We heard the words of Jesus read from the New Testament on three occasions.[22]

Here is how professing Christian and president emeritus of Bethlehem University, Joseph Loewenstein, perceives America's number one fundamentalist minister: "Falwell comes to Jerusalem. There are [Palestinian] Christians all around him, but he refuses to see them. He closes his eyes and his heart to Christians who[se ancestors] have lived here since the time of Christ. He forsakes their suffering—to please the Zionists."[23]

Palestinian attorney and American citizen Jonathan Kuttab recently returned to his native land to assist Palestinians in Jerusalem with their legal affairs. Kuttab asserts, "The Israelis know that . . . Christians such as Falwell are with them all the way, regardless of what they do morally or ethically. No matter how oppressive they become, Israelis know the American Christian Zionists are with them and willing to give them weapons and billions of dollars and vote for them in the United Nations."[24]

Lynn Bozich Shetzer relates an incident involving other Christian tourists in the "Holy Land"

> One very large group—600 church people—came as part of a religious convention while I was there. Being both philosophically and financially supportive of the State of Israel, they were treated to special programs and meetings, some with government officials. One evening a briefing was scheduled with a military officer who made a special announcement. News had just reached him that a successful reprisal raid had been carried out against a Lebanese refugee camp. Nearly 50 Palestinians were killed in retaliation for a road mine incident in which one Israeli soldier had died and several others were wounded. In response to the announcement, the Christian assembly rose to its feet and cheered, "Hallelujah! Praise the Lord!"[25]

Many American Christians dream about visiting the Holy Land. Over half a million professing Christians tour Israel each year. That number translates into many shekels for Israel. Tourism is Israel's largest industry, grossing over $1 billion. And it's all because it is the land of the Bible, where Jesus lived. Few tourists to the Holy Land seem concerned that Israeli Jews, whose economy they are boosting, took the land from the Palestinians, confiscated their homes, disallowed their return and over 40 years later still won't give them one inch of ground, let alone a dime! Maybe if these Christians would feel convicted about economically supporting the Jews' occupation of this land at the Palestinians' expense, they would do something about pressuring Israel to resolve the dispute!

All the Promised Land Now?

In 1982 Falwell met with other leaders of the Conservative Evangelicals in Washington, D.C. to affirm their support of Israel. They declared, "We believe all of the Holy Land is the inalienable possession of the Jewish people." Falwell has explained: "Genesis 15 sets the boundaries of Israel and supports its claim to the land. . . . the Jews have the historical, theological and legal right to the land called Israel."[26] **Jerry**

Falwell, as well as many other Christian Zionists, confuse the historic land of Israel with the entire Promised Land of Genesis 15.

How can Falwell add, "I am not against Arabs or Palestinians,"[27] when he asserts that present Israel has the divine right not only to keep all of the occupied territories, but to take the remainder of the Promised Land now as well? If they do, that means they have a divine mandate to seize Jordan, Lebanon and most of Syria! What is more anti-Arab than that? Don't expect the world just to sit back and watch it happen.

The Scriptures are crystal clear that the Jews are not yet entitled to all of the Promised Land. When the Israelites were poised to cross the Jordan River and take the land of Canaan, Moses instructed them to set aside three cities of refuge therein for fugitives guilty of unintentional manslaughter (Deut 19.2-7). But we saw in Chapter 1 that Canaan did not comprise all of the land promised to the patriarchs. So Moses added, "And if the LORD your God enlarges your territory, just as He has sworn to your fathers, and gives you all the land which He promised to give your fathers—if you carefully observe all this commandment, which I command you today, to love the LORD your God, and to walk in His ways always—then you shall add three more cities for yourself, besides these three" (vv. 8-9). Moses was referring to land west of the Jordan River, not east, which they had already taken.

Moses believed that God would indeed enlarge his people's territory someday. But notice that Moses makes the Jews' final acquisition of the Promised Land contingent on their obedience to the Law, which has still never happened. God withheld Philistia and Lebanon for this very reason. **Therefore, it must be concluded from Deut 19.8-9 that neither are today's Israeli Jews, who for the most part are irreligious, entitled to any more land than that possessed by their forefathers.**

Moreover, many Christians claim from Scripture that the Jews are not entitled to the remaining Promised Land until they accept Jesus as their Messiah, which they think will not occur *en masse* until Christ's second coming.

International Christian Embassy

The most outspoken Christian Zionist organization in the world is located in Jerusalem. The International Christian Embassy was established there in 1982. Much of Israel's Christian community spurns this organization.[28]

In 1985 the International Christian Embassy sponsored the first Christian Zionist Congress. Held in Basel, Switzerland, 589 persons from 27 countries attended to voice their support for Zionism. Resolutions were passed to (1) encourage more Jews to migrate to Israel, (2) approve both Israel's annexation of East Jerusalem and the declaration of all of Jerusalem as its capital, (3) insist that "all nations" move their embassies from Tel Aviv to Jerusalem, (4) urge Israel to annex the West Bank and (5) demand that the U.S. "desist from arming Israel's foes."

A Paradox

The friendship between Christian Zionists and Israel is a paradox. Christian Zionists are staunchly conservative, both politically and economically. Jews, on the other hand, are well known for being politically liberal and social-minded. Many Israeli Jews, or their parents, immigrated to Palestine from Russia or Europe, bringing with them socialistic ideas. Israel's kibbutzim—collectivist farms—reflect these socialistic values.

Moreover, many Christian Zionists are fervently evangelistic. Jerry Falwell certainly is. Evangelical Christians usually decry laws against their evangelism as an offense to God. Yet Israel allows no Christian proselytizing.

Finally, Jews usually avoid evangelistic Christians like the plague! But Israelis restrain their aversion in order to receive the Christian Zionists' uncritical backing of their state. How true the old adage, "Politics make strange bedfellows."

No Partiality

God says repeatedly in Scripture that He shows partiality to no one, neither the rich, the famous, nor the ostentatiously religious, not even the Jews. God exhorts us to do likewise. He commanded through Moses, "You shall not show partiality in judgment" (Deut 1.17). King Solomon added, "To show partiality in judgment is not good. He who says to the wicked, 'You are righteous,' peoples will curse him, nations will abhor him" (Pr 24.23-24). Indeed, some nations have been cursing U.S. administrations because they have been partial to the Jews.

Christian Zionists seem to think that because the Jews are God's Chosen People, they can do no wrong. We saw in Chapter 1 that this is not the case. The Torah confirms Arthur Hertzberg's contention about the Jews, that **"the meaning of their chosenness is that they are subject to the most severe and searching of moral judgments."**[29]

Once the church has clearly renounced its anti-Semitic past, it needs to unite to sound a prophet's voice of warning in the ear of Israel. But Christian Zionists are a clanging noise that deafens Israel's ear and hardens its heart. If they continue giving uncritical support to

Israel, strengthening its intransigence toward the Palestinians, they could unwittingly be paving the way for a resurgence of anti-Semitism. Indeed, American Jews are concerned about this possibility. Chaim Weizmann wrote in his autobiography, "I am certain the world will judge the Jewish state by how it will treat the Arabs."[30]

Present Return Not God's Promised Ingathering
Christian Zionists claim that God is now accomplishing His promised ingathering of the Jews to the Promised Land. They conclude therefore that to criticize anything about this process is, in effect, to criticize God. Moreover, many exuberantly expect continued Jewish immigration and Israeli land expansion to speed up the return of Christ. Cheryl Rubenberg is right. Christian Zionists see the Palestinians only as obstacles to God's resettlement of His Chosen People.

Throughout the Diaspora, most rabbis had said that God would not regather the Jews until Messiah would come. In contrast, Christian Zionists are often careless in failing to recognize the context of these passages on the return of Jews. Many portions which depict God's promised ingathering clearly appear in a millennial context. Some dispensational scholars readily admit this. Similarly, those premillennialists who are not Christian Zionists have long cautioned that most of the OT scriptures which expressly declare God's restoration of Israel will be fulfilled only *after* the second coming of Christ. They believe that **the present return is indicated in only a few biblical passages and that these do not designate it as promised and blessed by God.** (See Appendix C: God's Promised Regathering of the Jews.)

Anti-Ecumenicalism
Christian Zionists and other Fundamentalists tend to denigrate peace negotiations between nations and dismiss the UN as a worthless organization. This is in part due to their misunderstanding of Jesus' prediction, "You will be hearing of wars and rumors of wars. . . . nation will rise against nation, and kingdom against kingdom" until the end of this age (Mt 24.6-7). Just because Jesus forewarned that wars would continue until His return does not mean that governments should forego efforts toward peace and justice in this world. Jesus predicted that Judas would betray Him, but He did not condone Judas' betrayal. In fact, Jesus had taught previously in His Sermon on the Mount, "Blessed are the peacemakers" (Mt 5.9). Early dispensationalists erred by applying this sermon only to the future millennium and not to the present church age.[31]

In addition, most Fundamentalists attend independent churches, which are noted for being anti-denominational and anti-ecumenical. Fundamentalists often take the opposite view from the WCC or the UN on some issue simply because they oppose these groups rather than considering their arguments. Their individualism leads to isolation. A lack of dialogue with Christians of other persuasions provides them no challenge to examine their own views more critically.

Fundamentalists oppose ecumenism in any form mostly because of their futuristic interpretation of Rev 17. The harlot riding a beast is interpreted to be an endtime apostate, one-world church led by the Catholic Church, or perhaps the WCC, and including many denominations. Fundamentalists therefore regard ecumenicalism as a precursor to the formation of a final, false church.

Other interpreters see the harlot as representing not the church in particular but organized, false religion in general, not only during the endtimes but throughout all of history as well. Its center in the last days is not the seven-hilled city of Rome, but Babylon.[32] This interpretation does not cause people to turn a deaf ear to what ecumenical organizations and church denominations are saying about the Israeli-Palestinian conflict.

Soviet Support of the PLO

We have already seen that the Soviet Union has clearly been pro-Palestinian and that it still refuses to have diplomatic relations with Israel. Furthermore, during the 1970s, some PLO resistance organizations held Marxist views and received arms from the Soviet Union. This connection between the Soviets and the PLO has caused Christian Zionists further to oppose the PLO, and therefore the Palestinians, not only because of Soviet atheistic communism but on account of another of their points of eschatology.

Because of their interpretation of Eze 38-39 as a Russian-led invasion of future Israel, Christian Zionists tend to oppose Soviet participation in any negotiations to settle the Palestinian-Israeli conflict.

The prophet Ezekiel predicted an awesome military invasion of the Jewish-occupied land of Israel by an enemy from the north during the last days. Ezekiel identified the ungodly leader of this attack as "Gog of the land of Magog, the prince of Rosh, Meshech, and Tubal" (Eze 38.2; cf. v.3; 39.1). Christian Zionists have adopted the interpretation, held by nearly all dispensationalists, that the proper name "Rosh" indicates Gog will be a Russian leader and that the Russians will be the primary invading force. To be against Russia, therefore, is to be on God's side.

This interpretation of Eze 38-39 is based rather tenuously on the similarity of the words Rosh and Russia, Meshech and Moscow and Tubal and Tobolsk. Biblical scholar and archaeologist Edwin Yamauchi asserts that such an identification "would be a gross anachronism." That is, the word "Rus", from which the name "Russia" derives, was unknown in that land until the Middle ages, well over a thousand years after Ezekiel wrote.[33] Moreover, some worthy English versions do not even include this word.

The Hebrew word *rosh* means "chief." This is why the KJV, RSV, NIV translate the Hebrew words in Eze 38-39 as "chief prince." The "Rosh" translation, which appears in the JB, NEB and NASB, originates with the LXX. That is, the LXX does not translate *rosh* but simply transliterates it as a proper noun. This "Russian" interpretation has been refuted by several able biblical scholars in this century.[34] Prominent dispensationalist Charles Ryrie notes at "Rosh" in Eze 38.2 in his *Ryrie Study Bible* in the NASB: "(better, the chief prince of Meshech and Tubal). The area of modern Turkey."

Aliens

When modern Israel was founded, many Jewish leaders hoped that the democratic nation would serve as a model of justice for the world. They reasoned that justice would be so indelibly imprinted on the consciousness of every Jew following the long Diaspora and the Nazi Holocaust. Besides, the Jews' religious heritage demanded it. Indeed, many Israeli Jews deplore the police brutality that has been used to quell *intifada*, as well as some other denials of Palestinian rights.

Christian Zionist leaders who fail to speak out against suppression of Palestinian rights have lost touch with the spirit of the biblical prophets. The Hebrew prophets were not only seized by the Spirit to predict future events; they were also concerned with contemporary social problems. Most prophets' primary mission was to denounce injustice, oppression, impoverishment and other immoralities, and to call the people back to God. How one treats his neighbor was, and is, of great concern to God and His prophets.

God commanded the Israelites through Moses, "You shall love your neighbor as yourself" (Lev 19.18). Today's Palestinians living in Israel and the occupied territories are more than just Israel's neighbors. Biblically, they are "aliens." The words "alien," "stranger," "foreigner" and "sojourner" appear frequently in the Hebrew Bible. They signify relatively the same type of person: "a non-Israelite who lived for a time, or possibly for his whole life, in the midst of the Israelitish nation, but without being incorporated into it by circumcision."[35]

Moses and later prophets instructed Israel concerning the alien:

1. "Show your love for the alien, for you were aliens in the land of Egypt" (Deut 10.19; cf. Ex 22.21; 23.9).

2. "The stranger who resides with you shall be to you as the native among you, and you shall love him as yourself" (Lev 19.34).

3. "You shall not pervert the justice due an alien" (Deut 24.17).

4. "If you do not oppress the alien. . . . and do not shed innocent blood in this place, . . . then I will let you dwell in this place, in the land that I gave to your fathers forever and ever" (Jer 7.6-7).

5. "You shall not wrong a stranger or oppress him, . . . If you afflict him at all, and if He does cry out to Me, . . . I will kill you with the sword; and your wives shall become widows and your children father-less" (Ex 22.21, 23, 24).

These are only a sampling of solemn biblical warnings for Israeli authorities to ponder regarding their treatment of the Palestinians. Have Israeli authorities been oppressing Palestinians in the occupied territories and shedding innocent blood? **May the church unitedly cry out to Israel, "Love the Palestinians as yourselves."**

Conclusion

Western Christians have been divided concerning the Palestinian-Is-raeli conflict. **Denominational churches have spoken out with a prophet's voice against Israel's failure to recognize the same rights for the Palestinians as for the Jews. On the other hand, due to their eschatology, Christian Zionists are providing uncritical support to Israel, support which encourages continued intransigence on the part of Israeli leaders and which could inadvertently fuel smoldering fires of anti-Semitism.** Their need to overlook oppression and injustice ought to signal to the Christian Zionists that their scenario for the endtimes is seriously defective.

Chapter 9

PROPOSED SOLUTIONS

Throughout the past generation, the Israeli-Palestinian conflict has continued to loom as the most serious threat to peace in the Middle East. The problem has contributed an enormous arms build-up there. In 1977 Egyptian President Sadat summed up the Palestinian problem well, "If this question is not solved there will be no peace" in the Middle East.[1]

A solution to the Israeli-Palestinian conflict has eluded peace negotiators throughout the 20th century. Many solutions have been offered by kings, presidents and statesmen. Those offered before 1947 were presented in Chapter Three. First the League of Nations, then Great Britain, then the UN have all persistently applied themselves to resolving this problem. In its nearly 45-year history, the UN has not concerned itself with any problem more, or for a longer period of time, than the Israeli-Palestinian conflict.

UN Partition Plan (1947)
Perhaps no solution offered so far appears more reasonable than the UN Partition Plan of 1947. (See Chapter 3.) But its patch-work division of the land was a drawback. Why was the proposed line of demarcation so irregular? It was drawn according to demographics. Except for the sparsely-populated Negev, those portions of Palestine to be granted to the Jews were only the areas which contained a Jewish majority in population.

Over 40 years later, it seems little known that these irregular borders drawn up by UNSCOP were only intended as a starting point for negotiation. It was expected that the two parties would negotiate boundaries acceptable to each.

After the UN Partition Plan was passed in late 1947, hostilities between Jews and Palestinians in the region intensified. This led to the Jews' Proclamation of Independence and war with the Arabs, resulting in Israeli statehood. Thereafter, the UN Partition Plan became a dead issue. However, some analysts think that, according to international law, it is still applicable.

The Jews had accepted the UN Partition Plan until they preempted it by declaring statehood in May, 1948. The Palestinians rejected it, still hoping to regain all of Mandate Palestine.

Forty years later there has been a shift in sentiment. The PLO now accepts the concept of two independent states in Palestine. Nearly all Israeli leaders have rejected the idea. Some hope to retain all of Palestine.

UN Security Council Resolutions 242 and 338

No major proposal for resolving the Arab-Israeli conflict was offered for the twenty years following the UN Partition Plan.

Soon after the 1967 War, the UN Security Council drafted a brief resolution which still remains the most important document in the history of the conflict. **Resolution 242 demanded that Israel withdraw from the occupied territories and acknowledged the right of each state in the region to have "secure and recognized boundaries."** (See Appendix D: UN Security Council Resolution 242.) Israel, of course, did not withdraw.

Jews and Arabs disagreed over the interpretation of Resolution 242. **The Israelis contended that in order for them to live within secure, defensible borders, the resolution only required their partial withdrawal from the occupied territories.** This view provided the basis for the Labor Party's policy of trading "land for peace." The Arabs, on the other hand, argued that the resolution demanded that Israel withdraw from **all** of the occupied territories. Despite these disagreements, most parties involved still recognize Resolution 242 as a legitimate basis for negotiation.

The Jews and Arabs remained at an impasse because of their opposing preconditions for negotiation. Israel refused to negotiate with the Arab states until they stopped their belligerency toward Israel and recognized its legitimacy, a condition which was indeed presupposed in the resolution. The Arabs enjoined Israel first to show good faith by engaging in the negotiating process. The Arabs also required that the Palestinians be included in negotiations as if they were a sovereign state. But Israeli authorities had always denied that the Palestinians constituted a national entity. For many years Jewish leaders had argued that the Palestinians relinquished any aspirations for statehood when they rejected the UN Partition Plan. They had alleged that the Palestinians were strictly refugees and that they should be resettled in Arab states. Some had named Jordan as the Palestinian state.

The PLO rejected Resolution 242 because it called the Palestinians "refugees," which was received as an insult, and because it failed to recognize the Palestinians' right to a sovereign state.

On the day of the first ceasefire of the 1973 War, the UN Security Council met and passed the even more brief Resolution 338. It reaffirmed Resolution 242, adding that negotiations to achieve peace should begin "under appropriate auspices." (See Appendix E: UN Security Council Resolution 338.)

In 1974 Yasser Arafat indicated a policy shift when he said he would support Resolutions 242 and 338 "if a complementary resolution is passed which calls for a national homeland and Palestinian national rights," ensuring a comprehensive settlement.[2] These requirements by Arafat were being included in General Assembly resolutions, though not in those of the Security Council.

Another UN resolution in 1974 clarified that "no territorial acquisition or special advantage resulting from aggression is or shall be recognized as lawful."[3] Israel refused to recognize this definition as retroactive and therefore applicable to its 1967 seizure of the occupied territories.

The General Assembly, however, consisting of the entire UN membership, lacks the authority of the Security Council. The Security Council has never affirmed the Palestinians' right to an independent state in Palestine. Nevertheless, it is conceivable that a Palestinian state could be achieved through Resolutions 242 and 338, since most parties understand "appropriate auspices" in Resolution 338 to mean an international conference. Israel refuses to accept an international conference, fearing that the big powers would try to force it to relinquish territory to the Palestinians for their state.

Israel's Concern for Security
Security has always been a chief concern of Israeli authorities. Apart from the occupied territories, much of the State of Israel is so narrow (9-15 miles) that it lacks enough strategic depth to be adequately defended. This elongated coastal region, from Haifa to Ashqelon (Hebrew spelling), contains 80% of all of Israel's Jewish population. Most of Israel's industry is located here, as well as seaports

and its main airport—Lod Airport servicing Tel Aviv and Jerusalem.

The irregular border between Israel and the West Bank makes matters worse. It stretches nearly three times longer than the Jordan River border, which separates the West Bank and Jordan. If the West Bank became Israeli territory, the Jordan River would serve as a clear physical barrier separating Jews from Arabs. A U.S. military briefing which opposes establishing a Palestinian state in the occupied territories states:

> The introduction of sophisticated weapons systems into the Middle East arena. . . . makes it almost impossible to ensure an effective defence of Israel, with acceptable loss, from the pre-1967 boundaries. . . . Had the Arab attack of Yom Kippur 1973 been launched from the pre-1967 armistice lines, Israel would have been sliced in two, Jerusalem severed from the rest of the country, and the major centers of population would have been overrun by enemy forces.[4]

With pre-1967 borders, i.e., without the West Bank, most of Israel was vulnerable to an air strike from the east. Much of Israel consists of the low, coastal plain, whereas the West Bank is elevated hill country. Flying in low from the east, today's fighter planes could avoid Israeli radar detection until they reached the central mountain range in the West Bank. Israel would have only precious seconds to react. Under the threat of war, pre-1967 Israeli borders would make preemptive air strikes absolutely essential. Dayan adamantly maintained that the pre-1967 border with Jordan was indefensible. U.S. defense experts have always agreed that Israel's return to pre-1967 borders would only heighten tensions in the region. **It seems that autonomy is the best that Israeli leaders can allow for the West Bank if Israel is to maintain defensible borders.**

Geneva Peace Conference (December 1973)

The Geneva Peace Conference was held soon after the 1973 War, in which Egypt, Jordan and Syria fought Israel. Jointly sponsored by the UN, U.S. and USSR, it has come closest to being an international conference. But a comprehensive settlement was impossible; Syria refused to attend because the PLO was not invited.

Only one meeting was held. A decision was reached to support U.S. Secretary of State Henry Kissinger in his new approach to peace negotiations in the Middle East. Called "shuttle diplomacy," it consisted of his scurrying back and forth between Arab capitals and

Jerusalem, holding private discussions with heads of state. Kissinger's diplomacy led to the later Camp David Accords.

In 1977 the Soviets and Americans issued a joint communique calling for a reconvening of the Geneva Conference, this time with participation of all parties involved. The effort was discontinued when Egyptian President Sadat began his peace initiative soon afterwards.

Ever since the 1973 Geneva Conference, peace negotiators have favored one of the following methods of pursuing peace between Israelis and Arabs: (1) an international peace conference, in which all pertinent parties are represented and all issues addressed or (2) bilateral discussions, which only address issues relating to those parties involved. Israel's Likud Party opposes an international conference. It maintains that the superpowers would attempt to coerce Israel into an undesirable settlement. Neither does Likud recognize the PLO as a legitimate and pertinent party. The Labor Party advocates such a conference, although party head, Shimon Peres, has opposed PLO participation. The PLO and most Arab states want an international conference. The Reagan administration never pursued the conference idea in the '80s.

Kissinger Commitment (1975)

Two years after the 1973 War, a Sinai disengagement agreement was signed by Israel, Egypt and the U.S. Henry Kissinger, then secretary of state, attached a statement to it. **This "Kissinger Commitment" promised Israel that the U.S. would not recognize or negotiate with the PLO until it recognized Israel's existence and accepted Resolution 242.** Many observers believe that this U.S. pledge considerably hindered later negotiations.

In 1979 an action by U.S. ambassador to the UN Andrew Young caused a commotion because of the Kissinger commitment. It led to his forced resignation. He met "inadvertently" with a PLO representative at the UN. Israel charged that this meeting was a violation of the Kissinger commitment. Accusations of espionage, intelligence leaks, and many questions of legality surfaced as a result of this incident. Clyde R. Mark, prominent foreign affairs researcher for the U.S. Congressional Research Service, maintained:

> Legally, the United States is not committed to Israel not to meet or negotiate with the PLO. In fact, the Congress specifically stated that it did not approve the U.S.-Israeli understandings of September 1975 or March 1979 . . . which included the Kissinger pledge not to meet with the PLO. Those understandings have

not been submitted to the Congress as executive agreements or treaties.

His rationale was that, without congressional approval, the Kissinger commitment lacked the force of law.

Israeli Autonomy Plan (December 1977)

In late 1977 Israeli Prime Minister Begin proposed to the Knesset that some form of limited self-government (autonomy) be allowed in the West Bank and Gaza. His proposal provided for the following:

1. Israel to maintain sovereignty over the territories.

2. Israeli troops and police to remain in the territories to keep peace.

3. Election of an Israeli-Jordanian Administrative Council to administer eleven government departments and decide which existing laws would be applied in the territories.

4. Palestinians to decide between citizenship in Israel or Jordan. (The Likud Party later dropped this offer of citizenship in Israel.)

Israel's Labor Party opposed this plan and advocated trading part of the occupied territories for peace.

Camp David Accords (September 1978)

In a state visit to Washington in early 1977, Egyptian President Anwar el Sadat privately shared with the new U.S. President, Jimmy Carter, his desire to pursue peace with Israel. Carter thereafter became intensely involved in peace negotiations between Egypt and Israel.

In late 1977 Sadat made a daring and dramatic overture toward achieving peace. Without little advance notice, he visited Jerusalem and even spoke to the Knesset. Israel's Prime Minister Begin reciprocated by visiting Egypt the next month. Sadat had achieved a thaw in relations between the two countries.

President Carter invited the two men and their advisers to the presidential retreat center at Camp David, Maryland, for peace negotiations. They met for two weeks in September, 1978. Begin and Sadat clashed severely. Carter kept them separated much of the time by meeting with their advisers. Carter's Christian convictions provided him with an extra stimulus for facilitating the tough negotiations.

The Camp David Accords, as they came to be called, became Carter's legacy as U.S. president. They provided the framework for the Egypt-Israel Peace Treaty signed by Sadat and Begin six months later. **In the accords, Israel agreed to return the Sinai Peninsula to Egypt**

and remove its armed forces and settlements. The U.S. would compensate Israel for $3.3 billion spent on a military airfield there by financing a new airstrip in the nearby Negev desert. Egypt could use the Israeli-built airstrips for non-military purposes only. Egyptian police and international peacekeeping forces would be stationed on the south side of the border in a buffer zone. Egypt also pledged to allow Israeli ships freedom of passage through the Suez Canal, Gulf of Aqaba and Straits of Tiran.

Of major importance in the Camp David Accords was the fact that for the first time, Israel recognized "the legitimate rights of the Palestinian people." Palestinian residents would elect a self-governing authority and select a police force to replace Israeli police, though a few would remain. This point did not accord with Resolution 242, which requires the complete withdrawal of Israeli forces. Five years later the final status of the West Bank and Gaza would be decided and implemented by a committee consisting of members from Israel, Egypt, Jordan, and the self-governing authority, but not the PLO.

Proposals were made in the accords for achieving a peace treaty between Israel and Jordan. Arguments would ensue as to whether or not the accords placed a moratorium on additional Jewish settlements in the territories.

One month after Camp David, the Arab League met at Bagdad, Iraq, to condemn Egypt, the U.S. and the accords. Sadat was branded a traitor to the Palestinians' cause and to Arab unity. Threats were issued to punish him and boycott Egypt. Egypt was ousted from membership, and the League transferred its headquarters from Cairo to Tunis. The Arab world was split.

The Arabs dismissed the Camp David Accords as fundamentally flawed. The Palestinians had always argued that "legitimate rights," which Israel recognized in the accords, include self-determination and therefore sovereignty, not just autonomy. Neither did the accords address the problem of the dispossessed Palestinians, who constituted over half of all Palestinians. Finally, the agreement did not recognize the Palestinians' choice of the PLO as their representative.

Egypt-Israel Peace Treaty (March 1979)

Despite the expected opposition, Sadat and Begin signed the treaty in March, 1979, and began autonomy talks. Sadat broke them off the next year when the Knesset declared Jerusalem as Israel's "eternal and undivided capital." Soon after Sadat resumed the talks, Egypt and the world lost a courageous statesman. The personable Sadat was assassinated in October, 1981, in his own country by Moslem radicals violently opposed to the treaty.

Both Syrian President Assad and Jordanian King Hussein are convinced that the treaty only aggravated the Palestinian situation.

Carter and Begin soon differed over interpretation of the accords. Its language was ambiguous, which is sometimes the case in order for parties to achieve an agreement. Begin claimed it permitted Jewish settlements in the occupied territories after a three-month moratorium; Carter claimed that Begin agreed to a five-year delay. The settlements were supposedly designed to enhance Israel's security, yet former Defense Minister Dayan argued that they provided no military advantage whatsoever. He and other Israelis charged that they were solely for gaining a foothold toward achieving permanent possession of the West Bank. Believing Begin had no intention of granting real autonomy to the Palestinians, Israel's war hero, Dayan, resigned from Begin's cabinet in late 1979.

The autonomy plan was never instituted due to Palestinian and Jordanian opposition. Carter later accused Begin of reneging on the agreement when he proclaimed before the Knesset, "I, Menachem, son of Ze'ev and Hana Begin, do solemnly swear that as long as I serve the nation as prime minister, we will not leave any part of Judea, Samaria, the Gaza Strip or the Golan Heights."[5]

Carter wrote in 1985 that "without American leadership, an international forum under U.N. Resolution 338 is the only logical alternative." He also advised abolishing conditions for negotiation, including the Kissinger commitment.[6]

European Community Declaration (June 1981)

The European Community (EC) met in Venice in June, 1981, and issued an eleven-point declaration for settling the Palestinian problem. Also called the Venice Declaration, it demanded Israel's withdrawal from the occupied territories and condemned both the settlements therein and Israel's making Jerusalem its capital. The declaration asked all parties involved to recognize Israel's existence and the Palestinians' right to self-determination. Finally, it called for a comprehensive peace conference, with PLO participation, rather than Camp David's bilateral approach.

Arab states and the PLO welcomed this initiative, but Israel rejected it.

European nations have differed on the issues and their influence has been minimal. Nevertheless, in early 1988 EC members reaffirmed their Venice Declaration and reiterated a call for an international conference under UN auspices "as early as possible." They stated that "the status quo in the occupied territories is not sustainable" and that they "deeply deplore the repressive measures taken by Israel, which are in violation of international law and human rights."

PLO Plan (August 1981)
Through a representative, Yasser Arafat proposed a three-stage plan at a UN regional meeting in August, 1981. It was similar to the EC proposal and one offered later by Saudi Arabian King Fahd. It called for Israeli withdrawal from the occupied territories and the establishment of an independent Palestinian state therein, with peace guarantees by a UN peacekeeping force. This PLO plan received little media coverage.

Reagan Statement (September 1982)
Israel's 1982 pounding of the PLO in Beirut brought much attention to the Palestinian problem and several proposals for its solution.

On September 1, 1982, President Reagan affirmed U.S. support of the Camp David Accords. He declared, "America's commitment to the security of Israel is ironclad." **He also acknowledged "the legitimate rights of the Palestinians," but denied recognition of the PLO. The president urged proceeding with autonomy talks but not an international peace conference. He also endorsed associating the territories with Jordan.**

Reagan had some European support. Britain had earlier announced its rejection of the PLO as a terrorist organization. France withdrew its endorsement of the Venice Declaration due to its inclusion of the PLO in a comprehensive peace conference.

To Begin's chagrin, Reagan also demanded a freeze on Israeli settlements in the occupied territories. The Jewish Agency had earlier announced its "master plan" for placing 1.2 million Jewish settlers in the West Bank in the next 30 years. By 1982 there were 120 Jewish settlements, with a total population of approximately 65,000, in the West Bank. In the Gaza Strip there were eight settlements, with about 2,700 people. Begin yielded. No settlements were added until two small ones in 1989.

All of these settlements violate the Fourth Geneva Convention (1949), which Israel rejects. It forbids an occupier to settle, or annex, any newly-acquired territory. The U.S. has always considered these settlements as monstrous "obstacles to peace."

Reagan also declared that "the United States will not support the establishment of an independent Palestinian state in the West

Bank and Gaza, and we will not support annexation or permanent control by Israel." It may be noted that the Reagan statement rejected a Palestinian state in the West Bank/Gaza, but it left open the possibility of its being located in some other territory in Palestine. Reagan later said of the Palestinians, "We can't go on with these people in not providing something in the nature of a homeland," adding that he did not mean a sovereign state.[7]

The PLO rejected the Reagan statement, insisting that a Palestinian state be formed first, with later confederation with Jordan.

Jordan's King Hussein is perhaps the most experienced and respected dignitary in the Middle East. He is very tentative in his decisions regarding the Palestinians. Two years before ascending the throne—his father was mentally incompetent—17-year old Hussein witnessed the assassination of his grandfather, King Abdullah, on the temple mount at Jerusalem. Palestinians were suspected; it was rumored that King Abdullah had been meeting secretly with the Israelis.

Hussein's association with Arafat and the PLO improved after stormy years in the early 1970s. Now, the king vows he will only carry out the wishes of the Palestinian people, doing nothing without the approval of Arafat and the PLO. Hussein believes Israel's intent is to stall negotiations regarding the future status of the territories and eventually to annex at least the West Bank.

King Hussein has endeared himself more to the Palestinians than has Syrian President Assad. For several years Assad rejected Arafat's PLO leadership and seemed inclined toward becoming the sole leader of the Palestinians himself.

One week after Reagan's statement, Israeli Prime Minister Begin shouted before the Knesset, "No one will determine for us the borders of the Land of Israel. No one will determine for us what is our homeland. . . . This is our homeland! It is our country, the land of our fathers and the land of our sons."[8] Both Begin and present Prime Minister Yitzhak Shamir have frequently made such assertions. Yet we have already seen in Chapter 2 that historical Israel did not include the Plain of Philistia.

In early 1983 President Reagan questioned how long Israel could go on "living as an armed camp," with 130% inflation.[9] Every young Israeli Jew must serve three years in the military and many years thereafter in the reserves.

During the '80s, one-fourth of Israel's annual budget was spent on defense. The U.S. averaged $3 billion per year in foreign aid to Israel, much of it in military equipment. The past few years, over one-fourth of all U.S. foreign aid has gone to tiny Israel.

Fahd-Fez Plan (September 1982)
A week after PLO evacuation from Beirut, the Arab League met at
Fez, Morocco, for its Twelfth Summit. Arafat was welcomed as a hero.
A brief eight-point declaration was issued addressing the Palestinian
problem. Features included those put forward a year earlier by Saudi
King Fahd, derived completely from past UN resolutions. But it dif-
ferred by affirming PLO leadership. It proposed that an independent
Palestinian state be established in the West Bank/Gaza under PLO
leadership, with Jerusalem as its capital. It also requested UN
peacekeeping guarantees and compensation to all dispossessed Palestinians.
Except for Israel and the U.S., reactions to the Fez plan were generally positive.

Soviet Plan (September 1982)
Except for the 1973 Geneva Conference, the Soviet Union has virtually
been excluded from peace negotiations in the Middle East. Nevertheless, in mid-September, 1982, Soviet Secretary General Brezhnev announced a six-point plan similar to the Fahd-Fez Plan. It proposed
reconvening an international conference, co-chaired by the Soviets
and Americans, this time with PLO participation. Brezhnev criticized
the Camp David Accords for dividing Egypt from the Arab world and
declared the right of Palestinians to "their own state." This plan was
later clarified, requiring Israel's complete withdrawal from the occupied territories and the creation therein of a sovereign Palestinian
state. It was endorsed by all Arab states and the PLO.

Jordan-PLO Initiative (February 1985)
In early 1985 Hussein and Arafat released a joint agreement calling
for an international conference, consisting of the five permanent members of the UN Security Council and a joint Jordanian-Palestinian
delegation with PLO members, to establish a Palestinian state in the
territories in confederation with Jordan. That summer Hussein
formed the Jordanian-Palestinian delegation. In contrast to Likud,
the Labor Party's Prime Minister Peres had campaigned in the 1984
elections for such a conference. He now added that all participants
should have diplomatic relations with Israel. This was aimed at the
Soviet Union. Peres surprisingly revealed intentions to relinquish up
to 70% of the West Bank in a policy called "trading land for peace."
Unfortunately, this effort collapsed in October that year when Israel
bombed PLO headquarters in Tunisia. More than 70 people were
killed. Some accused Israel of purposely torpedoing the peace pro-

cess, and the U.S. was criticized for failing to promptly condemn the attack.

Recent Developments
In the mid-'80s, disharmony erupted in PLO ranks between moderates and radicals. By then, Arafat was considered a moderate. He survived this instability and publicly renounced terrorism in late 1985. For awhile, the PLO still carried out some terrorist acts.

In early 1986 Arafat reiterated his disapproval of UN Resolutions 242 and 338. He again requested UN clarification to insure Palestinian self-determination in the occupied territories.

Also in early 1986, Prime Minister Peres proposed ceding parts of the West Bank to the Palestinians under the administration of Jordan. Shamir and other Likud members of the coalition government adamantly objected.

In early 1988, U.S. Secretary of State George Schultz conducted whirlwind tours of the Middle East to get autonomy talks started. He proposed a rehash of the Camp David Accords at an international conference without PLO attendance. While in Jerusalem, Schultz offered to meet with any Israeli Palestinians. Due to PLO disapproval, none showed. The same thing had happened in 1977 to U.S. Secretary of State Cyrus Vance. Moderate Israeli Palestinians refuse to defy the PLO in fear for their lives. Palestinian collaborators are sometimes killed. Schultz himself escaped an assassination attempt by PLO elements. Such deplorable acts by the PLO, especially against the U.S. Secretary of State, only hurt the Palestinians' cause.

American policy seemed to shift when Schultz met in the U.S. with two members of the PNC who are also U.S. citizens. These two distinguished Palestinians, Edward Said and Ibrahim Abu-Lughod (both referenced in this book), are prominent professors at high-ranking American universities. The meeting was first approved by Arafat. Shamir accused Schultz of violating the Kissinger commitment. Schultz denied the charge on the basis that the two men were not members of the PLO.

In mid-1988 President Reagan seemed to direct his remarks to Shamir when he said, "Those leaders, who . . . consistently reject new ideas and fail to exploit realistic opportunities to bring about negotiations make progress impossible and in the end, they will have to answer to their own people for the suffering that will inevitably result."[10]

After meeting all its demands, in late 1988 the Reagan administration began holding talks with the PLO for the first time.

In mid-1989 the new U.S. Secretary of State James Baker stunned 1,200 members of the most powerful Jewish pro-Israel lobby in America by saying, "For Israel, now is the time to lay aside, once and for all, the unrealistic vision of a greater Israel." Baker did not appear to be using the term "greater Israel" to mean the entire Promised Land, but that Israel must abandon hope of ever annexing the occupied territories. He condemned Jewish settlements in the territories and affirmed Palestinian "political rights."[11] Shamir called the speech "useless."

Soon afterwards, Shamir drew on the Camp David concept by proposing open elections for Palestinians in the occupied territories. Those elected would begin autonomy talks with Israeli officials. He ruled out an independent Palestinian state. As did his predecessor, Menachem Begin, Prime Minister Shamir vowed Israel would retain permanent control of the occupied territories. He also forbade Palestinians of East Jerusalem from voting. Shamir further alienated the U.S. administration by announcing that the settlements program would be resumed. He added that over the next several years the expected influx of Russian emigres would be settled in the West Bank.

In early 1990, hardliner Ariel Sharon resigned from the Likud cabinet over objections to Shamir's proposed peace plan. Sharon had demanded that the Palestinians end *intifada* as a precondition to negotiations. He further announced plans to challenge Shamir as head of Likud and to campaign for prime minister of Israel.

For the first time in the history of U.S.-Israel relations, President Bush announced in early March, 1990, that the U.S. would reduce aid to Israel if it began new settlements in the West Bank and East Jerusalem. As a result of this and disagreement over the election plan, Israel's coalition government collapsed.

Also, the U.S. Congress was hotly debating whether or not to slightly reduce its financial aid to Israel and others and give it to the democratically-emerging Eastern European countries. Adding to the controversy, in April the U.S. Senate contradicted established government policy by passing a resolution recognizing Jerusalem as Israel's capital.

Conclusion
The many proposals for settling the Israeli-Palestinian conflict reveal that numerous world leaders have expended much effort toward resolving this complex problem, yet to no avail. **It seems everything possible has been tried except the most promising possibility: a comprehensive, international peace conference including all parties to**

the conflict, especially the PLO. Until this occurs, it appears that the Palestinian problem will continue and may worsen.

Since 1971, a Harvard University team of negotiators, directed by social psychologist Dr. Herbert C. Kelman, has conducted numerous workshops on conflict resolution. Several have been attended by Israeli and Palestinian scholars. Rarely have Israelis and Palestinians met face to face to discuss their conflict, even in Palestine. After several years' experience as a facilitator in these workshops, here is the sum of Kelman's conclusions: **There can be no resolution of the Israeli-Palestinian conflict unless each party gets its own state in a portion of Palestine.**[12]

Since 1967, all the major plans offered for resolving the Palestinian-Israeli conflict have focused on the West Bank/Gaza as the land for the Palestinians. There are so many strikes against this territory ever going to the Palestinians. **It's time to consider another alternative.**

Chapter 10

A NEW PROPOSAL

How can anyone hope to propose a meaningful solution to the Israeli-Palestinian conflict when so many able statesmen have tried so hard yet failed to achieve peace? The proposal in this chapter is not original with this author. It was discovered as a by-product of the author's lifelong study of Bible prophecy.

Some of the Hebrew prophets seem to imply the existence of a Palestinian state in their predictions of endtime events. The last four chapters of this book deal with these scriptures in detail. But for now, let us not appeal to the prophets but to history and to reason for a solution.

Historical Precedent

The claim that Jews are divinely entitled to the entire land of Palestine is obviously unacceptable to a secular world. Besides, most Zionists are irreligious. Therefore, in attempting to establish their right to Palestine, the Zionists' primary argument has been ancient historical precedent: their forefathers possessed the land nearly 3,500 years ago.

On the other hand, the Palestinians' primary claim to the land is based on more recent property ownership. In contrast to the Jews, many Palestinian families owned deeded land in Palestine, some for hundreds of years prior to their dispossessions in 1948 and 1967.

Palestinians also assert a claim to historical precedent. Their claim, however, is usually considered to date back only 1250-1750 years, to either the Arabian conquest (A.D. 638) or to the Romans' expulsion of the Jews (A.D. 135). Yet we saw in Chapter 5 that Palestinians have **some** connection to Palestine farther back in history.

We have also seen that the Jews' claim to historical precedent in the land of Palestine was recognized by both the League of Nations and the United Nations. However, the League of Nations, like the previous Balfour Declaration, only recognized the Jews' right to a national home **in** Palestine. And the UN's decision was to divide Palestine into two separate states.

West Bank and Gaza Strip?

Most of the proposals thus far offered for resolving the Palestinian-Israeli conflict have focused on giving the Palestinians the West Bank and the Gaza Strip. Why these particular territories? Slightly enlarged versions of these were suggested in the UN Partition Plan of 1947 because the Arab population was concentrated mostly there. From 1948 to 1967, most parties in the Middle East recognized the West Bank and the Gaza Strip as the Palestinians' land, even though it was controlled by Jordan and Egypt, respectively.

It should be remembered that the UN Partition Plan's division of the land of Palestine was only a suggestion. It was intended as a starting point for negotiations between the Jews and Palestinians in determining the final borders of the two states.

A Palestinian state in two separate parcels of land is impractical. The continuing focus on giving the West Bank and the Gaza Strip to the Palestinians should be abandoned.

Besides such a state being unfeasible, most Israeli Jews reject the idea of relinquishing the West Bank to the Palestinians. **For many Jews, forfeiting Judea and Samaria (the West Bank) would be like cutting the heart out of ancient Israel. Indeed, giving the Palestinians the West Bank would not be in accord with ancient historical precedent.**

Philistia for the Palestinians

As was made clear in Chapter 2, throughout its ancient history Israel never decisively possessed the Plain of Philistia. The very few years during which the ancient Israelites occupied and settled part of the Plain of Philistia do not support modern Jewish claims to that area.

The conflict might be resolved by dividing the land of Palestine into two separate parcels for the two states on the basis of historical precedent. Indeed, if historical precedent were followed for all of the land of Palestine, the Plain of Philistia would have to be severed from Israel. Who is more deserving of its possession than the Palestinians? Since the Palestinians have some connection to the ancient Philistines by more than name, as seen in Chapter 5, they deserve consideration as having ancient historical precedent in the land as well.

If the land of Palestine were divided according to historical precedent, a fairly straight line of demarcation would separate the two
countries into two relatively elongated areas, lying side by side. This
would greatly simplify the border differentiation between the two
countries. The Jews would keep the Galilee, the Haifa District, the
coastal plains of Sharon and Dor, Samaria and Judea (the West Bank)
and most all of the Negev; **the Palestinians would obtain the entire
Plain of Philistia.** The State of Israel would thus be restricted to that
territory which its ancestors possessed throughout most of their ancient history.

Some might say of this simple division of the land, "Why hasn't
this been thought of before?" In all of this author's research, he has
discovered only one writer who has suggested this specific division
of the land for resolving the Israeli-Palestinian dispute. Wesley G.
Pippert was the senior correspondent in the Middle East for United
Press International (UPI) in 1983-1986. In his book, *Land of Promise,
Land of Strife* (1988), Pippert provides this interesting remark:

> I often have shocked audiences—of either Israeli or Palesti-
> nian sympathizers; it doesn't matter—by proposing my own
> somewhat jocular solution to the Middle East controversy. We
> must pay attention to ancient claims, I say. Thus, the West Bank,
> because it contains so many Jewish holy sites—Hebron, Nablus,
> and even Bethlehem—clearly goes to Israel, the Jewish state.
> This satisfies many Israeli sympathizers. The territory of the
> five ancient Philistine cities and the rich farmland and coastal
> plain south of Tel Aviv, go to the Palestinians. This outrages the
> Israeli sympathizers![1]

Maybe Pippert's solution will one day not be such a joke after all. This
will become evident when the writings of the Hebrew prophets are
examined in the closing chapters of this book.

"Palestinians Are Not Philistines!"

Some will object that the Palestinians are not descendants of the
ancient Philistines. Indeed, the Palestinians do not originate solely
from the ancient Philistines. However, it cannot be denied that there
is **some** genetic link between today's Palestinians and the ancient
Philistines. It seems that following the Jews' exile to Babylon, many
Philistines spread east to settle in Judah, and this is partly why the
whole area was called *Palaestina* by the Greeks.

The Romans kept Philistia separate from Judah, indicating that its people were distinguished from the Jews. Some historians as late as the Roman period still identified the inhabitants of the Plain of Philistia as Philistines. These points suggest that some Philistine ancestry may well be prevalent among Palestinians today.

Nevertheless, the ancient Philistines themselves should not be reckoned as a racial group, but as a geographic people. **Since the word "Palestinian" is derived from a geographic designation, the Palestinians should be reckoned in the same manner as the ancient Philistines—people of a land and a common culture, not necessarily of common ancestry.** The Palestinians are Arabs only culturally, not genetically.

Jews Not a Genetically Pure Race
If it is argued that the Palestinians are not pure Philistines, it must be recognized that neither are the Jews pure Hebrews, although the Palestinians are certainly a more racially-mixed group than today's Israeli Jews. Throughout history there was continual intermarriage of Jews with Gentiles. The following are a few examples:

1. From earliest times, some of the immediate sons of Israel (Jacob) married Gentile women. Judah married "Bath-shua the Canaanitess," with whom he had three of his five sons (1 Chron 2.3; cf. Gen 38.2-5). Joseph's Egyptian wife, Asenath (Gen 41.50-52), was the mother of Manasseh and Ephraim. These two largest tribes of Israel were genetically half Jew and half Egyptian.

2. "A mixed multitude" of Gentiles chose to join the Israelites in their exodus from Egypt (Ex 12.38; cf. 9.20). They must have eventually been absorbed into the Jewish population.

3. The Torah provides for Gentile converts to live in the land of Israel and be included in the Jewish religious community. Such a policy must have resulted in some intermarriage.

4. As discussed in Chapter 1, the Jews failed to drive out the Canaanite nations as instructed. Their intermarriage with the Canaanites eventually resulted in God's judgments in the Assyrian and Babylonian captivities.

5. The Assyrians left more of the ten tribes than is commonly thought, especially the women. Assyrian soldiers married these Jewish women and resettled the region between the Galilee and Judea, called "Samaria." Their descendants, half Jew and half Gentile, were called "Samaritans." The Samaritans were known for practicing an altered form of Judaism which considerably pre-dated the Assyrian conquest. Some small sects remain in Samaria today, tracing their lineage back to the ancient Samaritans.[2]

Mostly because of their mixed breeding, Judeans hated the Samaritans and did not regard them as Jews. Ironically, by modern Israel's definition of a Jew—one born of a Jewish mother—most of the Samaritans must be regarded as Jews.

6. Upon their return from the Babylonian exile, both Ezra and Nehemiah separately condemned the widespread practice in Judea of Jewish men—descendants of those who had remained behind following the exile—marrying foreign women (Ezra 9.2; 10.44; Neh 13.23-30).

7. It was inevitable that the more than 1800 years of the Jewish Diaspora would result in considerable intermarriage of the Jews with the native Gentiles of their host countries. This was especially true of those Jews who advocated assimilation as a means of escaping the scourge of anti-Semitism. Orthodox Jews continued to denounce intermarriage of Jews with Gentiles, but they constituted only a minority. Reformed and Conservative Judaism, which allows for intermarriage with Gentiles, is more prevalent in the U.S. Secular Jews have always made up the majority of Jewry.

The genetic effect of the Jews' intermarriage with Gentiles during the Diaspora is readily witnessed by viewing Jewish immigrants to Israel. They often exhibit racial features corresponding to the peoples of the nations from which they emigrate. A recent and classic example is the Ethiopian Jews, called "Falashas." At the end of 1984 the Israelis began secretly to fly out these 7,500 starving Jews from drought and famine-stricken Ethiopia. Their origin had long been disputed. They are indeed Jewish. But over two millennia of intermarriage with the Ethiopians have made the Falashas look more Ethiopian than Jewish: dark-skinned, tall and slender.

To conclude, God has certainly kept his promise thus far, that Abraham's physical seed would be perpetuated. Yet God never predicted that the chosen nation of Israel, which was to be His witness to the other nations, would remain separate from them and thus keep genetically pure.

Advantages of the "New Philistia" Proposal
There are numerous advantages to be gained by dividing the land of Palestine into two separate states having the same borders as those of ancient Philistia and Israel. Such a state will be referred to herein as "New Philistia," since it seeks to approximate the extent of ancient Philistia.

The proposed borders would be in accordance with historical precedent. That is, they would be those boundaries which Israel and

Philistia maintained throughout most of their rivalry. The trend in international law is to award national rights to land on the basis of historical precedent.

The stated goal of the Palestinian Charter is to regain all of Palestine. Indeed, any settlement which would give the Palestinians a portion of Mandate Palestine is still regarded by some PLO leaders as only a first step toward recovering the remainder of Palestine. This is perhaps the greatest fear of Israelis in permitting a Palestinian state. But settling the dispute according to historical precedent might help persuade the Palestinians against designs of further expansion.

The proposed borders would be much more simple, natural and recognizable than the border separating Israel from the West Bank and the Gaza Strip. Philistia was somewhat rectangular, running in a north-south direction parallel to the Mediterranean coast. One problem with the proposed West Bank/Gaza entity is that it has no natural boundaries separating it from Israel. On the other hand, ancient Philistia was divided from Israel by the easily-recognized Shephelah. Meaning "lowlands" in Hebrew, the Shephelah ascends from the eastern edge of the Philistine plain to connect with the elevated Judean hill country to the east. All of Philistia was located in the southwestern coastal flatland, whereas Judah usually included the Shephelah. Except for the early centuries, Judah also included the plain to the north of the Sorek valley. The Sorek also served as a natural northern border between the two countries.

The Palestinian state would simply consist of a considerably expanded Gaza Strip. This additional land would provide relief from the overcrowded conditions in the miniscule Gaza Strip, which measures only 25 miles long and 4-6 miles wide. **The Palestinian area would be extended north of the Gaza Strip another 25 miles to the Sorek Valley, not much farther than was proposed under the UN Partition Plan.** From about the time of the monarchy, the Nahal Sorek was the usual northern border of ancient Philistia.

Eastward, the Gaza Strip would be widened from its 4-6 mile width to include all of the Plain of Philistia, about 15 miles in width. The eastern Shephelah would probably remain with Israel as the border between the two countries, just as it was between Judah and Philistia in antiquity. More on this later.

From the current southern border of the Gaza Strip, the Palestinian state would therefore extend northward approximately 50 miles in length and stretch from the Mediterranean Sea eastward to about 15 miles in width. The Gaza Strip would therefore be increased six-fold, from its present 140 square miles to about 840 square miles. Israel would give up the Gaza Strip, as well as 700 square miles of its own territory, in exchange for receiving the 2,000 square miles of the entire West Bank. Israel would receive a net gain of nearly 1,200 square miles.

A Palestinian state in only 840 square miles may be insufficient to accommodate an estimated high figure of 3.5 to 4 million Palestinians. Of course, not all of the Palestinians would transfer to the new state of Palestine. One study, recognized by the U.S. government, projected an estimated additional inflow into a West Bank/Gaza entity for the first five years of only 1.25 million Palestinians.[3] However, if the state of Palestine were located in the more developed Plain of Philistia, this territory would probably attract more Palestinians than would the West Bank. An inadequate size of territory could be the biggest drawback to this proposed solution.

But there is ample evidence that ancient Philistia extended farther south, about twenty-five miles beyond the Gaza Strip to the Wadi el Arish. The Wadi el Arish usually served as Egypt's northeastern border. According to a literal understanding of the Genesis record, the Philistines occupied at least a part of this additional territory as early as the period of the patriarchs, in 1950-1750 B.C. (See Appendix A: Early History of the Philistines.)

During Israel's early history, this territory between the present Gaza Strip and the Wadi el Arish seems to have been occupied by the Cherethites. The Cherethites are mentioned ten times in the Hebrew Bible, usually in association with the Pelethites, believed to be the Philistines. It is generally thought that the Cherethites were incorporated into the Philistine nation, so that their territory came to be included in Philistia.

In addition, Joshua implied that this small portion of the Sinai was Philistine land when he allotted the Promised Land to the tribes of Israel. After specifying that Judah would receive the Philistine region that included Ekron, Ashdod and Gaza, he added, "as far as the brook of Egypt," the Wadi el Arish (Josh 15.47).

The Camp David Accords provide that "Egypt, Israel, Jordan and the representatives of the Palestinian people should participate in negotiations on the resolution of the Palestinian problem in all its aspects." Perhaps both Egypt and Jordan could contribute toward a solution.

Egyptian President Mubarak is intent on finding a solution to the Palestinian problem, especially since the Arab world has so heavily criticized Egypt for its treaty with Israel. He might agree to relinquish this small, unused portion of the northeastern Sinai to the Palestinian state. An international peacekeeping zone, approximately 25-40 miles in width, runs along the south side of the entire Israel-Egypt border, in the Sinai. In the northeastern Sinai, it encompasses over half of this territory between the Gaza Strip and the city of El Arish. El Arish, the only city in the region, is located adjacent to the Wadi el Arish, but on the west side. The zone is patrolled by an international peacekeeping force and by Egyptian police. If Egypt were to relinquish this territory to the Palestinians, it would comprise about one-third of the Palestinian state proposed herein.

Although the northeastern Sinai is arable, sparse rainfall makes it agriculturally undesirable. Only a few Arab villages exist in the region, along the coast. Yet Israel was in the process of successfully settling the northwestern portion of the area until its 1982 withdrawal. It had eight settlements near the Gaza border. During this time the Kinneret-Negev Conduit (National Water Carrier)—Israel's underground agricultural lifeline—was extended to these Sinai settlements. After the

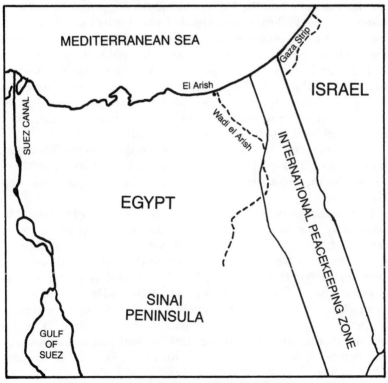

MAP 10: INTERNATIONAL PEACEKEEPING ZONE

settlements were dismantled, the region reverted to desert. A renewed extension of the conduit, but farther into the Sinai, could make this region blossom like a rose for the Palestinians.

As its contribution to resolving the dispute, perhaps Jordan would agree to allow extra water to be diverted from the Jordan River, passing through the conduit to this corner of the Sinai. Indeed, diverting a large volume of irrigation water from the Jordan River has already been considered. Though never implemented, Jordan's 1964 plan to divert Jordan River waters for itself was a factor that led to the 1967 War. Such an agreement would seem to be in the best interests of Jordan. It would relieve the Hashemite Kingdom of much of the Palestinian population in Jordan, where many live in refugee camps.

Such agreements with Jordan and Egypt would represent a comprehensive regional settlement, which is the yet unachieved goal of the Camp David Accords, as well as that of many proposed settlements.

Another possibility would be to enlarge the Gaza Strip even farther eastward into the Negev, beyond the suggested fifteen mile range. Indeed, Philistia often extended inland in its southern extremity, where the Shephelah ends and the Judean hill country becomes less pronounced. We have already seen that the UN Partition Plan included an L-shaped portion of territory for the Palestinians which extended well into the Negev. The current Gaza Strip represented the major part of the vertical leg of the L, and the horizontal leg extended from the southern end of the Gaza Strip southeast along the present border between Israel and the Sinai.

Such arrangements would add needed territory to the Palestinian state, making this proposal more viable. This expanded territory would give the Palestinians almost as much land as that of the West Bank/Gaza.

Israel's requirements for secure and defensible borders would be adequately met by this proposal, perhaps more than by any other conceivable division of the land of Palestine. Certainly, a Palestinian state in the West Bank/Gaza area, or in the division of land proposed by either the Peel Plan or UN Partition Plan, would pose grave security risks for Israel. Israel's populous narrow coastland is very vulnerable to attack from the West Bank. Its military authorities therefore cringe at the prospect of giving up any part of the West Bank. The fact remains that Israel cannot give up the West Bank and maintain secure and defensible borders, as provided for in UN Security Resolutions 242 and 338.

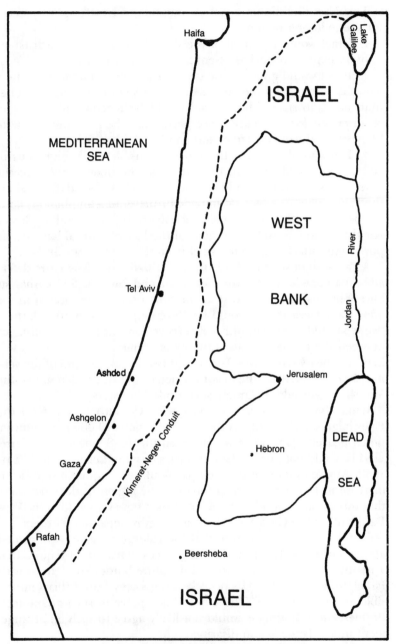

MAP 11: KINNERET-NEGEV CONDUIT

This New Philistia proposal accommodates Israel's security needs for the following reasons:

1. Israel would retain all of the West Bank, most of which Israeli military experts regard as essential to Israel's security.

2. Israel would give up a slender portion of land on its southwest, which is bordered on the other side by the Mediterranean Sea rather than an Arab state. Thus, Israel would be meeting an important requirement for its security: not permitting the Palestinian state to be positioned between Israel and another Arab state.

3. Israel would possess the more defensible rocky highlands of Judea and the Shephelah, in contrast to the open flatland of the lower Philistine plain. In addition, wide stretches of sand dunes along the Palestinians' coast would impede or prevent an amphibious landing by forces with tanks to assist the Palestinians in assaulting Israel. For this reason, as well as because of the lack of natural harbors, no power ever attacked ancient Israel from the Mediterranean Sea.

A Palestinian state in the Plain of Philistia would be more defensible than one located in the West Bank and the Gaza Strip. Analysts have long maintained that if a Palestinian state were located in the West Bank/Gaza that it would be absolutely necessary to link these two separated territories with a travel corridor. The minimum distance between the two territories is twenty-one miles. In the event of war between the two countries, Israel might easily take control of the very narrow corridor. Also, the major portion of the Palestinian state—the West Bank—would be largely surrounded by Israel.

What about UN peacekeeping forces? Couldn't they protect the Palestinian state? Hardly! Although the region's 10,000-man international peacekeeping force was awarded the 1988 Nobel Peace Prize, UNFIL could not prevent Israel's incursions into Lebanon in 1978 or 1982. Any resolution of the conflict should not require a significant increase in UN peacekeeping forces in the region. It does not seem that this could be avoided if the Palestinian state is located in the West Bank and in the Gaza Strip, with its lengthy, separated borders.

Could a settlement require that the Palestinian state be disarmed and protected by UN peacekeeping forces? This would require that a neutral zone be created around its entire border contiguous with Israel, fully guarded by UN peacekeeping forces. Surely this is impossible and preposterous. The UN is not capable of such guarantees. Besides, the Palestinians would not likely agree to such an arrangement unless Israel is also disarmed.

The length of contiguous border between the two states would be considerably shorter under this New Philistia plan than that of a West Bank/Gaza entity. A West Bank/Gaza border, contiguous with Israel, would measure about 210 miles. In addition, it would be extremely irregular and difficult to defend. On the other hand, if the Palestinian state were located in the Plain of Philistia, the total length of border contiguous with Israel would be no more than 80 miles. Thus, the West Bank/Gaza contiguous border with Israel would be 2.6 times longer than a Philistine Plain border.

Furthermore, the New Philistia border would follow the natural topography of the region. It would begin at the mouth of the Nahal Sorek in the north, follow it to the Shephelah and turn south, continue in a fairly straight line running along the western edge of the Shephelah and down to the Sinai at the present Egypt-Israel border. This line of demarcation would be more defensible for both states and presumably limit border incidents.

Another reason Israelis have rejected a Palestinian state in Palestine has been fear that the Soviets could become allied with it and therefore destablize the region. This is recently becoming less likely due to the social and political changes occurring in the Soviet Union, its weakening economy and its decreasing military commitments in foreign lands.

Israel would be better off without the volatile Gaza Strip. The over-populated and turbulent Gaza Strip is peopled almost entirely by Palestinians, and mostly impoverished, embittered ones at that. As with the present *intifada*, Palestinian hostilities have always begun in the Gaza Strip. When Israel first seized the Gaza District from Egypt in 1956, Israeli Prime Minister David Ben Gurion insightfully warned, "Gaza as part of Israel could be like a cancer. . . . To take a small territory with a vast Arab population would be the worst possible exchange."[4] Israel soon withdrew.

A Palestinian state located on the Plain of Philistia would be more economically viable than one in the West Bank/Gaza region. The Ashqelon/Ashdod sector to the north of Gaza, which Israel would relinquish to the Palestinians under this plan, is already quite developed and includes industry. Admittedly, Israel would not be eager to surrender this territory.

The entire proposed area for the Palestinians would not require huge amounts of investment capital as would the less-developed West Bank. This would enable the Palestinian nation to become self-reliant more quickly.

Economists predict that a Palestinian entity in the separated territories of the West Bank and the Gaza Strip, joined by a necessary travel corridor, would be "no economist's dream."[5] Economist Don

Peretz claims, "A Gaza component in an Arab West Bank entity would not be an economic asset."[6] Indeed, it would create administrative problems and prove costly for transportation and commerce. U.S. Secretary of State George Schultz visited the region in early 1988 and announced, "We don't think an independent Palestinian state on the West Bank makes sense."[7] It would require more border patrols and passport and security checks. The corridor might be as difficult to manage as the Allenby Bridge.

The Allenby Bridge, near Jericho, is one of only two bridges crossing the Jordan River. By far the busiest, it is an annoyance to the Palestinians. They frequently charge that Israeli authorities purposely hassle them there. Long delays are commonplace, sometimes causing loss of Palestinian farmers' perishable goods. Such problems would be avoided with a unified territory.

The Palestinians would gain the second most fertile land in Mandate Palestine. The Jews would still retain the most fertile and agriculturally-productive land in Palestine: the Valley of Jezreel in northern Israel. The sandy loam soil of the coastal plain is much more fertile than West Bank soil. It is also more tillable because it is relatively flat, whereas the West Bank is hilly, with much rocky outcropping. The warm, temperate climate of the coastal region provides high yields of citrus fruits and winter vegetables. These are important reasons why the entire coastal plain is more populated than the West Bank. The West Bank will therefore require large amounts of investment capital and take longer to develop, a burden that the Palestinians would avoid.

The present underground Kinneret-Negev Conduit would provide the necessary irrigation for the southwestern coastal region to realize its rich agricultural potential. Some agreement guaranteeing an uninterrupted water supply through the conduit would have to be worked out. The UN Partition Plan provided for "joint economic development [between the two states], especially in respect of irrigation."

The Palestinians would obtain the modern port at Ashdod, the second largest port in present Israel, something they would not have with the West Bank/Gaza alternative. Being spread along the Mediterranean coast would provide good access for the Palestinians to the lucrative European winter markets for fruits and vegetables. The additional Mediterranean beachfront, with its tourist and recreational opportunities, should also aid the Palestinian economy.

The cost of resettling approximately 1.5 million Palestinians from the West Bank and other places in Israel to the New Philistia would no doubt be high. It is a drawback to this solution. Under UN administration, the major portion of this expense might be borne by the oil-rich Arab states, and perhaps the industrial nations as well, as a necessary price for achieving a measure of peace in the region. Persian Gulf states are already committed financially to the Palestinian cause.

Israel's thoroughly-planned West Bank settlements program will accommodate the necessary transfer of Jews from the Ashqelon/Ashdod area. Israel's ambitious plan for resettling the West Bank underscores its intent to keep that territory. This plan will accelerate settlement of the West Bank, one of Israel's primary goals. The Israeli government would no longer have to offer financial and other incentives to attract settlers to the West Bank. The cost of this Jewish resettlement program should not be excessive, since it does not affect a large number of people. The West Bank would also accommodate the estimated 500,000 Russian Jews expected over the next 3-5 years.

As provided in the UN Partition Plan, the state of Palestine could allow Jews, and Israel could permit Palestinians, to remain as citizens if they so desire. Arafat stated in his 1974 UN speech that the PLO's goal for a democratic Palestinian state would include "all Jews living in Palestine today and willing to live together with us without discrimination on Palestinian territory."

An enlarged Gaza Strip would solve its problem of overpopulation. Of course, the Palestinians would assume ownership of abandoned Jewish houses in the surrounding territory. The transfer of Jewish houses and industry in the Ashqelon/Ashdod area to the Palestinians would possibly be regarded as part of Israel's necessary compensation to the dispossessed Palestinians, a debt long overdue.

Zionist Jews would get what they want: secure borders, Judea and Samaria and a completely Jewish state. More than any other portion of Mandate Palestine, the Jews are historically and emotionally connected to Judea, the very heartland of ancient Israel. The continuing growth of Israeli right-wing political and religious parties makes it increasingly unlikely that Israel will ever give up the West Bank. Polls reveal that half or more of Israeli Jews prefer that Israel keep the West Bank rather than give it to the Palestinians in exchange for peace.[8] **It would seem that if the Israelis were faced with the two alternatives, they would much prefer to give the Palestinians the territory of ancient Philistia than to give them the West Bank.**

If the "land of Israel" were more clearly defined according to history, under this plan Israeli Jews would get the "ancestral land" they

claim in their Proclamation of Independence. (See Appendix C.) This
document obviously identifies Eretz Israel generally as the land of
their forefathers, a land which clearly did not include the Plain of
Philistia. In fact, it is most ironic that the Proclamation was signed in
Tel Aviv, which was the capital of Israel for the next thirty-four years.
Yet in the early centuries of Israel's existence in Canaan, the territory
of present Tel Aviv was part of northernmost Philistia.

What about Jerusalem? If historical precedent were the guide for
it too, the entire city would remain with the Jews. Some arrangement
would no doubt have to be worked out to insure protection of, and
free access to, the holy places and shrines. (The issue of Jerusalem
is a full subject in itself, one which the author plans to address from
the perspective of biblical prophecy in a forthcoming volume.)

Israel would fulfill *halakhic* requirements to retain Eretz Israel.
Judaism requires that Jews be bound to *halakhah*—the complete body
of religious, civil and legal laws of rabbinic tradition. It is generally
accepted that Jews of every generation, including those of the Jewish
state, must adhere to *Mitzvat Yishuv Eretz Yisrael*—the divine command
to settle the land of Israel (e.g., Num 33.52-53). The territory involved
is generally recognized as historical Israel, which includes the West
Bank. So this *mitzvat* (Hebrew for "command") religiously obligates
today's Jews to settle that land.

Furthermore, Jews are supposedly prohibited from irrevocably
transferring any portion of Eretz Israel to Gentiles, a *mitzvat* called
Lo Tohennem in Hebrew. However, some Jewish authorities argue that
Lo Tohennem does not apply because King Solomon gave King Huram
of Tyre twenty cities in the Galilee as payment for supplying Solomon
with building materials with which he constructed the temple at
Jerusalem (1 Kgs 9.11). The retort to this is that those cities were
inhabited by Canaanites (cf. 2 Sam 24.7), the cities displeased Huram
(v. 12), and he gave them right back (2 Chron 8.2).

Another problem over which rabbinical scholars disagree is whether
pikuah nefesh (Hebrew for "the saving of human life") takes precedence
over both *Mitzvat Yishuv Eretz Israel* and *Lo Tohennem*. That is why
several members of Israel's Labor Party propose trading some West
Bank land for peace. They claim that, in the long run, it would save
lives by avoiding war.

This religious dilemma could be resolved if Israel relinquished the
Ashdod/Ashqelon/Gaza region to the Palestinians and in turn incorporated the West Bank into Israel. As we have seen, the Plain of Philistia
cannot be considered as historical Israel and therefore should not be
subject to *halakhah*.

The Palestinians would realize their aspirations of having their own independent, sovereign state in Palestine. The Palestinian National Charter demands all of the land of Palestine for the Palestinians. If the word "Palestine" were redefined according to its ancient use, this proposal would also provide the Palestinians with what they claim: all of Palestine, which means Philistia.

Menachem Begin once warned an Israeli Jewish audience against conceding that Israel is Palestine. "If this is Palestine," Begin asserted, "then it belongs to a people who lived here before you came."[9] Exactly! If the word "Palestine" designated only the Plain of Philistia, it would belong to the Palestinians because some of their ancestors lived there before the Hebrews came.

Population Transfers in Modern Times
Can population transfers really work? In ancient times, population transfers were practiced frequently by conquering nations in order to guard against rebellion. There is precedent for population transfers in modern times as well.

World War II left the majority of Europeans embittered against the Germans. Many Germans resided in other European countries before the war broke out. Under the 1945 post-war Potsdam Conference agreement, entitled "Orderly Transfers of German Populations," a total of 11.5 million Germans were expelled from mostly eastern European countries and transferred to Germany. They were forced to give up their homes without compensation from the host countries. Later, they received financial assistance under the U.S. Marshall Plan.

About the same time, the British were reluctant to grant independence to Gandhi's India. They feared increased strife between its approximately 68% Hindu and 22% Muslim populations. Indeed, following India's independence, massacres became widespread. Consequently, in the late '40s, there was a voluntary exchange of about 18 million Hindus and Muslims between India and its neighbor, the predominantly Muslim Pakistan.[10]

Thus, history reveals that it should be possible to resettle Palestinians in a significantly enlarged Gaza Strip.

Conclusion
It now appears inevitable that the Israeli-Palestinian conflict will only be resolved by establishing two independent states in the land of Palestine. A Palestinian state in the two separated territories of the West Bank and the Gaza Strip is economically unfeasible and would render both countries indefensible. International focus on this pro-

longed land dispute should shift to restoring boundaries in the region according to ancient historical precedent. **That is, let the Jews have the historical land of Israel, which includes the West Bank, and give the Palestinians the Plain of Philistia in which to establish their independent, sovereign state.**

Part III

THE
NEAR
FUTURE

Chapter 11

REESTABLISHMENT
OF PHILISTIA

*"And they will swoop down on the slopes of the Philistines
on the west"* (Isa 11.14).

Now we turn to the major concern of this book: a detailed discussion
of certain biblical prophecies related to the New Philistia proposal in
Chapter 10. For Bible students, it is essential that interpretations
herein interact with opposing views held by biblical commentators.

**Just as the Bible predicted the modern reestablishment of Israel,
it also indicates the revival of other ancient countries in the Middle
East, one of these being Philistia.** Perhaps as many as seven prophetic
scriptures in the Hebrew Bible indicate a rebirth of Israel's ancient
arch rival—Philistia. Two passages which clearly signify the reestablishment of Philistia are Isaiah 11.14 and Zechariah 9.5-8. Others that
can be put forward with varying degrees of certainty are Joel 3.4-8,
Obadiah 19, Zephaniah 2.4-7 and Psalms 60 and 108.

Interpretation of Biblical Prophecy
There are two kinds of Bible prophecies. There is prophecy which
communicates God's message to people, called preaching or **forthtel-
ling**. And there is prophecy which predicts the future, called **foretel-
ling**. Old Testament prophets did both.

There are two kinds of predictive prophecy in Scripture: fulfilled
prophecy, which has already happened, and unfulfilled prophecy,
which has not yet occurred. The remaining chapters of this book will
concern mostly unfulfilled predictive prophecy, to which the words
"prophecy" and "prophecies" will henceforth refer.

There are at least four crucial principles to which the prophetic student must adhere in order to understand biblical prophecies:

1. Consider the context in order to establish the time of the event being prophesied.

2. Interpret prophecies literally unless there is clear evidence indicating otherwise.

3. Compare Scripture with Scripture.

4. Accept the possibility of multiple fulfillments, usually dual fulfillments, i.e., a partial fulfillment in a time near the prophet and a more complete fulfillment in the far, distant future.[1]

The context often reveals if a fulfilled prophecy has a more complete fulfillment yet to be accomplished. Careful analysis and interpretation are required. With regard to Messianic prophecies, the apostle Peter claims that the scriptural prophets themselves "made careful search and inquiry, seeking to know what person or time the Spirit of Christ within them was indicating as He predicted the sufferings of Christ and the glories to follow" (1 Pt 1.10-11).

Unfulfilled prophecies are the most difficult portions of the Bible to interpret. Indeed, an appeal to various biblical commentaries on unfulfilled prophecies often presents a bewildering myriad of conflicting interpretations. There are three primary reasons for this:

1. Some critical scholars reject the supernatural and therefore the predictive element in prophetic writings.

2. Most Christian commentators have tended to suppose an exaggerated significance of the church in prophecy. They consequently regard many OT prophecies concerning Israel as non-literal and symbolically identifying the NT church.

3. Many students of prophecy attach undue importance to contemporary times and thus sometimes err in interpreting prophecies according to current events.[2]

Over the past century, there have arisen a growing number of biblical scholars who either do not accept the supernatural or accept it very sparingly. One way or another, they dismiss prediction as impossible. Many therefore assign the time of authorship of a book like Daniel to a date later than has been held traditionally. Thus, they regard the text as history when written rather than prediction of the future. This procedure is especially typical of radical form and redaction critics, who hold liberal views of the inspiration of Scripture.

In addition, throughout church history there have been many very capable, conservative biblical scholars who interpreted the Bible literally except when it came to prophecy. To appeal to any of these, or especially to either form or redaction critics, for their interpretation of the passages about to be considered will prove of little value to those who accept the supernatural inspiration and predominantly literal interpretation of the scriptures.

Even if the above principles are followed, there will be differences of interpretation among the best of teachers on the prophetic scriptures. In addition, the student will be well-guided in attempting to distinguish between those biblical prophecies whose interpretations are more clearly discernible and those which remain obscure. Students ought to seek to be tentative with their opinions regarding the latter.

History of Prophetic Interpretations

We saw in Chapter 8 that the church was predominantly premillennial in belief during the first three centuries. Later, Roman Catholic and most Protestant scholars dismissed the literal interpretation of OT prophecies indicating Israel's future triumph. Instead, they interpreted these allegorically as signifying the church's general victory over evil.

The results of allegorizing prophecy have sometimes proved tragic. One example was the "Holy Crusades" of medieval times. One reason for the Crusades was that it was thought that the church needed to regain the Holy Land, especially Jerusalem, in order to fulfill OT prophecies of "Israel's" worldwide rule through the church.

Throughout church history, two practices have brought biblical prophecies into disrepute: (1) predicting the exact time of the second coming of Jesus, which was clearly forbidden by Jesus Himself (Mt 24.36) and (2) both amillennialists and postmillennialists interpreting Israel in the OT allegorically.

Literal Method of Interpreting Prophecy

In contrast to Roman Catholic and Protestant scholars, premillennialists have always agreed with past eminent Jewish commentators on many points of prophecy, especially the reemergence of a literal nation of Israel in its former homeland before Messiah's coming in glory. (Of course, they do not agree on the crucial subject of the identity of Messiah.) In fact, post- and amillennialists often referred disparagingly to premillennialism as the "Jewish theory." But the mid-20th century establishment of the State of Israel proved this "theory" correct. Here is solid evidence that premillennialists, and often Orthodox Jews, are more reliable interpreters of OT prophecies regarding Israel than either amillennialists or postmillennialists.

Thus, it is best to interpret prophecy literally, according to the historical-grammatical method of interpretation. Unless **clear** evidence indicates otherwise, names of historical persons, tribes, nations, cities and other geographical locations, along with numbers, do not constitute symbols but are to be understood literally.

The interpreter of biblical prophecy is wise to consider how prophecy has been quite literally fulfilled in the past. The following are some examples:

1. It was foretold that the kingdom of Israel would be divided in two. One division would consist of two tribes (1 Kgs 11.11-13) and the other division of ten tribes (vv. 29-31).

2. Judah was prophesied to go into captivity in Babylon for 70 years (Jer 25.11; Dan 9.2; 2 Chron 36.21; Ezra 1.1).

3. Moses predicted the Diaspora, in which, because of their sins, God would remove the Jews from their land and scatter them throughout the nations of the world (Deut 4.26-27; 28.64; 30.1).

4. Hosea foresaw the Diaspora, predicting that "the sons of Israel will remain for many days without king or prince, without sacrifice or sacred pillar, and without ephod or household idols" (Hos 3.4).

5. Ezekiel envisioned modern Israel when he predicted that "in the latter years" many Jews would return from the Diaspora to the land of Israel, "which had been a continual waste" (Eze 38.8).

6. The NT interprets many OT Messianic prophecies as being literally fulfilled in Jesus: He was born in Bethlehem (Mic 5.2), rode into Jerusalem on a donkey (Zech 9.9), was rejected by the Jews (Isa 53.3), was sold for 30 pieces of silver, with which they bought the potter's field (Zech 11.12-13), died by crucifixion with casting of lots for His clothing (Ps 22.14-18; Zech 12.10) and rose from the grave (Ps 16.10).

7. In A.D. 30 Jesus predicted that Jerusalem and its temple would be destroyed within a generation. It happened in A.D. 70., exactly one generation later.

The list could go on. The evidence is overwhelming that most prophecy is to be understood literally.

Introduction to Isaiah 11

The prophet Isaiah predicted more about the promised Messiah and His kingdom than any of the other writing Hebrew prophets. Most of his writings concern the time when Messiah will come to deliver Israel, destroy its enemies and establish His worldwide kingdom on earth, with its center at Jerusalem.

The eleventh chapter of Isaiah is one of the primary Messianic passages in the Hebrew Bible (OT). The majority of Jewish commentators regard its entire contents as Messianic.[3] The chapter concerns

Messiah's deliverance of Israel and the establishment of His kingdom. **In Isa 11.14 the prophet Isaiah provides the clearest indication in Scripture that at the time of the coming of the conquering Messiah, an adversary of Israel will exist in the southwestern coastal plain of Palestine.** This adversary is called "the Philistines." Most commentators, however, interpret the passage figuratively and/or regard it as already completely fulfilled in history. Thus, they neglect the prospect that a people whom the prophet called the Philistines (Palestinians) might yet be reestablished in "the land of the Philistines."

It must first be established, however, that the context of Isa 11.14 concerns the yet future Messianic destruction of Israel's neighbors, the Philistines (Palestinians) and the Jordanians.

Isaiah 11

1 Then a shoot will spring from the stem of Jesse, and a branch from his roots will bear fruit.

2 And the Spirit of the LORD will rest on Him, the spirit of wisdom and understanding, the spirit of counsel and strength, the spirit of knowledge and the fear of the LORD.

3 And He will delight in the fear of the LORD, and He will not judge by what His eyes see, nor make a decision by what His ears hear;

4 But with righteousness He will judge the poor, and decide with fairness for the afflicted of the earth; and He will strike the earth with the rod of His mouth, and with the breath of His lips He will slay the wicked.

5 Also righteousness will be the belt about His loins, and faithfulness the belt about His waist.

6 And the wolf will dwell with the lamb, and the leopard will lie down with the kid, and the calf and the young lion and the fatling together; and a little boy will lead them.

7 Also the cow and the bear will graze; their young will lie down together; and the lion will eat straw like the ox.

8 And the nursing child will play by the hole of the cobra, and the weaned child will put his hand on the viper's den.

9 They will not hurt or destroy in all My holy mountain, for the earth will be full of the knowledge of the LORD as the waters cover the sea.

10 Then it will come about in that day that the nations will resort to the root of Jesse, who will stand as a signal for the peoples; and His resting place will be glorious.

11 Then it will happen on that day that the Lord will again recover the second time with His hand the remnant of His people, who will remain from Assyria, Egypt, Pathros, Cush, Elam, Shinar, Hamath, and from the islands of the sea.

12 And He will lift up a standard for the nations, and will assemble the banished ones of Israel, and will gather the dispersed of Judah from the four corners of the earth.

13 Then the jealousy of Ephraim will depart, and those who harass Judah will be cut off; Ephraim will not be jealous of Judah, and Judah will not harass Ephraim.

14 And they will swoop down on the slopes of the Philistines on the west; together they will plunder the sons of the east; they will possess Edom and Moab; and the sons of Ammon will be subject to them.

15 And the LORD will utterly destroy the tongue of the Sea of Egypt; and He will wave His hand over the River with His scorching wind; and He will strike it into seven streams, and make men walk over dry-shod.

16 And there will be a highway from Assyria for the remnant of His people who will be left, just as there was for Israel in the day that they came up out of the land of Egypt (emphasis added).

Israel's Promised Messiah

Isaiah begins his chapter eleven by announcing that "a shoot will spring from the stem of Jesse." Jesse was King David's father. Jewish and Christian commentators unanimously concur that this phrase identifies the Messiah's physical line of descent. The Hebrew prophets frequently predicted that Messiah would descend from the tribe of Judah, the tribe to which Jesse and David belonged, and that He would sit on David's throne as King of Israel. That is why He was called "the son of David."

Next, Isaiah describes how "the Spirit of the LORD will rest on Him" (v. 2). This suggests that either there would be a greater measure of the Spirit on Messiah than on anyone before (cf. Col 1.19: "fullness") or that the Spirit would rest on Him permanently, or both. Jesus identified Himself as the One Whom Isaiah here presents (Lk 4.17-21; cf. Isa 61.1-2). (See also Isa 42.1; cf. Mt 12.18.)

It could only be the Messiah that is in view here. In the remainder of our consideration of Isaiah 11, our purpose will be to discover the time to which the prophet refers. Upon establishing this context, we will then be able to see clearly the time of fulfillment of the reference to the Philistines in v. 14, the ultimate focus of this chapter.

Messiah and His Glorious Kingdom

In vv. 3-4 Isaiah reveals that Messiah will judge the poor with fairness and will destroy the wicked. Following the Messianic destruction depicted in v. 4 ("He will strike the earth . . . and . . . slay the wicked"), the prophet pens one of the most beautiful and beloved passages in all of Scripture. It describes peace on earth among the animals and implies the same among men (cf. vv. 6-9 with 9.6-7). Such universal peace and knowledge of the LORD can only identify the future Messianic (millennial) kingdom (cf. 2.2-4). For Christian believers, this means the second coming of Jesus Christ.[4]

Isaiah writes in v. 10 a pivotal phrase which identifies the time period prophesied. The words, "Then it will come about in that day," refer both to the time when Messiah initially comes to judge (v. 4) and when Edenic conditions are restored to earth (vv. 6-9). Consequently, "that day" cannot be reckoned as a twenty-four-hour period of time. "That day," like the phrase "the day of the LORD," translates technical words frequently used by the Hebrew prophets. It can refer to any period of judgment by Yahweh. But it usually identifies that final "day of the LORD" when Messiah comes in His kingdom and apparently includes the time period of His subsequent reign. Herein, that final day of the LORD is distinguished by capitalizing it, e.g., "the Day," "the Day of the LORD," or "the Day of Yahweh."

Final Return of Jews to Eretz Israel

Isaiah reveals that the nations will come to worship Messiah, who will sit on His glorious throne (v. 10). At the same time, Yahweh will gather the surviving Jews "the second time" to the land of Israel (vv. 11-12). This second ingathering points to God's regathering of the Jews at the coming of Messiah to deliver Israel. So far, God has **taken** the Jews to Palestine twice: at the initial conquest following the exodus and at their return from the Babylonian exile. But God has only "**recovered**" (v. 7) the Jews to their land once: the return from Babylon in 537 B.C. God's second promised regathering awaits the coming of Messiah in power and great glory.

Some more liberal commentators interpret that Isaiah's regathering in v. 11 does not refer to the Messianic age but only the post-exilic return.[5] This passage shows three evidences against this view:

1. This regathering will occur "on that day," i.e., the final Day. Only then will all the conditions in vv. 3-10 transpire, including universal justice and peace.

2. This regathering is not from one particular region, as was the return from Babylonia. Instead, Isaiah names many other lands from

which Jews will return (v. 11), as well as "the four corners of the earth" (v. 12). This expression, which denotes the earth's four continental land masses with Israel as the center, indicates a worldwide regathering.

3. This regathering is not partial. The return from Babylonia consisted of only a minority of Jews from the tribe of Judah. In contrast, this final regathering includes both divisions of the kingdom: Israel (Ephraim) and Judah (vv. 12-13).

In addition, Isaiah repeats these two themes—the complete recovery of the Diaspora and the conversion of the Gentile nations—in other parts of his book within a Messianic kingdom context (e.g., 2.2-3; 27.13). He even relates these events to each other, showing that the Gentile nations will come to Jerusalem to worship Yahweh, bringing the dispersed Jews with them (42.2; 43.5-6; 49.22-23; 60.4, 9; 66.20). Such a dramatic event can occur only in the Messianic kingdom.

Isaiah next reveals in v. 13 that following this regathering of the Jews, "Ephraim will not be jealous of Judah, and Judah will not harass Ephraim." Ephraim was one of the two sons of Joseph. His tribe later became the most powerful of the ten tribes of the northern kingdom. Following the monarchy, either "Ephraim" or "Israel" were frequently used to identify the northern kingdom. "Judah" stood for the southern kingdom, which consisted of the tribes of Judah and Benjamin. Will the distinction, and perhaps some of the strife, that existed between the two divisions of ancient Israel someday recur in Israel (cf. Eze 37.15-28)?

Isaiah adds that at this time "those who harass Judah will be cut off." This apparently refers to the defeat of the nations at the end of the age, when they gather to destroy Judah and Jerusalem (Isa 29.7-8; Joel 3.2, 12; Zech 12.2-9; 14.2).

Thus, throughout vv. 3-13 Isaiah prophesies of a time that can only be understood as the coming of Messiah at the end of this age to destroy the wicked, to gather dispersed Jews worldwide and to unite them in a glorious kingdom of peace on earth.

For a moment, let us skip the focus of our study, v. 14, and consider the time depicted in the remaining verses of Isa 11.

In v. 15 the prophet reveals that Yahweh will destroy the "tongue of the Sea of Egypt," probably the Gulf of Suez but maybe the Suez Canal. About the same time, God will strike the Euphrates River with a scorching wind. Seven shallow streams will remain, enabling men to cross over dryshod. These acts are reminiscent of Yahweh's parting

of the waters of the Red Sea. The purpose of these wonders is either
to provide Israel with a route of attack on its southern and northern
neighbors (cf. 27.12) or to make a passage for the Jews of the Diaspora
to return to Israel, or perhaps both. There is no evidence in Israel's
history that anything like this has ever happened to these waters.
Surely this prophecy refers to no other time than the coming of
Messiah in victory.

In v. 16 Isaiah indicates that some Jews of the Diaspora will return
via an elevated highway extending from Assyria to Israel. This, too,
can only be fulfilled during the millennial kingdom (cf. 19.23; 35.8;
40.3; 62.10).

Many contemporary writers rightly regard Isa 12 as a hymn of
thanksgiving which anticipates the Messianic age, the ultimate time
of thanksgiving, comfort and joy.

To sum up, except for v. 14, it has been established that Isa 11.3—
12.6 pertains exclusively to the coming of Messiah to deliver Israel
from its enemies and establish the promised kingdom. **Because of
this context, Isa 11.14 can refer to no other time than the Messianic
age.**

Messianic Destruction of Philistia and Jordan

Now we turn to Isa 11.14, which reads, "And they will swoop down
on the slopes of the Philistines on the west; together they will plunder
the sons of the east; they will possess Edom and Moab; and the sons
of Ammon will be subject to them." The Hebrew word translated
"swoop" is usually used to depict a bird of prey swooping down upon
its victim. (See Hab 1.8.) The Hebrew word rendered "slopes" is
literally "shoulder." It signifies the sloping Shephelah ("lowland"),
which connects the elevated Judean hill country with the relatively
flat, Philistine coastal plain.

In v. 14 Isaiah continues with his previous theme, that of Ephraim
and Judah being united. Together, these Israelites will make a surprise
attack on a people dwelling on their west. Like a bird of prey, they
will swoop down upon the shoulder (Shephelah) of their victim. They
presumably continue their assault upon the inhabitants of the coastal
plain.[6] This is implied in the remainder of the verse, in which the
Israelis are seen plundering and subjugating their eastern adversary.
These eastern ancient place names of Edom, Moab and Ammon
comprise modern western Jordan. It must be concluded that the
Israelis would not attack those dwelling to the west if they themselves
possessed that territory.

The language of Isa 11.14 therefore requires that Israel will not possess the ancient land of the Philistines in the last days preceding the Messianic kingdom.

Isaiah does not specifically identify Israel's western enemy in Isa 11.14. Yet the language, "slopes of the Philistines," implies that the Philistines (Palestinians) will then possess the coastal plain and perhaps part of the Shephelah. (See, however, remarks on Obad 19 in Chapter 13.)

Thus, according to Isa 11.14, the Philistines will become reestablished on the southwestern coastal plain of Palestine. **This requires that Israel will someday release the Gaza Strip, either voluntarily or involuntarily, as well as adjacent land eastward and northward.**

Synthesis of the Last Days
A synthesis of the Hebrew prophecies concerning the last days provides the following scenario:

1. At the end of this age the nations' armies will converge on Israel to annihilate it (Isa 29.7; Eze 38-39; Joel 3.2, 12; Mic 4.11—5.1; Zech 12.3, 9; 14.2).

2. A Jewish remnant will gather at the temple in Jerusalem to repent of their sins and pray to God for deliverance (2 Chron 6.24-25; Joel 2.12-17).

3. Messiah will come in glory to deliver the surviving remnant in Jerusalem and throughout all of Israel (Isa 59.19-20; Zech 9.14-16; 14.3-5).

4. Physically strengthened and united, these Israelites will join Messiah in destroying the nations' armies in their land (Isa 11.13; 41.11-16; Mic 5.7-9; Zech 9.13-15; 10.3-7; 12.6-8; 14.14).

5. The Israelites will expand their conquest by destroying neighboring nations (Isa 11.14; 19.16; 34.5-6; 63.1; Zeph 2.4-5).

6. Gentiles who survive a worldwide earthquake, fire and other calamities attending the Day of the LORD will bring all remaining Jews of the Diaspora to Israel. There they will bow down and worship Yahweh and His Messiah (Isa 14.2; 49.22-23; 60.3-4).

7. The earth's curse will be removed and the earth will be restored to pre-Fall, Edenic conditions (Isa 35; 65.17-25).

8. Israel will be glorified as head of the nations and a blessing to all Gentiles (Deut 28.13; Zech 8.13).

Objections
Some Christian and Jewish commentators who interpret Israel literally in Isa 11.13-14 regard the entire chapter as chronologically ar-

ranged. They maintain that an attack by Israel on its neighbors in v. 14 cannot follow either the kingdom of peace, described in vv. 6-9, or the conversion of Gentiles and the final regathering of the dispersed Jews, in vv. 10-12. Consequently, they usually interpret v. 14 as a literal Israel in spiritual supremacy over the Gentiles during the Messianic kingdom.[7]

However, Isaiah, like many biblical prophets, here employs the typical pattern of skipping back and forth in time in order to elaborate on themes mentioned previously. The prophets were like artists, who first sketch an outline on canvas and afterwards fill in the colors. Thus, in v. 14 Isaiah returns to the theme he first presented in v. 4, showing that the Israelites will accompany Messiah in defeating the nations' armies gathered against Jerusalem and Judea (Zech 10.3-7; 12.3-9; 14.3-4; Joel 3.2, 12) and afterwards in destroying their surrounding neighbors. Throughout vv. 3-16, however, Isaiah remains within the timeframe of "that day," i.e., the Day of the LORD.

Most Christian commentators dismiss altogether a literal interpretation of Isa 11.13-14. This is typical of non-premillennarians, who usually interpret allegorically those OT prophecies regarding Israel's final destruction of its enemies and the promised kingdom. For example, John Calvin provides the traditional allegorical interpretation that "Israel is regarded as the church and the Philistines, Edomites, Moabites and Ammonites as enemies of the church."[8] Thus, Israel attacking its enemies is interpreted to be the church spiritually triumphing over its enemies through the preaching of the gospel.

J.A. Alexander, whose father founded Princeton Theological Seminary, was one of the leading Presbyterian scholars of America. He observed that both the Jewish Targum (Aramaic translation/paraphrase of the OT) and most Jewish commentators have regarded the eleventh chapter of Isaiah as Messianic. He wrote concerning v. 14:

> the Jews explain this as a literal prediction having respect to the countries formerly possessed by the races here enumerated. Most Christian writers understand it spiritually of the conquests to be achieved by the true religion, and suppose the nations here named to be simply put for enemies in general, or for the heathen world.[9]

The same kind of thing is alleged about other verses. One notable Christian commentator on Isaiah takes vv. 15-16 to mean that God will bring His people out of the prison house of spiritual bondage and sin to the "highway from Assyria," which represents Jesus Christ as the Way, the Truth and the Life (Jn 14.6).[10] This is an example of how non-premillennial commentators strain to apply prophetic scripture to the Christian life and thereby lose the true meaning of the text. All Scripture does not apply to every circumstance or time in history. It is better to let the words stand as to their normal meaning and derive life applications from more appropriate texts.

Reestablishment of Philistia

Like the Jews, many premillennial commentators have not only interpreted from the Bible that Israel will be reestablished before the triumphant coming of Messiah, but that Israel's ancient neighbors will reemerge as well.

Premillennialist William Kelley was the close associate of J.N. Darby, the "father of dispensationalism."[11] In 1871 Kelley expounded on Isa 11.14, maintaining that Israel's neighbors in antiquity would in the future become reestablished in their respective lands:

> As for [Israel's] plotting neighbors, they may reappear. . . . It is a favourite infidel argument against the literal accomplishment . . . that the people mentioned in verse 14 have disappeared from the stage of history, and therefore that neither the restoration of Israel nor the events growing out of it can be so understood. But this is sheer unbelief of the power of God and of the reliability of scripture. **The God Who will bring His hidden ones of Ephraim out of the darkness that still veils them will disclose the descendants of their old adversaries in due time, and among these of their neighbours** (emphasis added).[12]

Thus, Kelley foresaw the reestablishment of Israel, Jordan and Philistia. This successor to the father of dispensationalism cannot therefore be regarded as a Christian Zionist, as are some dispensationalists today.

After affirming that Isa 11.4 refers to Christ's coming in judgment, premillennialist W.E. Vine (author of Vine's *Expository Dictionary of New Testament Words*) claims that "the rest of this chapter depicts millennial conditions." Concerning vv. 14-15, he explains that the Jews "will subdue surrounding foes."[13]

E.H. Plumptre provides a summary of the entire chapter as it relates to v. 14:

> The seer has had revealed to him the glory of the Messianic kingdom as a restored Eden, full of the knowledge of Jehovah,

the Gentiles seeking light and salvation from it. Suddenly, he blends this with anticipations that belong to the feelings and complications of his own time. He sees Philistines, Moabites, Ammonites, in that far future. They will be then as they were in his own times, the persistent foes of Israel (comp. Zeph. ii. 7-9), but will be, at last, subdued.[14]

In more recent times, J. Barton Payne has authored the most useful English resource for prophetic students. In his *Encyclopedia of Biblical Prophecy* (1973), Payne interprets Isa 11.14 literally, that at the second coming of Christ, "Israel will despoil the territories of Philistia, Edom, Moab . . . and Ammon."[15]

Thus, these men had not only foreseen from Scripture that Israel would become a nation again, but that Philistia would as well. **It must be concluded from Isa 11.14 that the ancient land of Philistia will in the future become reestablished. What else can it be but the Palestinian state?**

Chapter 12

RETRIBUTION UPON THE PHILISTINES

"All the regions of Philistia. . . . I will return
your recompense on your head" (Joel 3.4).

The Hebrew prophet Joel wrote about that grand theme of Holy Scripture—"the day of the LORD," or "the day of Yahweh." In that final Day, Yahweh will manifest His awesome power by destroying the nations that come against Israel and consummating His plan not only for Israel, but for all mankind.

In Joel 3 the prophet implies that Philistia will exist as a separate entity from Israel at the end of this age. As in Isa 11, this can only be determined by analyzing the context.

Israel's Repentance
Joel begins his little book by depicting an unprecedented invasion of locusts (grasshoppers) over the land of Israel (1.4). To this pestilence are added drought, fire and famine. The prophet exhorts Israel to follow King Solomon's instruction to assemble at the temple during such times of distress and pray to Yahweh for deliverance (1.13-14; cf. 1 Kgs 8.23-61). Joel himself interprets this invasion of insects as a harbinger of a future military invasion of the land of Israel. "A great and mighty people" will attack Israel from the north (2.2, 20) as divine punishment for Israel's sins.

To what army and time does the prophet refer? If the book of Joel was written before King Hezekiah's time, as conservative scholars generally believe, part of Joel 2 was no doubt fulfilled by Assyrian King Sennacherib's assault on Judah in 701 B.C. (2 Kgs 18-19). Because good King Hezekiah prayed at the temple, Jerusalem was delivered when "the angel of the LORD" destroyed 185,000 Assyrian troops.

Yet some parts of Joel 2 can refer only to that future invasion of the land of Israel by all the nations' armies at the end of the Tribulation,[1] as depicted in Joel 3. For instance, after the invasion from the north (2.1-9), the gathering of the Israelites at the temple to repent (vv. 12-17) and the removal of the enemy (v. 20), God says:

> **19** . . . I will never again make you a reproach among the nations.
> **26** . . . Then My people will never be put to shame.
> **27** . . . And My people will never be put to shame.

When will God remove forever the reproach of the Jews? It will not be until the coming of the Messianic kingdom (Isa 25.8). Thereafter, Jews will never be put to shame (Isa 45.17; Eze 39.26).[2] **Joel 2.1-27 must therefore be presenting a dual prophecy which, in addition to predicting the Assyrian invasion, anticipates the future Messianic deliverance.**

Outpouring of the Spirit and Heavenly Signs

Joel 2.28-32 is further evidence that all of Joel 2 refers to the latter days, as the following verses attest:

> **28** And it will come about after this that I will pour out My Spirit on all mankind.
> **31** The sun will be turned into darkness and the moon into blood.

The Spirit of God has never been poured out on all mankind. This will not happen until the Messianic kingdom comes.[3] The words "after this," in Joel 2.28, indicate that the outpouring will occur just after the time previously described, when the invading army will have been removed (v. 20).

The prophet Joel is increasingly concerned with the subject of the last days, especially the Day of Yahweh. The same events recorded in Joel 2.10-11 and 30-32 are further delineated in Joel 3 in a context which indisputably concerns that final Day (3.14). While Joel 2.1-27 seems to continue the theme presented in the previous chapter—the invasion of locusts—the language appears figurative, pointing to an invasion of the nations in the last days. Indeed, an invasion of Israel by its enemies is definitely the theme of Joel 3.[4]

Cataclysmic disturbances in the sun and moon in Joel 2.10 and 30-31 are mentioned again in Joel 3.15 (cf. Isa 13.9-10; Mt 24.29; Rev 6.12). These astronomical signs have never yet occurred. In that

Day Yahweh will utter His voice before His army (2.11; cf. Isa 42.13; 1 Th 4.16) from Mount Zion in Jerusalem (3.16). Those who call upon Yahweh will be delivered and escape the final onslaught (2.32). They are the same ones who find refuge in Him in Joel 3.16.

Joel 3.1-8

> **1** "For behold, in those days and at that time, when I restore the fortunes of Judah and Jerusalem,
> **2** I will gather all the nations and bring them down to the valley of Jehoshaphat. Then I will enter into judgment with them there on behalf of My people and My inheritance, Israel, whom they have scattered among the nations; and they have divided up My land.
> **3** They have also cast lots for My people, traded a boy for a harlot, and sold a girl for wine that they may drink.
> **4 Moreover, what are you to Me, O Tyre, Sidon, and all the regions of Philistia? Are you rendering Me a recompense? But if you do recompense Me, swiftly and speedily I will return your recompense on your head.**
> **5** Since you have taken My silver and My gold, brought My precious treasures to your temples,
> **6** and sold the sons of Judah and Jerusalem to the Greeks in order to remove them far from their territory,
> **7** behold, I am going to arouse them from the place where you have sold them, and return your recompense on your head.
> **8** Also I will sell your sons and your daughters into the hand of the sons of Judah, and they will sell them to the Sabeans, to a distant nation," for the LORD has spoken (Joel 3.1-8; emphasis added).

Valley of Jehoshaphat

The words in Joel 3.1, "in those days and at that time," refer to the time period last referred to in Joel 2. It is the time immediately preceding and including the "day of the LORD." Joel maintains that God will draw all the nations' armies to the land of Israel. Their purpose will be to exterminate all the Jews (Joel 3.2; cf. Isa 29.7; 34.2; Zech 12.3; 14.2). Instead, God will gather them into the "valley of Jehoshaphat" (meaning "Yahweh judges;" 3.2, 12). There, Yahweh will destroy the nations for assaulting Israel, dividing its land and selling Jews into slavery (3.2-3, 12).

Since the 4th century A.D., the Valley of Jehoshaphat has been identified as the Kidron Valley, located just outside Jerusalem on the east, between the temple grounds and the Mount of Olives. It is called a "winepress" or "wine trough" in the Bible because this is where Messiah will trample the nations' armies as men trample grapes in a winepress (Joel 3.13; Isa 63.1-6; Rev 14.18-20; 19.15).

Gentile nations have a long history of possessing and dividing Yahweh's land. Although God has used the nations in disciplining Israel, He will nevertheless hold them responsible for what they have done to His people. On account of the crimes mentioned by Joel, Yahweh says to Tyre, Sidon and Philistia, "I will return your recompense on your head" (3.4, 7). With this mention of Philistia we have arrived at the critical passage relating to our theme.

Future of Tyre, Sidon and Philistia
Most biblical commentators regard Joel 3.4-8 as having been fulfilled in Israel's past, with no future fulfillment remaining, yet they admit that the surrounding context clearly concerns the last days.[5] There has probably been **some** fulfillment of Joel 3.4-8 in Israel's history, though most evidence offered for it is weak. The following reasons suggest that Joel 3.4-8 also awaits a future fulfillment:

1. Tyre, Sidon and Philistia seem to be included among the nations which attack Israel in the last days. Tyre and Sidon were the foremost cities of the Phoenicians. The Phoenicians and Philistines were infamous slave traders in antiquity.[6] The word "They," which begins v. 3, suggests that many of the nations to be gathered into the valley, not just Phoenicia and Philistia, sold and scattered the Jews and divided their land. History affirms this. The word "They" also seems to disallow severing vv. 4-8 from the context of the last days and restricting these verses to a past fulfillment.[7] A.C. Gaebelein, while admitting a possible past fulfillment of vv. 4-8, remarks on vv. 7-8, "But the words must also have their final fulfillment when the nations are in the valley of Jehoshaphat."[8]

2. It is doubtful that the prophet would interrupt the flow of this important prophetic chapter, which otherwise describes exclusively the last days, with vv. 4-8 if they refer only to events long past.

3. For those who would argue that the Philistines will not exist in the last days, v. 4 only specifies "all the regions of Philistia," i.e., the geographic area, and does not identify the Philistines themselves. **Note that the future Philistia will encompass all of its former territory, not just the Gaza Strip. Here is evidence that Egypt will relinquish its northeastern corner of the Sinai, between the Gaza Strip and the Wadi el Arish.**

Following the depiction of the Messianic destruction, God's retribution on Tyre, Sidon and Philistia is described. The Philistines and others took God's silver and gold from Jerusalem (Joel 3.5; cf. 2 Chron 21.16-17; 36.10). Now they will honor the Jews with gifts of silver, gold and other wealth (Isa 60.6, 9, 11, 17). With these, the fourth (millennial) temple will be built (Zech 6.12-15; cf. Isa 60.10), just as the tabernacle in the wilderness was constructed with gold from Egypt (Ex 12.35-36; 30.12-16).

Joel 3.4-8 is no doubt the most difficult Philistia passage to fit into a yet future scenario. Yet it is certain that it cannot refer to the Babylonian exile because of v. 6, which portrays Jews being sold as slaves to the Greeks.

Because of their selling Jews as slaves, God says to Tyre, Sidon and Philistia, "I will sell your sons and your daughters into the hand of the sons of Judah, and they will sell them to the Sabeans" (v. 8). Selling slaves at the beginning of the Messianic kingdom may seem preposterous, but a characteristic of Messiah's government is justice. As the nations did to Israel, so at this time will Israel do to the nations (Obad 15).

Isaiah provides further insight into how this justice will be meted out during the Messianic kingdom. Like Joel, he foresees the Jews enslaving some Gentiles. Gentiles will gather the remaining Jews of the Diaspora, "take them along and bring them to their place, and the house of Israel will possess them [those Gentiles] as an inheritance in the land of the LORD as male servants and female servants; and they [the Jews] will take their captors captive, and will rule over their oppressors" (Isa 14.1-2; cf. 49.22-23).

This prophecy by Isaiah can be fulfilled only in the Messianic kingdom. It was not fulfilled by the returning exiles from Babylonia. The Persian forces that escorted the Jewish exiles from Babylon to their former homeland did not include women. Neither did the Persians remain to become the Jews' servants (Ezra 8.22; Neh 2.9). The returning exiles never took their captors—the Babylonians—captive nor ruled over them.

Moreover, this prophecy by Isaiah refers to a time when Yahweh's hand will be stretched out against all the nations and a king of Assyria will be trampled on the mountains of Israel (Isa 14.25-26). This cannot refer to any other time than the Day of Yahweh. That is when He will destroy the Antichrist, an Assyrian (Isa 10.12, 24; 14.25; Mic 5.5-6), by the hand of Christ.

It is conceivable that God will bring this retribution of Joel 3 on the inhabitants of Tyre, Sidon and Philistia on Judgment Day, which immediately follows the Messianic destruction. Perhaps it is then when the Israelis will sell some of their former enemies to the Sabeans, who were ancient traders. The Sabeans were inhabitants of Sheba, located on the southwestern coast of the Arabian peninsula in present South Yemen. Maybe the Sabeans will be spared enslavement because they will not participate with the nations in the final attack on Israel (Eze 38.13).

The prophet Zephaniah writes of a time when all the nations will bow down to Yahweh (Zeph 2.11). This can only refer to the time of the Messianic kingdom. Just before this, the prophet relates concerning Israel's neighboring foes, Moab and Ammon, "The remnant of My people will plunder them, and the remainder of My nation will inherit them" (2.9). Thus, the Messianic victory will result in Israel's acquiring some citizens of both Philistia and present western Jordan as their servants.

Yet God is not only just, but merciful. Assuming that the Mosaic civil law prevails throughout the Messianic kingdom, perhaps these Philistine servants and others will be loosed in the 50th year, the Year of Jubilee (Lev 25.10). That is when all slaves were freed under the Levitical law.

In Israel's early history, no people "divided up" Israel's territory by possessing it more than did the Philistines. The implication of Joel 3.2-8 is that, in turn, God will give the land of the Philistines to Israel as a portion of the Promised Land. Indeed He will, a subject which the prophet Zephaniah addresses, and to which we now turn.

Chapter 13

ANNEXATION OF PHILISTIA TO JUDEA

"And the coast will be for the remnant
of the house of Judah" (Zeph 2.7).

Like Joel, Zephaniah is a prophet of the "day of the LORD." The two books are similar and should be compared. Because of its indefiniteness, however, the small book of Zephaniah has been regarded as one of the most difficult prophetic books in the Bible to interpret.[1] Zephaniah provides a sweeping general summary of the future.

Many biblical commentators think that Zephaniah's "day of the LORD" in his first two chapters does not refer to any specific time-period, but can be applied to various times of calamity future to the prophet. Most regard the end of the book, Zeph 3.8-20, as depicting yet future conditions at the final Day of the LORD, when Messiah comes in glory. However, some material in the first two chapters of Zephaniah directly corresponds to Zeph 3.8-20, as well as endtime material in other prophetic books. This suggests that much of Zephaniah's book concerns the last days as well.

Our interest in Zephaniah centers on the prophet's mention of the Philistines in Zeph 2.4-7. What time is the prophet writing about? An analysis of the preceding verses is necessary in order to grasp the context of Zeph 2.4-7.

Zephaniah 1
In the first chapter of Zephaniah, the prophet describes in vv. 2-3 and 14-18 a worldwide destruction. If understood literally, these events can only describe the end of the world, on the eschatological Day of the LORD.[2] Note the following examples from Zeph 1, with direct parallels to other endtime passages added in brackets:

> **2** I will completely remove all things from the face of the earth. [Cf. Isa 24.3.]
> **3** I will remove man and beast; I will remove the birds of the sky and the fish of the sea, . . . and I will cut off man from the face of the earth. [Cf. Isa 24.6b.]
> **14** Near is the great day of the LORD, near and coming very quickly. . . .
> **18** And all the earth will be devoured in the fire of His jealousy, for He will make a complete end, indeed a terrifying one, of all the inhabitants of the earth. [Cf. Zeph 3.8; Mic 7.13.]

Zephaniah 1.4-13 portrays God judging sinful Judah and Jerusalem. These verses have no doubt had some remarkable literal fulfillment in the assaults on Jerusalem by Babylon's King Nebuchadnezzar and Rome's General Titus. Nevertheless, because vv. 2-3 and 14-18 were not fulfilled during those times, Zeph 1 must await a final and complete fulfillment in the endtime.

The Great Day of the LORD
In Zeph 1.14 the prophet adds a qualifying word to the expression, "the day of the LORD." He specifies "the **great** day of the LORD." Like "the great tribulation," "the great day of the LORD" distinguishes it from any previous "day of Yahweh." On all of those days Yahweh exercised His power in judgment, yet always with restraint. In contrast, on "the great day," the Almighty will pour out **all** His wrath without holding back. It must be concluded that that great day will be "near," as Zephaniah says in v. 14, when Judah and Jerusalem will be assaulted by the nations at the end of the age.

Israel's Call to Repent
When the nations attack Jerusalem, Zephaniah exhorts sinful Israel to gather at the temple, humble itself and repent (cf. Joel 2.12-17). If the Israelites do this, they may escape the onslaught and be hidden in the day of the LORD's anger (cf. Joel 2.32; Zech 14.5).

Zephaniah 2.1-3

> **1** Gather yourselves together, yes, gather, O nation without shame,
> **2** Before the decree takes effect—the day passes like the chaff—before the burning anger of the LORD comes upon you, before the day of the LORD's anger comes upon you.
> **3** Seek the LORD, all you humble of the earth who have carried out His ordinances; seek righteousness, seek humility. Perhaps you will be hidden in the day of the LORD's anger.

Zephaniah 2.1-3 cannot apply to the Babylonian conquest in the 6th century B.C. Despite the greatest reforms in Israel's history under King Josiah, which occurred immediately beforehand, God said he would still remove the Southern Kingdom as He had the Northern Kingdom (2 Kgs 23.25-27). Long before the Babylonian advance, God's decree of judgment on those Judeans was irrevocable. Zephaniah's call to repentance here clearly refers to the time of Israel's destruction at the end of the yet future Tribulation.[3]

Neither was Zeph 2.1-3 fulfilled by the Romans' destruction of Jerusalem in A.D. 70. All of those Jews closed up inside became victims of the siege and final onslaught. Many erroneously thought they could "be hidden in the day of the LORD's anger" (v. 3). Josephus witnessed it all. He reports that Jerusalem's citizens hid themselves "in the caves and caverns under ground; whither, . . . they did not expect to be searched for; but endeavoured that, after the whole city should be destroyed, and the Romans gone away, they might come out again, and escape from them. This was no better than a dream of theirs; for they were not able to lie hid either from God or from the Romans."[4]

Hiding Place

How appropriate that God would choose Zephaniah to write about His hiding place on the Day of the LORD! Zephaniah means "Yahweh hides." Sometimes God has a hiding place for the humble who seek Him. The final Day of the LORD is one of those times. This theme in Zeph 2.3 is repeated in 3.12, "I will leave among you a humble and lowly people, and they will take refuge in the name of the LORD." The context of this verse exclusively concerns the endtime. The repentant Jews will be hidden from the awesome wrath that Yahweh will pour out on the earth at the end of the Tribulation (cf. Zech 14.4-5).

With this context established, we now turn to the focus of our study.

Zephaniah 2.4-7

4 For Gaza will be abandoned, and Ashkelon a desolation; Ashdod will be driven out at noon, and Ekron will be uprooted.

5 Woe to the inhabitants of the seacoast, the nation of the Cherethites! The word of the LORD is against you, O Canaan, land of the Philistines; and I will destroy you, so that there will be no inhabitant.

6 So the seacoast will be pastures, with caves for shepherds and folds for flocks.

7 And the coast will be for the remnant of the house of Judah, they will pasture on it. In the houses of Ashkelon they will lie down at evening; for the LORD their God will care for them and restore their fortune.

Messianic Destruction of Philistia

Following the predicted invasion of Judah and Jerusalem and the exhortation to repent, in Zeph 2.4-5 the prophet describes an invasion and destruction of Philistia on the Day of the LORD (cf. v. 2). Only four cities of the Philistine pentapolis are mentioned. By Zephaniah's time, Gath had declined (cf. 2 Chron 26.6). The Cherethites of v. 5 lived just south of the Philistines, on the coastal plain toward Egypt. As mentioned in Chapter 2, they are probably to be regarded as a branch of the Philistines.

As in Zeph 1, the destroying power is not specifically identified. Could it be the aforementioned Jews at Jerusalem, who will have escaped destruction on account of their repentance? Indeed, this becomes evident in the verses which follow, and it corresponds with other prophets.

In Zeph 2.4-15 it is not only the nation of Philistia that Yahweh will destroy, but also Moab and Ammon (present Jordan), Ethiopia and Assyria. These are Israel's enemies according to the four directions of the compass.

Concerning the inhabitants of the land presently known as Jordan, Zephaniah proclaims: "The remnant of My people will plunder them, and the remainder of My nation will inherit them" (v. 9). It is therefore the Jews who will destroy Jordan. They are likely, then, the same power who will overtake Philistia. But could these predicted destructions of Philistia and Jordan have already been completely fulfilled in the Hasmonean era, under Alexander Jannaeus, and therefore require no further fulfillment? Not at all![5]

Following Jordan's destruction, Zephaniah claims "all the coastlands of the nations will bow down to Him [Yahweh], everyone from his own place" (v. 11; cf. Isa 45.23; Rom 14.11; Phil 2.10-11). This is unmistakably the universal worship of Yahweh during the Messianic kingdom. Therefore, all these judgments will mostly likely occur at the same endtime. H.A. Ironside regards all of Zeph 2 as

> a picture of the time of the end. Judah then will be much in the position she occupied in Zephaniah's day—in the land, surrounded by enemies, a feeble remnant, crying "How long, O Lord?" the mass, apostate and swayed by Antichrist . . . and their enemies who have glorified over their helplessness shall become the objects of [the LORD's] avenging wrath, preparatory to the ushering in of the world-kingdom of our God and His Christ.[6]

Coastland for Judah

The Hebrew word *chebel*, which appears three times in vv. 5-7, is translated "seacoast" and "coast." It means "a measuring cord," and here it denotes a "country" or "region."[7] The district of the Philistines is intended, with its four cities bound together as one whole.[8] Thus, prior to the Messianic destruction, the entire Philistine coastal plain will designate a region separate from Judea, a nation of the Philistines.

Verse 7, "the coast will be for the remnant of the house of Judah" implies that this region is not possessed by the Judeans immediately prior to the Day of the LORD. Only after Philistia is conquered on that Day will it belong to the remnant of Judah forever. This passage cannot be regarded as completely fulfilled during Israel's past. Even during the Hasmonean occupation of most of the Plain of Philistia, the Jews never retained the enlarged district of Ashkelon.

Furthermore, Zechariah relates concerning the Jews, that "in the houses of Ashkelon they will lie down at evening" (v. 7). Israel's physical security and financial blessing, indicated in v. 7, is so complete that it cannot pertain to either the post-exilic return or modern Israel, but only to the Messianic kingdom. The "lying down" is also mentioned in Zeph 3.13 in an exclusively Messianic context. Only at that time "Israel will do no wrong and tell no lies," and there will be "no one to make them tremble." Verse 7 is echoed at the end of Zephaniah: "I will give you renown and praise among all the peoples of the earth, when I restore your fortunes before your eyes" (3.20). The contexts of these verses, as well as their similarities to Zeph 2.7, suggest that Zeph 2.7, indeed, all of Zeph 2.1-7, awaits an endtime fulfillment.

Annexation of All the Promised Land

The prophet Isaiah prophesied concerning the annexation of the remaining Promised Land in the early days of the glorious Messianic kingdom:

> **26.1** In that day this song will be sung in the land of Judah: . . .
> **26.15** "Thou hast increased the nation, O LORD,
> Thou hast increased the nation,
> Thou art glorified;
> **Thou hast extended all the borders of the land.**"
>
> **54.3 For you will spread abroad to the right and to the left.
> And your descendants will possess nations,** and they will resettle the desolate cities (emphasis added).

The Messianic destruction will encompass the entire Promised Land. "The LORD will start His threshing from the flowing stream of the Euphrates to the brook of Egypt" (Isa 27.12; cf. 9.4-5).

The Messianic destruction will be immediately followed by the promised ingathering. He will "multiply the nation" (Isa 9.3), gathering all Jews remaining from the Diaspora (Isa 27.13). Upon their arrival they will say, "The place is too cramped for me; make room for me that I may live here" (Isa 49.20).

Then Yahweh will extend the borders of Israel to include all of the Promised Land (Mic 7.11). He will settle Jews east and north, in "the land of Gilead and Lebanon, until no room can be found for them" (Zech 10.10). They will "feed in Bashan and Gilead [present northwestern Jordan] as in days of old" (Mic 7.14), when the two and a half tribes lived east of the Jordan River. But Israel will not only annex territory to the east.

Isaiah says the Israelites will spread both right and left, meaining east and west (Isa 54.3). Although the entire western border of land which modern Israel now controls is the Mediterranean Sea, this cannot mean that the present return fulfills Isa 54.3. Isaiah 54 clearly portrays the Messianic kingdom. Only then will Israel no more feel humiliated or disgraced (v. 4), or will Israel's sons be taught the LORD and be far from oppression and fear (vv. 13-14).

Israel cannot spread to the left if its western border is the Mediterranean Sea, as it is presently. Therefore, **between now and the coming of the Messianic kingdom, a portion of the Mediterranean coast will be severed from the State of Israel, presumably to form the Palestinian state (Philistia).**

Thus, when Messiah comes to establish His glorious kingdom, Israel will be extended in every direction. The following lands will be annexed: the Sinai in the south, western Jordan to the east, Lebanon and much of Syria in the north and Philistia on the west.

Zephaniah 2.4-7, combined with Isa 54.3 and 26.15, makes it certain that **the State of Israel will not possess the Philistine Plain in the endtimes preceding the Messianic kingdom. Yet Israel will thereafter be enlarged by the LORD to include all of Philistia.**

Psalms 60 and 108: Defeat of the Philistines

The book of Psalms was the Hebrews' hymnal. It consisted of 150 poems set to music. King David composed many of them out of his own experiences. God sometimes spoke through David as He did through the prophets. Accordingly, some of these psalms go beyond David's life to predict the sufferings and triumphs of Messiah.

A subtitle appended to Psalm 60 reveals that it was occasioned by the most notable victory in David's military career. This battle against the Mesopotamians in Syria may prefigure Messiah's "battle on the great day of God Almighty" (Rev 16.14 NIV; cf. 19.11-21), known popularly as Armageddon.

Psalms 60.6-12 and 108.7-13 are almost identical. They celebrate military victories by the Jews over their neighbors. Verses from Ps 60, also in Ps 108.7-9, read as follows in the RSV:

> **2** Thou hast made the land to quake, thou hast rent it open; repair its breaches, for it totters.
> **6** God has spoken in his sanctuary: "With exultation I will divide up Shechem and portion out the Vale of Succoth.
> **7** Gilead is mine; Manas'seh is mine; E'phraim is my helmet; Judah is my scepter.
> **8** Moab is my washbasin; upon Edom I cast my shoe; **over Philistia I shout in triumph"** (emphasis added).

Such victories by Israel over its neighbors have never occurred. In v. 8, "casting the shoe" is an idiom signifying possession. Israel will indeed conquer and possess Edom (southwestern Jordan) when the Messianic age begins (cf. Isa 34.5-17; 63.1; Joel 3.19; Obad 18-19). Likewise, shouting over Philistia indicates God's victory, accomplished through a united Ephraim and Judah (vv. 7, 9-12), over the inhabitants of the Plain of Philistia. And we have already seen that during the Messianic age, Israel will possess Gilead, Bashan, Ammon and Moab (northwestern and central western Jordan).

Psalm 60.2 identifies the time of this psalm. It pictures a great earthquake that causes huge cracks in the earth's surface. This bears striking similarity to cataclysmic disturbances depicted in other apocalyptic scriptures (e.g., Isa 24.18-20; Rev 6.12; 16.18). These suggest that Ps 60 pertains to the endtime as well. In that case, Yahweh will accomplish these victories in vv. 6-8 by Messiah's leading Israel in battle on the final Day of the LORD.

If Ps 60 and 108 refer to Messianic victories, they indicate that Philistia will exist in the latter days as a country separate from Israel. As with the other conquered neighbors, it too will be annexed to Israel.

Obadiah 15-21: Israel Will Possess Philistia
Obadiah 15-21 depicts Yahweh's judgment at the end of this age. Portions of this passage appear below.

> **15** For the day of the LORD draws near on all the nations.
> **16** Because just as you drank on My holy mountain, all the nations will drink and swallow, and become as if they had never existed.
> **17** But on Mount Zion there will be those who escape, and it will be holy. And the house of Jacob will possess their possessions.
> **19 Then those of the Negev will possess the mountain of Esau, and those of the Shephelah the Philistine plain;** ...
> **21** ... And the kingdom will be the LORD's (emphasis added).

Near the end of the Tribulation, all the nations' armies will gather at Armageddon to attack Israel (Rev 16.16). What they won't know is that God will be gathering them there and into the Kidron Valley to destroy them (Joel 3.14). Upon taking Jerusalem, the nations' leaders will celebrate with a toast on Mount Zion (Obad 16). But the tide will turn. At the coming of Messiah in glory, Mount Zion will become the rallying place for Israelis who survive the nations' slaughter. Following the Messianic destruction of the nations' armies, Israelis will possess the spoil (Zech 14.1, 14; Eze 39.10). Only then can it be said that Zion "will be holy" (Obad 17).

Obadiah 19-21 means that Israelis living in southern Israel ("those of the Negev") will take possession of their neighbors' lands to the east and west. Was this scripture fulfilled by the Hasmonean Kingdom in the early 1st century B.C.? That was certainly not a time in which it could be said, "Mount Zion ... will be holy" or "the kingdom will be the LORD's" (vv. 17, 21). We saw in Chapter 2 how Hasmonean

King Alexander Jannaeus, who accomplished much land expansion, was a cruel and godless tyrant. Instead, this passage more aptly describes the Messianic era, as is generally maintained by Jewish commentators.[9] Only then will the kingdom of Israel truly belong to Yahweh. Even non-premillennialist C.F. Keil concludes concerning Obadiah, "the fulfillment of vv. 17-21 can only belong to the Messianic times, . . . in a complete fulfillment at the second coming of our Lord."[10]

Obadiah 19 indicates that the Israelis will already possess both the Negev and the Shephelah near the end of the Tribulation, but **not** southwestern Jordan or the Philistine Plain. Messianic victories, however, will result in Israel's annexing both of these territories as part of the Promised Land.

Turning to the present Israeli-Palestinian conflict, **Obadiah 19 is the only biblical passage which expressly identifies the future border between Israel and the Palestinian state as the western edge of the Shephelah**, their common border in ancient times. Here is additional evidence that the land dispute between the Israelis and the Palestinians will be resolved according to historical precedent.

Conclusion

On the final Day of Yahweh, Messiah will come to lead the Israelis in conquering their enemies. Neighboring lands, including Philistia, will afterwards be annexed to Israel. Then all Jews will realize that neither they nor their forefathers could obtain the Promised Land by their own shrewdness and strength. **Instead, the Jews will know that Yahweh, their Sovereign God, gives them all the land He promised, including the Plain of Philistia. But it will only happen according to His timing and plan, when they repent and turn to Him.**

Chapter 14

CONVERSION OF THE PHILISTINES

"I will cut off the pride of the Philistines. . . . Then they also will be a remnant for our God" (Zech 9.6-7).

The tears and sorrow are not over yet. Much suffering remains to be experienced by the people of the Blessed Land. But incredible as it may seem, the prophets of Yahweh have foreseen a "happily ever after" ending to the Palestinian-Israeli conflict. These seers not only predicted the reestablishment of Philistia, followed by its conquest and annexation to Israel; they also predicted a glorious reconciliation of the Philistines (Palestinians) with the Israelis and with God. This is clearly seen in the ninth chapter of the book of Zechariah.

Zechariah provides more information than any other prophet about the nations' future invasion of Israel immediately before the Jews' final deliverance. As the Gentiles will be slaughtering a multitude of Jews in their worst suffering ever, it will seem that God has forgotten His Chosen People. Yet, as Israel repents, "Yahweh remembers"—the very meaning of Zechariah's name.

Although much, if not all, of Zech 9-14 concerns the endtime, some of it has already seen fulfillment. For example, most commentators regard all of Zech 9.1-8 as having been thoroughly fulfilled during the 4th century B.C. in the military campaigns of Alexander the Great. Indeed, it is amazing how Alexander's movements correspond in precise detail to much of this prophecy. But there are some important aspects in this passage which clearly cannot be reconciled with the exploits of Alexander.

What we want to know from Zech 9 is this: Were vv. 1-8 completely fulfilled in the past? Or do they require a yet future revival of the ancient country of Philistia, first nationally, then spiritually?

Zechariah 9.1-8

1 The burden of the word of the LORD is against the land of
Hadrach, with Damascus as its resting place (for the eyes of
men, especially of all the tribes of Israel, are toward the LORD),
2 And Hamath also, which borders on it; Tyre and Sidon,
though they are very wise.
3 For Tyre built herself a fortress and piled up silver like dust,
and gold like the mire of the streets.
4 Behold, the Lord will dispossess her and cast her wealth into
the sea; and she will be consumed with fire.
**5 Ashkelon will see it and be afraid. Gaza too will writhe in
great pain; also Ekron, for her expectation has been con-
founded. Moreover, the king will perish from Gaza, and Ashkelon will not be inhabited.
6 And a mongrel race will dwell in Ashdod, and I will cut
off the pride of the Philistines.
7 And I will remove their blood from their mouth, and their
detestable things from between their teeth. Then they also will
be a remnant for our God, and be like a clan in Judah, and
Ekron like a Jebusite.**
8 But I will camp around My house because of an army, because
of him who passes by and returns; and no oppressor will pass
over them anymore, for now I have seen with My eyes (emphasis
added).

Zechariah begins chapter 9 with a pronouncement called, "a burden
of the word of the LORD." It is a judgment proclaimed against the
cities of Damascus and Hamath in Syria (vv. 1-2); Tyre, Sidon and
Hadrach in Lebanon (vv. 2-4) and Gaza, Ekron, Ashkelon and Ashdod
in Philistia (vv. 5-8).

Alexander the Great (356-323 B.C.) of Macedonia was the greatest
military conqueror in history. The Hebrew biblical prophets, all of
whom lived before Alexander, predicted much about him and his
kingdom. One of Alexander's notable feats was his siege and destruction of the wealthy Phoenician city of Tyre, in present Lebanon. It
certainly seems that Zechariah's prophecy against Tyre was fulfilled
by Alexander, when he burned it with fire and thoroughly destroyed it.

After destroying Tyre, Alexander continued his march south along
the Mediterranean coast. We would expect Zechariah to have listed
these four Philistine cities as they appeared geographically in the
conqueror's path. Instead, they are arranged in a different order:

Ashkelon, Gaza, Ekron and Ashdod. This variation is the first hint that Alexander's expedition against Philistia only partially fulfilled Zech 9.5-8. This order may indicate that during the Messianic destruction of Israel's neighbors, from the east Judah will first attack the cities of Ashqelon and Gaza because these will be the most developed and/or militarily strategic.

It seems that the people living in these Philistine cities braced themselves for Alexander's advance and that Zechariah's words then came true, "Ashkelon will see it and be afraid." All but Gaza surrendered to Alexander. Zechariah portrays the inhabitants of Gaza as squirming in great pain, an accurate picture of the suffering resulting from their resistance.

Alexander wanted to establish a world empire. To accomplish this, he tried to create mixed populations in many of his conquered territories. His purpose was to extinguish nationalism and thereby prevent rebellion. Verse 6 seems to indicate this policy, since "a mongrel race will dwell in Ashdod." The Septuagint renders it "a mixed population."

Such a population in Ashdod may, however, depict the heterogeneous Palestinians living there in the last days, since the context which follows requires a futuristic interpretation.

Conversion of the Philistines to Yahweh
After implying the assault on the four Philistine cities, the prophet summarizes on behalf of Yahweh, "I will cut off the pride of the Philistines" (v. 6). Following this Philistine downfall, Zechariah adds that "they also will be a remnant for our God" (v. 7). That is, the Philistines will worship Yahweh, the God of Israel. Zechariah's inclusion of the Philistines as the people of God echoes his theme elsewhere of the nations' universal worship of God during the Messianic kingdom (2.11; 8.20-23; 14.16).[1]

To be sure, the Philistines never converted to faith in Yahweh during the days of Alexander, nor at any other time in their history. They were devotees of Dagon and other pagan deities. Therefore, Zech 2.5-7 was not completely fulfilled by Alexander; it still requires a future fulfillment. Jewish Christian expositors David Baron and Charles Feinberg claim that vv. 7-8 require a future, literal fulfillment at the second coming of Christ.[2] C.F. Keil lists the exploits of Alexander, then explains that

> Koehler has already replied . . . that the prophecy in ver. 7 was not fulfilled by the deeds of Alexander, since neither the

remnant of the Phoenicians nor the other heathen dwelling in the midst of Israel were converted to Jehovah through the calamities connected with Alexander's expedition; and on this ground he merely regards the conquests of Alexander as the commencement of the fulfillment, . . . But we must go a step further and say that the commencement has not yet reached its end.[3]

In order for Philistines (Palestinians) living in the Plain of Philistia to be conquered and converted to Yahweh at the coming of Messiah in glory, they must first become reestablished there.

Incorporation of the Philistines into Israel

The remainder of Zech 9.7 refers exclusively to the Messianic kingdom. Then the Philistines will "be like a clan in Judah, and Ekron like a Jebusite." The Jebusites were the residents of Jerusalem (Jebus) before David conquered that city. They were afterwards assimilated into the Hebrew population. Apparently, the same will be true of the Philistines at Ekron, situated near the border with Judah.

The Philistine Plain will thus be annexed to Judea in the Messianic kingdom, and the Philistine (Palestinian) remnant will be incorporated into the Jewish population. Being "like a clan in Judah," they will enjoy a greater status than the alien or sojourner did in ancient Israel (e.g., Ex 12.45; 20.11; Lev 25.35). Philistine (Palestinian) sons will be like native-born Jews in Israel.

The prophet Ezekiel claims that during the Messianic kingdom, aliens will receive an inheritance of land in Israel, just as the Jews will:

> So you shall divide this land among yourselves according to the tribes of Israel. And it will come about that you shall divide it by lot for an inheritance among yourselves and among the aliens who stay in your midst, who bring forth sons in your midst. And they shall be to you as the native-born among the sons of Israel; they shall be allotted an inheritance with you among the tribes of Israel. And it will come about that in the tribe with which the alien stays, there you shall give him his inheritance (Eze 47.21-23).

Thus, each surviving Palestinian family will be allotted its inheritance of land in expanded Eretz Israel. Palestinians will probably be allotted land in their homeland of Philistia. Thereafter, Yahweh will no longer permit Israelis to buy and keep Palestinian land, as they have done in the 20th century. Instead, every 50th year, during the Year of Jubilee, everything, including real estate, will revert to its original owner (Lev 25.10).

"I Will Camp Around My House"

Zech 9.8 offers overwhelming evidence that this prophecy regarding the Philistines has never been completely fulfilled in history. Nonetheless, Alexander's activities remarkably fit this verse.

Josephus provides a fascinating account of Alexander the Great. When he was about to destroy Tyre, the Macedonian king sent messengers to Jerusalem requesting provisions for his army and promising reward. Jaddua, the honorable high priest, refused on account of his previous oath to Persian King Darius.

Alexander became enraged. He swore he would do to Jerusalem what he was about to do to Tyre and in this way teach all men to whom they ought to perform their oaths.[4] After destroying Tyre, however, he passed by Jerusalem on his way south along the Philistine coast to Gaza.

Except for Gaza, all of the Philistine cities surrendered to Alexander. Gaza, which means "strong," had a history like that of Tyre, of surviving long sieges. Yet after a two-month siege, Alexander's troops stormed Gaza. In v. 5 Zechariah had predicted that "the king will perish from Gaza." In a brutal display of triumph, Alexander dragged the king of Gaza behind his chariot throughout the city.

After destroying Gaza, Alexander headed hastily northeast to fulfill his threat against Jerusalem. Josephus explains that when Alexander approached Jerusalem, he saw the high priest in his priestly attire coming out to meet him. Alexander's troops thought him mad when he dismounted and bowed down to the high priest.

Josephus relates that when Alexander had earlier been contemplating how he might overtake Asia, he had had a dream. In it someone in priestly garments and headdress, exactly like this priest, assured the warrior that God had given him Asia. Thus, the priest appeared to Alexander as a divine portent, and the warrior changed his mind about destroying Jerusalem.

Whether or not Josephus' account is accurate, history verifies that Alexander befriended the Jews and did no harm to Jerusalem.

Alexander's movements in relation to Jerusalem appear to fulfill remarkably the first half of Zech 9.8, "but I will camp around My house because of an army, because of him who passes by and returns."

Most commentators think "My house" refers to the temple at Jerusalem or to the city itself. God did indeed "camp around [His] house" when Alexander passed by and returned.

The Jewish Targum, however, maintains that Zech 9.8a is an amplification of the security of Jerusalem during the Messianic kingdom, described earlier in Zech 2.4-5, 10.[5] In these verses an angel assures Zechariah: "Jerusalem will be inhabited without walls, because of the multitude of men and cattle within it. 'For I,' declares the LORD, 'will be a wall of fire around her, and I will be the glory in her midst' " (cf. Eze 39.26). Zechariah 2.11 also depicts the same conversion of the nations during the Messianic kingdom as described in Isa 2.3 and Mic 4.1-2. Kimchi, eminent medieval Jewish commentator, comments on the entirety of Zech 2, "It is certain that this vision is of the future, referring to the days of Messiah."[6] Accordingly, the similarity of Zech 2.4-5 to 9.8a suggests that the latter describes the Messianic kingdom as well. Unger and Tatford regard all of Zech 9.8 as being fulfilled exclusively in the endtime.[7]

The Antichrist: Israel's Last Oppressor
The one who "passes by and returns" in v. 8 not only refers to Alexander the Great but also to Israel's last and worst oppressor—the final Antichrist. The Antichrist will one day make a seven-year covenant with Israel but break it with three and a half years left (Dan 9.26-27). Near the end of this period, the Antichrist will pass through "the Beautiful Land" of Israel on his way to subdue Egypt, then return (Dan 11.40-45). Then he will lead all the nations in an effort to destroy helpless Israel. Suddenly, Messiah will appear and destroy the great oppressor—the Antichrist. Henceforth, Yahweh will "camp around His house" forever.

No More Oppressors
The second half of Zech 9.8 certainly never came to pass following Alexander's visit to Jerusalem. It reads, "and no oppressor will pass over them anymore." The Jews continued to suffer under various Gentile oppressors, even some of their own, like Alexander Jannaeus.

Furthermore, if Zechariah meant for his prophecy in v. 8b to refer to any period other than the endtime, he would be contradicting himself in Zech 12.3 and 14.2. There, the prophet relates that all the Gentile nations will besiege Jerusalem and Judah in the endtime, destroying two-thirds of the population (13.9). Then Messiah will come to deliver the surviving Jewish remnant (14.4-5). Until then it cannot be said that "no oppressor will pass over them anymore."

For a long time God "hid His face" from Israel (Deut 32.20; Isa 8.17; Hos 5.15), turning the sinful nation over to domination by the Gentiles. God no longer "shined His face" upon Israel, a Hebrew idiom indicating divine blessing and protection. Thus, the Messianic deliverance of Israel is immediately preceded by Yahweh turning His face back upon Israel to view with compassion the suffering, penitent nation (Eze 39.23, 29). This is the meaning of Yahweh's words, "For now I have seen with My eyes" (Zech 9.8b).

Reestablishment of the Philistines
The least that can be said of Zech 9.1-8 is that, despite some fulfillment in Alexander's career, vv. 7-8 still await a future, complete consummation. In sum, three things prophesied in Zech 9.7-8 have not yet happened:
1. The conversion of the Philistines to the God of Israel.
2. The assimilation of the Philistines into the Jewish population.
3. God's establishment of perfect and everlasting security for the nation of Israel.
These points suggests that not only vv. 7-8, but the entire section of vv. 1-8 awaits a complete fulfillment at the end of this age. Accordingly, a people called the Philistines must again become a recognizable people dwelling in their ancient homeland.

Indeed, this is the interpretation provided by perhaps the preeminent American premillennial expositor of the early 20th century. A.C. Gaebelein claimed not only that Israel would someday be reestablished in its ancient homeland, but that Israel's ancient neighbors would reemerge in their lands as well. Gaebelein wrote about Zech 9.1-8:

> This puts before us again the final deliverance of Jerusalem and Israel's land . . . A final destructive visitation will be upon the enemies of Israel and Jerusalem; **in fact, many of the ancient foes of Israel are seen revived in prophecy in the latter days**, then to be swept away, while Jerusalem will again be miraculously saved (emphasis added).[8]

Premillennialist H.A. Ironside agreed substantially with Gaebelein's comment on Zech 9.1-8. He remarked that these verses "evidently have a double application, setting forth, as they do, the past overthrow of the kingdoms ere the first coming of the Lord . . . as well as the future doom of the powers which will be in those lands when comes the final triumph of the King of kings."[9]

Premillennialist Charles Feinberg concurs concerning all of Zech 9.1-8: "The section before us has a double application: it sets forth the past judgment upon the kingdoms surrounding Israel as well as the future punishment that awaits the enemies of God's people which will be living in lands contiguous to Palestine."[10]

Israel's Destruction of Philistia

Much of Zech 9.9-17 relates to the same period of time as that of vv. 1-8.[11] Consequently, these two sections of Zech 9 should not be separated from one another, as is frequently done by commentators. The Hebrew prophets often wrote thematically rather than chronologically. They would fade in and out between a near and a far-distant future event. Such is the case with Zech 9.7-17.

The Messianic destruction is depicted in vv. 7-8. In v. 9 the prophet presents Messiah riding in humility into Jerusalem on a donkey, a prediction which Christians believe was fulfilled by Jesus. In vv. 10-17 Zechariah returns to the time-frame of vv. 7-8, when the Jews will take possession of all of the Promised Land and Messiah's "dominion will be from sea to sea" (v. 10).

Most interpreters, even some premillennialists,[12] exclusively restrict fulfillment of Zech 9.11-17 to the Maccabean era in the 2nd century B.C. However, the *Scofield Bible*, both the old and new editions, correctly notes that "after the King is introduced in v. 9, the following verses look forward to the end time and the kingdom."[13] Zechariah 9.11-15 no doubt finds some fulfillment in the wars of the Maccabees. Yet vv. 13-17 bear such striking resemblance to chapters 12 and 14 that they must also depict the Messianic victory in which the Jews will participate.[14]

It therefore seems that nearly all of Zech 9-14 applies to the last days. A chronological scenario of the events of these chapters appears to be as follows:

1. The nations will attack Israel in the last days (12.2-3, 9; 14.2, 16).

2. Yahweh will deliver the remnant of Israel through His Messiah (9.9-10; 10.11; 14.4).

3. Messiah will lead the invigorated Israelis in a crushing defeat of their neighbors (9.10-15; 10.3-7; 12.5-9; 14.14).

4. Israel will take possession of the entire Promised Land (9.5-7; 10.10).

Conclusion

The Hebrew prophets predict that in the end of this age the land of Philistia will belong to non-Jews, sometimes called "Philistines." It appears that today's Palestinians will fulfill the prophecy of those people designated Philistines, and that they will have their independent state in the Philistine Plain. When the State of Palestine becomes established in its land it will be one more sure evidence that Almighty God has spoken through His prophets. Only He knows and controls the future.

A Day is coming when God will remember the Jews. In the midst of their greatest suffering ever, He will turn to them with compassion, sending His Messiah to deliver them from their enemies and to bring the glorious kingdom to earth. God will finally give Israel all of the Promised Land, including the Philistine Plain. Eretz Israel will stretch from the Euphrates River to the Wadi el Arish and from the Mediterranean Sea to the Arabian Desert.

But Yahweh is not only the God of the Jews; He is the God over all the earth. When His kingdom comes, He will remember not only Israel but **all** who have ever bowed before His authority and put their trust in Him. They will all be rewarded in that Day.

In those days of universal peace and glory, Palestinians and Jews will live together as brothers and sisters in the Promised Land. Palestinians will be full citizens of Israel. They will be like a cherished clan in Jerusalem. And the Chosen People—the Jews—will fulfill their destiny to be a blessing to the Palestinians and to all the peoples of the earth forevermore.

Appendix A

EARLY HISTORY
OF THE PHILISTINES

The Palestinians derive their name from the Philistines. The contention of this book is that the Palestinians ought to be granted the land of the ancient Philistines in which to establish their independent state. An objection to this proposal might be, "But the Palestinians aren't the Philistines. They're Arabs," a response based on presumptions about ethnic origins. Appendix B reveals that the word "Arab" is not properly used as an ethnic term, but only as a cultural and linguistic one.

This excursus attempts to trace the early history of the Philistines. **Its two primary purposes are to establish that the Philistines were not a single ethnic people, but a heterogeneous group, and that their entrance into southwestern Palestine and the Sinai predates the Hebrews' entrance into Canaan.** These two points affect the Palestinians' claim to a portion of the land of Palestine.

The Origin of the Philistines

The origin of the Philistines remains uncertain. Their first mention in ancient literature or inscriptions is found in the early genealogical records of the Bible, in Gen 10.14 and 1 Chron 1.12. These two slightly ambiguous passages name the Philistines and the Caphtorim in a list of the descendants of Ham, one of Noah's three sons. Most English versions render these two passages as if the Philistines came from the Casluhim. Such a reading contradicts two passages which expressly identify the Philistines as former Caphtorites: "the Philistines, the remnant of the coastland of Caphtor" (Jer 47.4) and "the Philistines from Caphtor" (Amos 9.7). In addition, "the Avvites who lived in villages as far as Gaza, the Caphtorites coming out from Caphtor destroyed them and settled in their place" (Deut 2.23 NIV). The description, "as far as Gaza," apparently refers to that territory south of Gaza,[1] between Egypt and Canaan. This is evidence that the Philistines first lived south of Gaza.

Four divergent theories have emerged among biblical and secular scholars and archaeologists.

Some conservative biblical commentators allege that the Philistines are descendants of Ham because they are referred to in the list of Ham's descendants (Gen 10.14). The Philistines are therefore reckoned as originally migrating from Egypt to Crete and then to Palestine. However, there is uncertainty whether these passages mean that the Philistines were descendants of the Hamitic Casluhites (supposedly of Egypt), or only that they migrated from their land. Moreover, this view is totally unsupported from secular historical records and archaeology, and many lines of evidence are against it.

Some scholars suppose that the Philistines were Semitic and originated in Mesopotamia. This theory is based mostly on the fact that the Philistines used many Semitic place-names. But archaeology continually reveals that upon settling in Palestine, the Philistines assumed the more highly-developed Canaanite culture and presumably adopted Semitic names then common to the region.

Many have thought that the Philistines originated solely from the island of Crete, widely regarded as the biblical Caphtor. They claim that the present texts in Gen 10.14 and 1 Chron 1.12 are glosses. That is, these have been altered from their original, which portrayed the Philistines as migrating from Caphtor, not Casluh. For example, the Jerusalem Bible translates both passages: "Caphtor, from which the Philistines came." In this way these texts are harmonized with Jer 47.4, Amos 9.7 and Deut 2.23. But does this really settle the matter? The eminent 19th century geographer of Palestine, George Adam Smith, cautioned that "to have traced the Philistines to Crete is not to have cleared up their origin, for early Crete was full of tribes from both east and west."[2]

Modifications of this last view are now widely held. Primarily on the basis of Mycenaean pottery artifacts found at Philistine sites, archaeologists and **most historians allege that the Philistines originated from the region of the Aegean Sea, migrated to Crete and from there to Palestine. Recent mounting evidence, however, has led others to conclude that most of the Philistines traveled overland from the area now known as western Turkey to Palestine.** Some think "Caphtor," where the Bible says the Philistines came from, refers to ancient Cappadocia in central Turkey. Indeed, while the Masoretic Text has "Caphtor" in Amos 9.7 and Deut 2.23, the Septuagint, produced 1,000 years earlier, has "Cappadocia."

Cappadocia is where the Hittite Empire was centered. There is considerable evidence that later Philistines attacked Egypt in the early 12th century B.C. after having conquered the Hittites in central Turkey. It was from the Hittites that the Philistines learned the secret of how to forge iron, a technology which later made them formidable foes against the Israelites.

The Philistines: An Anachronism?
Perhaps the biggest problem to resolve concerning the time of the migration of the Philistines is whether or not they appear as an anachronism in the Genesis account.

Most secular historians and archaeologists, as well as many biblical commentators, maintain that **the Philistines did not migrate to Palestine until the 12th century B.C., when Rameses III of Egypt recorded an invasion from the north. The Bible, however, narrates that the Philistines lived there 600-700 years earlier, during the time of Abraham and Isaac** (e.g., Gen 21.32, 34; 26.1, 8, 14-15, 18; Exo 13.17; 15.14; 23.31). Most interpreters regard these Genesis accounts as anachronisms, i.e., references to that land or its people by the name of later inhabitants.

There are other examples of anachronisms in Genesis, where a later place name is employed in an earlier account. When this occurs in the Bible, both place-names are often given. An example is the city of Luz, which was changed to Bethel (Gen 12.8; 28.19; 35.6). But there is little or no evidence in the Bible of an anachronism being used for the actual people of a place, as "the Philistines." In this case, the supposed anachronism in Genesis regards not only the identification of the land as "the land of the Philistines" (Gen 21.32, 34), but it also refers to "the Philistines" themselves (Gen 26.14-15, 18). In addition, Abimelech is twice called "the king of the Philistines" (Gen 26.1, 8). Moreover, not only are the Philistines mentioned, but three times they are said to have interacted with Abraham and Isaac. For example, the Philistines stopped up their wells in the 18th and 19th centuries B.C., long before secular authorities claim the Philistines migrated to Palestine.

To conclude that the people dwelling in the land at that time were not really Philistines appears to many Bible readers as an error in the text. For them, this would deny the divine inspiration and historical accuracy of the Scriptures. Some conservative expositors are not willing to make this concession to historians.

Gerar: Center of the Early Philistines
The land of Canaan took its name from the descendants of Canaan who dwelt there. The word "Canaanites" often stands in the Hebrew Bible for the six or seven nations which derived their names from the descendants of Canaan. (See Gen 10.15-18.)

The Philistines are never included in any biblical lists of the Canaanite nations. This is because they were not descendants of Canaan and for a long time did not live in the land of Canaan.

It may be safely assumed that the writer of Genesis defines the general region of Canaan as it existed in the time of the patriarchs, c. 2,000-1,700 B.C. If mention in Genesis of the Philistines and their land is not an anachronism, it becomes apparent that at this early era the Philistines lived in a different part of the coastal plain, separate from Canaan, than in later centuries. Indeed, during the time of the patriarchs, "the territory of the Canaanite extended from Sidon as you go toward Gerar, as far as Gaza" (Gen 10.19). The words, "as you go toward Gerar," refer to the main caravan route southward from Sidon. At that time Gerar was probably a more notable city than Gaza in that region. Yet Canaan only extended to Gaza, not beyond, to Gerar. Thus, the Philistines could have lived only south of Gaza. This is implied in the Song of Moses, in which "the inhabitants of Philistia" are distinguished from "the inhabitants of Canaan" (Ex 15.14-15).

Gerar was a city located about eight miles southeast of Gaza. Abraham moved about in the region of Gerar in search of pasture for his herds. He came in contact with the Philistine "Abimelech king of Gerar" (Gen 20.2). (Scholars regard "Abimelech" as a kingly title, like "Pharoah" or "Caesar.") Abimelech invited Abraham to settle in "my land . . . wherever you please" (v. 15). Abraham accepted (Gen 21.22-34). Abimelech and Abraham soon consummated a peace pact in neutral territory, to the east in Beersheba.

Thus, neither Gaza nor Beersheba were Philistine cities during this period. After the pact, Abimelech "returned to the land of the Philistines" (v. 32). Then "Abraham sojourned in the land of the Philistines for many days" (v. 34). Apparently, Abraham pastured his herds a long time in this Philistine territory between Gerar and Beersheba.

So, during the period of the patriarchs, the Philistines were located south of Gaza and west of Beersheba, with Gerar likely their chief city.[3] If the Genesis accounts of the Philistines are not anachronisms, it must be concluded that at least **during the period of the patriarchs, the land of the Philistines was smaller and farther south on the coastal plain than in later times**. It probably stretched from just south of Gaza to the usual border of Egypt—the Wadi el Arish.

Thus, Philistia would not have originally included the three major coastal city-states of Gaza, Ashkelon and Ashdod. While archaeology reveals that these three existed first as Canaanite cities, this evidence does not prevent the Philistines from having dwelt just to the south.

Sea Peoples?

Since the rise of archaeology in the last century, the subject of the origin of the Philistines has received much attention.

Near the end of the 13th century B.C., a great upheaval of civilization began in the Mediterranean world which continued into the 12th century. Vast disruptions of population occurred in the region of the Aegean Sea, including the Dorian invasion of the Greek mainland and the sudden collapse of the Hittite Empire, located in modern Turkey and Syria.

In the eighth year of Pharoah Rameses III (reign: c. 1197-1158 B.C.), there was a notable hostile invasion by foreigners into the northern frontier of Egypt. To repel the assault, "the Egyptians exhausted their strength completely."[4]

According to numerous inscriptions on the famed Mortuary Temple walls in Medina Habu, Upper (southern) Egypt, the invasion "consisted of five groups: p-r-s-t (Philistines), t-k-r (Sikel?), s-k-r-s, d-n-n and w-s-s. Suggested names for these groups of people are, respectively, Peleset or Philistine, Tjeker, Shekelesh, Denyen, and Weshesh."[5] The groups other than the Philistines remain unknown. It is believed that because the Philistines were the larger of the five groups, the others became identified by that name after settling with them in the southwestern coastal plain of Palestine.

The Medina Habu inscriptions were first deciphered and published in 1881. The confederated attackers were called "Sea Peoples" because it was supposed that they crossed the Mediterranean Sea by boats and first invaded Egypt's Mediterranean shoreline.

Archaeologist Alassandra Nibbi claims that the designation Sea Peoples was premature. She maintains that close scrutiny of these inscriptions reveals that ym and "the Great Green" were mistaken for "the Great Sea." The Great Sea was the common name for the Mediterranean Sea in antiquity.

Egypt's Delta
Instead, Nibbi convincingly argues that these references identify the marshland of Egypt's Delta.[6] She claims that at that time Egypt's northern frontier was the Delta, not the Mediterranean coast, making Egypt an inland country. When the Nile rose in season, the entire Delta flooded except for the settlements of the foreigners living on natural hills and artificial mounds. Viewed from a distance, they would have resembled islands.[7] Nibbi claims the "islands of the Great Green do not refer to islands in the Mediterranean or Aegean Sea, from which it is supposed that the Philistines came, but to those small isles in the Delta marshland."[8]

These foreigners who lived in the Delta are often referred to in Egyptian inscriptions and documents as "Asiatics," a general term for people from present Turkey. On the other hand, the Egyptians' term "Northland" did not refer to Asia but to Lower (northern) Egypt, primarily the Delta.

Nibbi and others conclude that a confederation of people who came to be known as the Philistines settled in the less desirable Northland of the Delta, and from there they attacked the kingdom of Egypt.

Land Migration from Turkey
Rameses III tells us that before their attack on Egypt, these Asiatics ravaged both Alashia and the Hittite kingdom.[9] He says, "no land could stand before their arms." Furthermore, the famous city of Carchemish, in southwestern Turkey, is mentioned as one of the places they destroyed. Indeed, Carchemish was destroyed in about 1190 B.C.

Pictographs on the Medina Habu Temple include Philistine, ox-driven carts with heavy wooden wheels, loaded with women, children and possessions. The ox carts are identical to those still in use in Turkey and the Middle East today.[10] These pictures suggest that the Philistines invaded Egypt via the land bridge of Palestine rather than from the Mediterranean Sea, and that they first settled in the region prior to their attack.

But additional Egyptian evidence discloses that the Philistines existed in the area well before this attack. A long Karmak inscription shows that other attacks by Asiatics dwelling in the Delta had occurred throughout the earlier history of the kings of Egypt.[11] Many years before these invasions, Philistines were hired as mercenaries in the Egyptian army. It is known that Rameses III even placed some Philistines as guards on the northeastern Egyptian border.[12]

Dwelling in Palestine Before the Attack
The Egyptian South Stela reveals that these Asiatics (Philistines) who attacked Egypt in about 1190 B.C. were afterwards driven out of the Delta and back into their own lands, where they were later defeated by Pharoah's forces.[13] Their lands were identified as "the plains and hill-countries." This accurately describes southwestern Palestine, with its coastal plain and the hills of the Shephelah. The stela therefore confirms that Philistines had been established in Palestine well before their attack in the early 12th century B.C.

Assuming the widely-accepted latest possible date for the Hebrews' entrance into Canaan, about 1260 B.C, the Philistines would not have had ample time to possess their territory and become a formidable foe, as is presented in the books of Joshua and Judges, if they had not already been established there by the time of the attack on Egypt in 1190 B.C. during the reign of Rameses III.

Archaeology
While considerable uncertainty remains, archaeological excavations at Ashdod show that the Philistines' initial settlement there "preceded their great invasion and subsequent settlement associated with the eighth year of Rameses III."[14] This is also confirmed in other Philistine cities, like Ashkelon.[15]

Archaeologist Trude Dothan is recognized as the leading authority on the Philistines. Through her monumental work, she, along with M. Dothan, has discovered that these Philistines invaded Egypt in more than the one wave recorded by Rameses III. Trude Dothan shows that an earlier wave of the supposed Sea Peoples arrived prior to the reign of Rameses III and settled in the Nile Delta and the Egyptian southern frontier of Nubia (modern Sudan).[16] Relatives in these colonies corresponded and visited each other.[17]

Yohanan Aharoni has been an professor of archaeology and a distinguished authority on the history of the land of Israel and its neighbors. He claims that after the Egyptians pushed the Philistines outside the Egyptian northeastern frontier, beyond the Wadi el Arish, the Philistines "seized control over the whole southern coastal region and enforced their rule upon the local Canaanite populace. Most of the Canaanite towns continued to exist, though under new leadership, and their residents doubtless were absorbed by the Philistines with the passage of time."[18]

The major Canaanite cities which the Philistines took over were Gaza,

Ashkelon and Ashdod.[19] If the Philistines had been situated south of Gaza since the patriarchs' time, they had now expanded northward.

Later Philistine Expansion
It seems that Pharoah Rameses' repulsion of the so-called Sea Peoples resulted in their being pushed outside Egypt's northeastern frontier into southwestern Palestine. If Philistines already dwelt there, the defeated Sea Peoples must have assimilated with the already-established Philistine community. Perhaps this and other enlargements of the Philistine population became the occasions for expansion of the land of the Philistines northward. If the Genesis record is accepted literally concerning the Philistines, at some later period they must have pushed the neighboring Canaanites farther northward until the more familiar northern boundary of Philistia became established. Only then would the Philistines have possessed Gaza, Ashkelon and Ashdod.

The allotted inheritance of the tribe of Dan was the coastal plain from the Nahal Sorek northward to just beyond Joppa (Josh 19.40-46). But one of the Canaanite nations, the Amorites (Gen 10.16), pushed the Danites eastward into the hill country (Jud 1.34). For lack of space, much of the Danite tribe later migrated into present southeastern Lebanon (Jud 18). The conclusion must be that the Philistines lived farther south, not that these Amorites were actually the Philistines, as some have erroneously supposed. Yet during the period of Israel's judges the Philistines spread northward to establish themselves just beyond Joppa (Tel Aviv).

The settlement pattern of early civilization seems to substantiate further this Philistine expansion from south to north. Since Mount Ararat is located in Turkey, the descendants of Noah likely settled Canaan from north to south. The city of Sidon must have been where Canaan's first-born son, Sidon, settled (Gen 10.15). The southern extent of Canaan was probably less established, rendering it more vulnerable to an encroaching civilization like the Philistines.

Conclusion
There remains much uncertainty regarding the early history of the Philistines. **If the Genesis accounts of the Philistines are not anachronisms, their original migration into their land predates the Israelites' entrance into Canaan by several centuries.** The so-called Sea Peoples of the 12th century B.C. seem to have migrated from the region of the Aegean Sea, or western Turkey, to southwestern Palestine and to have joined earlier Asiatics who had settled there long before and become known as the Philistines.

Certain endtime biblical prophecies identify "Philistines" living in their ancient homeland. (See Chapters 11-14.) These people appear to be today's Palestinians, a heterogeneous group like their forerunners, the Philistines. **The Palestinians may be viewed as Philistines partially because of some genetic link, but mostly because their name derives from the Philistines.** (See Chapter 5.)

Appendix B

WHO ARE THE ARABS?

Palestinians are among the 165 million people in 21 countries of the Middle East and North Africa who identify themselves as Arabs. Whatever people think of the Arabs will affect their attitude toward the Palestinians.

The purpose of this appendix is to correct two popular misconceptions concerning Arabs and therefore concerning the Palestinians. **First, the term "Arab," as it is used almost universally today, does not identify an ethnic (racial) group but a culturally related people. Second, it cannot be established that the Arabs descended from Ishmael, the son of Abraham, so it is erroneous to call the Palestinians "Ishmaelites."**

Use of the Terms "Arab" and "Arabia"

The word "Arab" has undergone many changes throughout its complex history. The first literary source where the words "Arab(s)" and "Arabia"[1] appear is the Bible, in the account of the reign of King Solomon in the mid-10th century B.C. (1 Kgs 10.15; 2 Chron 9.14). The first secular sources are Assyrian annals, dating to 853 B.C. **The Bible distinguishes the Arabs from the Philistines** (2 Chron 21.16), as well as from the Ammonites, Moabites, Edomites and others of present Jordan and the Negev (e.g., Neh 2.19; 4.7; 6.1).

The term "Arab" originally referred to the wandering nomads, also called Bedouins, of the northern and central Arabian Peninsula as early as the late second millennium B.C. "'Arab' was the designation that the nomads applied to themselves."[2] The term distinguished the nomads from the permanent settlers of the desert oasis.[3] Many centuries later, Mohammed still refrained from calling the townsfolk of Mecca, Medina and other cities, Arabs. The Koran attests throughout that Mohammed applied the word "Arab" exclusively to the nomads.[4]

The land where most of these nomads wandered came to be called "Arabia."

The name first identified the northern and central peninsula we call the Arabian Peninsula, comprised mostly of present Saudi Arabia. The word was eventually applied to the whole peninsula, and even beyond by outsiders. For example, in the mid-5th century B.C., Herodotus included the Negev, Sinai and land reaching to the Nile River in his designation "Arabia." Centuries later, Roman historians Strabo and Pliny did likewise. The apostle Paul called the Sinai, "Arabia" (Gal 4.25).

The Arabs (nomads) were desert dwellers who raised camels and sheep, lived in tents and moved about seeking pasture for their flocks. Although the nomads of the northern and central Arabian Peninsula were Semitic, the word "Arab" originally identified only the nomadic way of life. Ironically, this meaning also describes the semi-nomadic life of Abraham. He too lived in tents and wandered about seeking pasture for his animals.

The term "Arab" does not appear in any of the thousands of inscriptions from the southern portion of the Arabian Peninsula until the 3rd century B.C. Even then, it only identifies the nomads of central and northern Arabia.

Those dwelling in the southern portion of the Arabian Peninsula were sedentary people who enjoyed a rich civilization dating from the late second millennium B.C. Their land received more rainfall than the peninsula's interior. They made it cultivable by developing an intricate dam and canal system. This region, later called Southern Arabia, was famous the world over for its spices and perfumes. Some of the Arabs (nomads) to the north became traders by developing caravan routes through the desert to transport these commodities northward.

Southern Arabian civilization collapsed in the third and fourth centuries A.D. Thereafter, the northern Bedouin tribes moved into southern Arabia; many settled permanently. Afterward, the term "Arab" gradually came to be applied to the whole population of the peninsula.[5] The entire Arabian Peninsula came to be called "Arabia," and "Arab" was used interchangeably with "Arabian."

Isolation of the Arabian Peninsula

The Arabian Peninsula is separated from its northern neighbors by the wasteland of the Syrian Desert. On the other three sides are seas. The Arabian Peninsula is therefore isolated from the rest of the world. That is why the Arabic name for the peninsula is *Jazirat al-Arab*, meaning "the island of the Arabs."

Throughout its history, very little immigration of foreigners into the Arabian Peninsula has occurred. This is attributed to its geographical isolation, sparse rainfall, harsh climate, largest sand deserts in the world and the earlier reputation of the Bedouins for raiding.

The Arabian Peninsula has never been conquered by outsiders. The Assyrians, Babylonians, Persians and Nabataeans only made temporary advances into the fringes of northern Arabia. Caesar Augustus sent a military expedition across nearly the entire length of Arabia. It ended in disaster, indicating how insurmountable the task was for outsiders to conquer the peninsula.

Such an isolated, hostile environment has enabled the population of the Arabian Peninsula to remain unusually pure, ethnically. Thus, when the word Arab, or Arabian, became applied to the entire population of the peninsula, this was the first time that the term acquired an ethnic meaning. But the use of the term changed after the Arab conquests.

Arab Conquests

In the 7th century A.D. Mohammed (Muhammed; A.D. 570-632) founded the monotheistic religion of Islam. He developed a political-religious community centered at Medina and Mecca in present Saudi Arabia. Adherents were called Muslims, or Moslems.

Following Mohammed's death from illness, tribal wars broke out as his successors sought to establish control over north and central Arabia. Their conquests spilled into the outskirts of Syria, then Palestine. In A.D. 636 the Arabs took control of all of Syria and Palestine, except Caesarea and Jerusalem, from the Byzantine Empire. These they stormed two years later. The populace in Palestine welcomed the Arab conquests as relief from Byzantine oppression.

Conquests of foreign lands solved economic problems for the Arabs. With their camels they were masters at hit-and-run raiding in the desert. They took booty from the rich Byzantine Empire: money, clothing, jewelry and women. (The Koran allows men to have up to four wives and an unlimited number of concubines.) The warriors distributed the spoils among themselves and sent one-fifth to the caliph (successor to Mohammed) in Arabia proper.

Twelve years after Mohammed's death, one-half million residents of the Arabian Peninsula had emigrated to these conquered lands in search of wealth and political power.[6] Within a century the new Arab empire included all of the Middle East and North Africa; it stretched from Persia (present Iran and Afghanistan) to Spain.

The Arabs ruled the new lands in the form of aristocracies. To govern successfully, they felt it necessary to remain separate from the indigenous population. Contrary to popular belief, for many years the Arab conquerors discouraged proselytization of the non-Arabian population to Islam. Historians therefore first identify the cultured arabization of these conquered peoples; their conversion to Islam followed years later.

Population Mix

By the 8th century A.D. the term "Arab" had undergone another transformation. Most of the conquered peoples came to be called Arabs because they spoke the Arabic language and shared a common culture. Most had also become Muslims. All of these features served to unify the developing empire. From then until this day, the word "Arab" has designated a cultural group. Nevertheless, "in the cities of the Arab world of today—Cairo or Khartoum, Damascus or Bagdad—the sedentary and civilized Arab is still apt to refer to the nomads as, specifically, 'the Arabs.' "[7]

Some peoples within Arabic countries have spurned the designation Arab, the Arabic language and Islam. These include the Kurds in northwestern Iraq, the Berbers in North Africa, the Christian sects of the Marionites in Lebanon and the Copts in Ethiopia.

In addition, even some Muslims in non-Arab countries do not call themselves Arabs. They do not speak Arabic. These include Turks, Persians (Iranians), Pakistanis and others.

In the conquered lands, intermarriage between the ruling Arabs and the local populations eventually resulted. But it is incorrect to deem the resulting population as ethnically Arab. Professor of the Middle East, Bernard Lewis, relates that intermarriage "produced a new governing class of administrators and traders, heterogeneous in race."[8] Professor of Arab history, Philip Hitti, explains, "Through their intermarriages with the conquering stock they served to dilute the Arabian blood and ultimately to make that element inconspicuous amidst the mixture of varied racial strain."[9]

But what about the Palestinian Arabs? In a historical analysis of Palestine published in 1920, the British Foreign Office concluded, **"the people west of the Jordan [River] are not Arabs, but only Arabic-speaking .... In the Gaza district they are mostly of Egyptian origin; elsewhere they are of the most mixed race"** (emphasis added).[10] Arab historian John of Wurzburg claims that the Palestinians are "the greatest human agglomeration drawn together in one small area of the globe."[11]

A further complication of the ethnic issue is the Turks, who are non-Arabs. Except for the brief era of the medieval Crusades, the Turks ruled Palestine and most of the Middle East from the 11th to the 20th century. Though mostly Muslim, Turks are not Arabs and do not speak Arabic. During this long period, the word Arab reverted to its original meaning, referring only to the Bedouins.[12] After the 1917 defeat of the Ottoman (Turkish) Empire, the word Arab regained its cultural meaning, which it maintains today the world over.

Negative Connotations about Ishmael

Many people are convinced that the current Palestinian-Israeli conflict will never be resolved. One reason is that they think the Palestinian Arabs are Ishmaelites. They believe the Bible predicts that the Ishmaelites will never be at peace with the Jews. Indeed, in the Jewish, Christian and Muslim faiths, the terms "Arab" and "Ishmaelite" have been regarded as synonymous.[13] The concept of an unending rivalry between these two lines of Abraham's offspring contributes considerably to many persons' perceptions of the Arab-Israeli conflict.

In the biblical tradition concerning Ishmael, there are several negative connotations which do not endear the Ishmaelites to the Hebrews. God's covenant promise was to give Abraham a multitude of descendants through his wife Sarah (Gen 17.19-21; 21.12). Before Isaac's miraculous conception, however, Sarah prodded Abraham to have sexual relations with her maid,

Hagar, in order to produce an heir. He did, and Hagar gave birth to Ishmael. Thus, Ishmael was the product of Sarah's initial unbelief in God's promise.

God announced to Hagar concerning her son Ishmael, recorded in Gen 16.12:

> "And he will be a wild donkey of a man,
> His hand will be against everyone,
> And everyone's hand will be against him;
> And he will live to the east of all his brothers."

Some versions render this last clause either, "And he will live in defiance of all his brothers," or, "And he will live in the presence of all his brothers." The NASB presents both as alternate readings. The same thing is stated in Gen 25.18, and versions vary here too. C.F. Keil renders both passages to mean the same thing: the Ishmaelites settled in the presence of their Hebrew brethren and remained separate from them.[14] Thus, it may very well be a mistake to deduce from two ambiguous scriptures the idea of a perpetual rivalry between the Israelites and the Ishmaelites.

The problem is further aggravated by an apparent contradiction between the Koran and the Bible. In the Koran's brief portrayal of Abraham's attempted sacrifice of his son, Chapter 37 does not explicitly identify whether Abraham offered Isaac or Ishmael. The promise of Isaac's birth follows this narrative as if it were a reward for Abraham's obedience in offering Ishmael. Thus, "it is the most received opinion among the Mohammedans that the son whom Abraham offered was Ishmael, and not Isaac, Ishmael being his only son at that time."[15] This view is affirmed in Islamic tradition. During mid-summer, Muslims celebrate *Eid Aladha* (Arabic for "the Feast of Sacrifice"), commemorating Abraham's near-sacrifice of Ishmael.

The Ishmaelites
Upon Sarah's demand, Hagar and Ishmael were forced to leave Abraham's household and live in the wilderness. Yet "God was with the lad." He grew up, became an archer and "lived in the wilderness of Paran" (Gen 21.20-21). This region was in the northeastern Sinai Peninsula. God promised to bless Ishmael, saying, "I will make him a great nation" (Gen 17.20; cf. 21.13, 18). Ishmael's Egyptian mother "took a wife for him from the land of Egypt" (Gen 21.21). Ishmael eventually had twelve sons (Gen 17.20; 25.16). If they were by his Egyptian wife, as it seems, the original stock of the Ishmaelites was 75% Egyptian!

The names of Ishmael's sons were preserved as names of places where they settled "by their villages, and by their camps, twelve princes according to their tribes. . . . They settled from Havilah to Shur which is east of Egypt as one goes toward Assyria" (Gen 25.16, 18). Though its exact location remains unknown, Shur was apparently an Egyptian military outpost situated just outside Egypt's northeastern delta. "The way to Shur" was the last segment

of a major caravan route in the northern Sinai. It either came through or
near the Wilderness of Paran, where Ishmael had settled.

The location of Havilah is uncertain. Various locations in the Arabian
Peninsula have been suggested. However, these do not accord with 1 Sam
15.7, which states that "Saul defeated the Amalekites, from Havilah as you
go to Shur, which is east of Egypt." Historians agree that Saul did not wage
war in the Arabian Peninsula. Furthermore, the tall Amalekites, descendants
of Esau, lived in the Sinai and Negev. Soon following the Israelites exodus
from Egypt, the Amalekites attacked them in the Sinai. All of this seems to
rule out Havilah being located much farther east, in the Arabian Peninsula.

Jewish scholar Israel Eph'al is a distinguished authority on the ancient
Arabs, one who is well acquainted with the literary sources. He claims that
the virtually identical description in Gen 25.18 and 1 Sam 15.7 "enables us
to locate Havilah definitely in southern Palestine although not pinpoint it."[16]
In agreement with Eph'al, some scholars claim that "Havilah" in 1 Sam 15.7
is a misspelling of a hill named "Hachilah," which is located somewhere
south of Hebron.[17] If so, the sons of Ishmael originally dwelt along a line
extending from the northwestern border of Egypt, through the Sinai Desert
and its Wilderness of Paran into the Negev, but not into the Arabian Peninsula.

On the other hand, Assyrian sources reveal that several of the names of
Ishmael's sons were place names in North Arabia. No such names are known
in the Negev and Sinai.

It is possible that all the sons of Ishmael first settled west of the Arabah—the
depression which divides the Negev from present southwestern Jordan—and
that their descendants later moved eastward to Arabia. Josephus writes that
the Ishmaelites "inhabited all the country from Euphrates to the Red Sea."[18]
This would support that the Havilah of Gen 25.18 was located near Assyria,
perhaps in northeastern Arabia.

Even if Josephus is correct, this does not mean that all of North Arabia
was populated by Ishmaelites. Classical Arab genealogies do place the
Ishmaelites in North Arabia but do not regard them as the original inhabitants, only as "arabized."[19]

Distinguished New York Times correspondent David Shipler writes in his
monumental work, *Arab and Jew: Wounded Spirits in a Promised Land*:

> There is nothing in the Bible to indicate that Ishmael was the forefather
> of the Arabs, nor was this a belief held by the ancient Arabs. The tribe
> of Ishmael disappeared early in biblical history, but the term Ishmaeli
> lived on, evolving into a designation of a desert people, and eventually
> extending to Arab peoples as a whole. The idea that Jews and Arabs
> were "cousins," descended from Isaac and Ishmael respectively, was
> accepted in Jewish writings and included by Muhammad in teachings
> that became the Koran, and it is an article of strong conviction among
> many Muslims today. Many Jews also accept the assumption.[20]

The Ishmaelites in Judith and Jubilees

All biblical mention of the Ishmaelites precedes the mid-10th century B.C.[21]
Eph'al claims that "the biblical terms 'Arabs' and 'Ishmaelites' are not used
concurrently" in the Bible and that this only occurs in extra-biblical sources,
long after the term Ishmaelite(s) had become obsolete.[22] In fact, the Ishmaelites are not mentioned in any non-Jewish literature as a recognized, existing
people until the Islamic era. Yet many civilizations of the intervening 1600-
year period provide much information on the peoples of the Arabian Peninsula.

Mention of the Ishmaelites first reemerges in the Jewish apocryphal Book
of Judith, written in Palestine during the 4th century B.C. The author, writing
over 200 years after the fact, alleges that King Nebuchadnezzar "spoiled all
the Children of Rasses, and the Children of Ishmael, which were against the
wilderness to the south" of Babylonia, viz., the Syro-Arabian desert (Judith
2.23).

Scholars have recently claimed that the author of Judith probably used as
a source the Babylonian Chronicle, which contains a passage corresponding
to the above. In contrast to Judith, it identifies the persons plundered as
A-ra-bi, the Babylonian word for "Arab." The romantic author of Judith was
fond of referring to present lands and people by their biblical names which
were no longer in use. Accordingly, he has substituted the word "Ishmaelites"
for Arabs. It is doubtful that by that time the Ishmaelites existed as a recognized people.

Jewish biblical scholar Doron Mendels heartily endorses the work of Israel
Eph'al. He also shows that the Jewish intertestamental literature contributed
to the erroneous belief that the Arabs are Ishmaelites. Mendels takes particular issue with the pseudepigraphical Book of Jubilees. It is a Jewish commentary on Genesis and Ex 1-12 produced in the late 2nd century B.C. Mendels
repudiates the Book of Jubilees' repeated assertion that the Arabs are descendants of Ishmael.[23]

Joktan

Abraham descended from Shem through Eber (Gen 21.24). Philologists believe that the word "Hebrew" may derive from Eber. Eber had two sons: Peleg,
from whom Abraham descended, and Joktan. Joktan fathered thirteen sons,
many of whose names, along with those of his grandsons, were perpetuated
as place names (Gen 10.30-31) in Arabia. Some can be identified with certainty
in South Arabia. Classical Arabic genealogies trace Joktan as the progenitor
of the Southern Arabians. Keil and Delitzsch comment that "Joktan is called
Kacktan by the Arabians, and is regarded as the father of all the primitive
tribes of Arabia."[24] Thus the sons of Joktan became established in Arabia
long before the Ishmaelites could have arrived there.

The Sons of Keturah

Eight lines of descent came from Abraham. Besides Ishmael and Isaac, Abraham had six sons by his concubine Keturah (Gen 25.1, 6; 1 Chron 1.32-33). Some of their names, and those of their sons, became place names in Arabia after Abraham sent them away from Isaac, "eastward, to the land of the east" (Gen 25.6). Of the sons of Keturah whose identity is certain, Dedan, Midian and Ephah can be located definitely in North Arabia.[25] The well-known Midianites usually lived on the eastern side of the Arabah, in far western Arabia. Moses fled from Egypt to Midian and stayed there 40 years; his wife was a Midianite.

Another son of Keturah was Shuah. Shuah was an international trade center near Mesopotamia. Eph'al shows that the sons of Keturah lived in North Arabia and were caravan traders of spices, gold, etc., from South Arabia.[26]

Conclusion

To summarize, the word "Arab" originally meant a nomad or Bedouin. Throughout most of history the word "Arab" has identified a cultural, not an ethnic, group. Today, the word "Arab" is used almost universally to signify a person who speaks Arabic. **Therefore, Palestinians are called Arabs, not because of ethnic derivation, but because they speak the Arabic language and share a common culture with other Arabic-speaking peoples.**

The original sons of Ishmael were not Arabian; they were 75% Egyptian. If the Ishmaelites lived in northern Arabia, they could only have represented a small portion of the total population of the Arabian Peninsula. They seemed to have been subsumed by those who lived in the peninsula, since their name vanished after the mid-10th century B.C.

The Arabians, who conquered and ruled Palestine beginning in the 7th century A.D., cannot be reckoned as Ishmaelites. Neither can today's Palestinians. Instead, the Palestinians are a very heterogeneous group. Like the original Ishmaelites, the Palestinians are more Egyptian than anything else.

No prejudice should be held against the Palestinians, on the grounds that they are Ishmaelites who will remain in defiance of their relatives, the Jews. Such an erroneous belief hinders resolution of the present Israeli-Palestinian conflict.

EXCERPTS FROM ISRAEL'S PROCLAMATION OF INDEPENDENCE[1]

The Land of Israel was the birthplace of the Jewish people. Here their spiritual, religious and national identity was formed. Here they achieved independence and created a culture of national and universal significance. Here they wrote and gave the Bible to the world.

Exiled from the Land of Israel the Jewish people remained faithful to it in all the countries of their dispersion, never ceasing to pray and hope for their return and the restoration of their national freedom.

Impelled by this historic association, Jews strove throughout the centuries to go back to the land of their fathers and regain their statehood. . . .

In the year 1897 the First Zionist Congress, inspired by Theordor Herzl's vision of the Jewish State, proclaimed the right of the Jewish people to national revival in their own country.

This right was acknowledged by the Balfour Declaration of November 2, 1917, and re-affirmed by the Mandate of the League of Nations, which gave explicit international recognition to the historic connection of the Jewish people with Palestine and their right to reconstitute their National Home.

The recent holocaust, which engulfed millions of Jews in Europe, proved anew the need to solve the problem of the homelessness and lack of independence of the Jewish people by means of the re-establishment of the Jewish State, which would open the gates to all Jews and endow the Jewish people with equality of status among the family of nations.

The survivors of the disastrous slaughter in Europe, and also Jews from other lands, have not desisted from their efforts to reach Eretz-Yisrael, in face of difficulties, obstacles and perils; and have not ceased to urge their right to a life of dignity, freedom and honest toil in their ancestral land.

On November 29, 1947, the General Assembly of the United Nations adopted a Resolution requiring the establishment of a Jewish State in Palestine. The General Assembly called upon the inhabitants of the country to take all the necessary steps on their part to put the plan into effect. This recognition by the United Nations of the right of the Jewish people to establish their independent State is unassailable.

It is the natural right of the Jewish people to lead, as do all other nations, an independent existence in its sovereign State.

ACCORDINGLY WE, the members of the National Council, representing the Jewish people in Palestine and the World Zionist Movement, . . .

. . . HEREBY PROCLAIM the establishment of the Jewish State in Palestine, to be called Medinath Yisrael (The State of Israel).

WE HEREBY DECLARE that . . . the National Council shall act as the Provisional State Council, and that the National Administration shall constitute the Provisional Government of the Jewish State, which shall be known as Israel.

THE STATE OF ISRAEL will be open to the immigration of Jews from all countries of their dispersion; will promote the development of the country for the benefit of all its inhabitants; will be based on the principles of liberty, justice and peace as conceived by the Prophets of Israel; will uphold the full social and political equality of all its citizens, without distinction of religion, race, or sex; will guarantee freedom of religion, conscience, education and culture; will safeguard the Holy Places of all religions; and will loyally uphold the principles of the United Nations Charter.

We appeal to the United Nations to assist the Jewish people in the building of its State and to admit Israel into the family of nations.

Our call goes out to the Jewish people all over the world to rally to our side in the task of immigration and development, and to stand by us in the great struggle for the fulfillment of the dream of generations for the redemption of Israel.

With trust in the Rock of Israel, we set our hand to this Declaration, at this Session of the Provisional State Council, on the soil of the Homeland, in the city of Tel-Aviv, on this Sabbath eve, the fifth of Iyar, 5708, the fourteenth of May, 1948.

Appendix D

RESOLUTION 242 (1967)

The Security Council,

Expressing its continuing concern with the grave situation in the Middle East,

Emphasizing the inadmissibility of the acquisition of territory by war and the need to work for a just and lasting peace in which every State in the area can live in security,

Emphasizing further that all Member States in their acceptance of the Charter of the United Nations have undertaken a commitment to act in accordance with Article 2 of the Charter,

1. *Affirms* that the fulfilment of Charter principles requires the establishment of a just and lasting peace in the Middle East which should include the application of both the following principles:

  (i) Withdrawal of Israel armed forces from territories occupied in the recent conflict;

  (ii) Termination of all claims or states of belligerency and respect for and acknowledgement of the sovereignty, territorial integrity and political independence of every State in the area and their right to live in peace within secure and recognized boundaries free from threats or acts of force;

2. *Affirms further* the necessity

  (a) For guaranteeing freedom of navigation through international waterways in the area;

  (b) For achieving a just settlement of the refugee problem;

  (c) For guaranteeing the territorial inviolability and political independence of every State in the area, through measures including the establishment of de-militarized zones;

3. *Requests* the Secretary-General to designate a Special Representative to proceed to the Middle East to establish and maintain contacts with the States concerned in order to promote agreement and assist efforts to achieve a peaceful and accepted settlement in accordance with the provisions and principles in this resolution;

4. *Requests* the Secretary-General to report to the Security Council on the progress of the efforts of the Special Representative as soon as possible.

Appendix E

RESOLUTION 338 (1973)

The Security Council

1. *Calls upon* all parties to the present fighting to cease all firing and terminate all military activity immediately, no later than 12 hours after the moment of the adoption of this decision, in the positions they now occupy;

2. *Calls upon* the parties concerned to start immediately after the cease-fire the implementation of Security Council resolution 242 (1967) in all of its parts;

3. *Decides* that, immediately and concurrently with the cease-fire, negotiations shall start between the parties concerned under appropriate auspices aimed at establishing a just and durable peace in the Middle East.

Appendix F

GOD'S PROMISED REGATHERING OF THE JEWS

Religious Israeli Jews anticipate "the redemption of Israel." By this term they mean the fulfillment of the the biblical promises of God's final ingathering (regathering) of the Jews to the land of their forefathers, the land's increased fruitfulness and the restoration of Israel's fortunes. These subjects are some of the most recurrent themes in the Hebrew Bible.

We have seen that Scripture repeatedly predicts that when God redeems Israel through His Messiah, Jews will acquire all of the remaining Promised Land. This includes the Plain of Philistia, Lebanon, part of present Jordan and Syria (Obad 19-20; Mic 7.14; Zech 10.10).

Israeli Expansionism
The U.S. has so heavily armed tiny Israel that it has reportedly become the fourth largest military power in the world. This military buildup, along with Israeli excursions across its borders, has caused Israel's neighbors to worry about possible Israeli expansionism. Former U.S. President Jimmy Carter sees the possibility of Israeli expansionism as a real, not imaginary, threat to stability in the Middle East.[1]

Right-wing Israelis advocate expanding Israel by annexing the occupied territories. Former Prime Minister Begin advocated expansionism throughout most of his career. Ariel Sharon often argues that Israel should seize more territory in Lebanon and Jordan. The former Israeli defense minister resigned from the Likud cabinet in February, 1990, in protest against Prime Minister Shamir's plan to negotiate a resolution of the Palestinian problem. Right-wing zealots like Sharon seek to recreate the greater Israel of David's and Solomon's monarchies. Some Jews and Christian Zionists think that the present return is that promised in Scripture, associated with the Messianic kingdom, and that Israeli Jews therefore have a divine entitlement to seize the remaining

Promised Land. This is a serious mistake! **It is imperative that Christians distinguish the present return of Jews to Eretz Israel from the future regathering promised by God.**

Distinguishing the Present and Future Returns

In Chapter 3 it was pointed out that most past rabbis have taught that God's final ingathering of the Jews would be preceded by a spiritual awakening. Walter Kaiser, of Trinity Evangelical Divinity School, correctly observes regarding isolated OT texts, "the question as to whether the return follows a national spiritual awakening and turning to the Lord or vice versa is difficult. Sometimes the prophets seem to favor the first, as in Deuteronomy 30, and sometimes it appears that the return precedes any general repentance, as in Ezekiel 36:1—37:14 and perhaps in Isaiah 11."[2] (See also Deut 4.29-30; 31.29.) An important question to ask is this: Does God require repentance before restoration?

We have already seen that God seemed to require a level of obedience to the Torah in order to give Israel the Promised Land. Considering the facts that Zionism has predominantly been a secular movement and that secularism continues to be the condition of the present State of Israel, it might be questioned whether or not God has created modern Israel at all! Indeed, some non-Israeli rabbis think that a pre-Messianic Jewish state is contrary to both Scripture and Judaism. Rabbi Yosef Becher explains:

> According to our belief, we [Jews] are not allowed to have a state. . . .
> The [earlier] rabbis were against a Jewish state because it was not the will of the Almighty. When it is his will, it will happen in a supernatural way—with the coming of the Messiah, when all kinds of miracles will be wrought. . . . until then we must remain among the peoples [Gentiles]. It is safer for us. If we have a state we could bring catastrophe upon ourselves, even if that state is religious and especially if it is irreligious, as the present state of Israel is.[3]

However, the closing chapters of this book show that several prophetic scriptures implicitly require a return of Jews to Eretz Israel before Messiah's coming in glory, and Eze 38.8 expressly declares it. Because God foretells a regathering does not necessarily mean He initiates or blesses it. Some of these passages reveal that God will redeem an Israeli nation already established in its land while simultaneously regathering all remaining Jews worldwide (herein called the "future return"). Such a view requires two returns: the present, partial return and a future, complete one at the coming of Messiah in glory.

Some Jews and zealous Christian Zionists, however, believe that the present return of Jews to the land of Israel is God's **final** regathering predicted in Scripture. They do not distinguish two returns following the long Diaspora.[4] This erroneous view both excuses and prolongs Israeli ill-treatment of the

Palestinians and fosters designs for their forced expulsion and for further Israeli expansionism. The main cause of this view is carelessness in considering the context of the pertinent biblical passages.

The present return of Jews to the land of Israel is not described in Scripture as God's promised regathering. The present and future returns can be distinguished in the following ways:

1. **The present return is partial.** In contrast, God's promised regathering will include every Jew throughout the world (Isa 43.5-7; 49.18; 66.20; Eze 36.10; 39.28).

2. **The present return has been a gradual process.** God's promised regathering will be accomplished in days, not decades, as the Gentiles bring the Jews back to the land (Isa 11.11-12; 60.9).

3. **The present return is a return in unbelief.** In contrast, the Jews of the future return will be called "the holy people" (Isa 62.11-12; cf. Zeph 3.9-10). Zionism is a secular movement. Furthermore, along with the rest of the world, Israel is predicted to apostatize (fall away from truth and righteousness) toward the end of the age (Deut 31.29).

4. **The future return will be preceded by the Jews' humility and repentance.** Unconverted Israeli Jews will begin to repent and seek God at the end of the age (Isa 59.20; Joel 2.12-17); Jews of the Diaspora will do likewise throughout the world (Deut 4.27-30; 30.1-5; Hos 3.4-5). Then God will gather the dispersed Jews back to the land of Israel (Isa 60.4, 9). Upon their arrival, their humility will become even more pronounced, after which they will realize total forgiveness (Zech 12.10; Eze 36.24, 32).

5. **The future return will be accompanied by an instantaneous conversion of the entire nation of Israel.** At the future return, Israel will be spiritually reborn in a day (Isa 66.8, 20). God will put both His Spirit and a new heart in every Jew, after which they will keep His commandments forever (Jer 31.31-34; Eze 36.26-27; 39.29).

6. **The present return is restricted chiefly to the historical land of Israel, whereas the future return will pertain to all of the Promised Land** (Isa 49.20; 54.3; Obad 19; Mic 7.11, 14; Zeph 2.7; Zech 10.10).

7. **The future return will begin during, or soon after, the Messianic conquest of the nations** (Isa 10.16-23; Jer 30.3-7; Dan 12.1; Zech 10.5-12).

8. **The future return will be accomplished by Gentiles escorting Jews back to their land. Many of these Gentiles will become their servants** (Isa 14.2; 35.10; 49.18-23; 66.20).

9. **God's promised regathering will commence the promised Messianic kingdom.** This is indicated by the context of many of the above passages.

Ezekiel 36-37

Perhaps the most prominent passage which is mistakenly applied to the present return is Eze 36-37.[5] These two chapters provide some of the most vivid and cherished prophecies in the Hebrew Bible: "O mountains of Israel, you will put forth your branches and bear your fruit for My people Israel;

for they will soon come. . . . O house of Israel, . . . I will take you from the nations, gather you from all the lands, and bring you into your own land. . . . everyone who passed by . . . will say, 'This desolate land has become like the garden of Eden' " (Eze 36.8, 10, 22, 24, 34-35).

The following features of the context of Eze 36 reveal that the regathering mentioned therein can occur only at the time of the Messianic kingdom, so that it does not apply to the present return:

1. It will be a complete regathering of "all of the house of Israel, all of it" (36.10).

2. There will be no more bloodshed in Israel and Jews will never again be bereaved of their children (36.14).

3. Israel will no longer hear insults from the nations nor bear any disgrace (36.15).

4. God will cleanse all Jews from their sins upon their arrival in the land of Israel, and He will enable them to keep His commandments (36.25-28; 39.29; Joel 2.28-32).

5. All Jews will thereafter worship God (36.11, 28, 38).

6. The nations will know that Yahweh is God (36.36; 37.28; 39.23).

Dispensational premillennialists persistently avow the necessity of interpreting biblical prophecy literally. Yet when it comes to Ezekiel's valley of the dry bones in Eze 37.1-14, most interpret it allegorically to mean the present political revival of Israel.[6] Ironically, most church fathers and commentators have regarded this portion literally, as the classic OT passage on the resurrection from the dead.[7]

Also to be considered is the scriptural principle that God hides His face from Israel until the nation repents (Deut 31.17-18; 32.20-21; Isa 6.9-10; 30.20; 45.15; 54.8; 64.7; Eze 39.29; Hos 5.15; Rom 11.25).[8] God hiding from Israel further precludes the present return being His promised ingathering.

Even though God has turned away from Israel, He still desires that individual Jews repent and turn to Him. "'Return to Me,' declares the LORD of hosts, 'that I may return to you' " (Zech 1.3; cf. Mal 3.7). When the nation of Israel does begin to repent at the end of this age, God will turn to shine His face on His covenant people. Then He will finally gather **all** Jews to the land of Israel and bless them abundantly, just as He promised to their father Abraham.

NOTES

PREFACE
[1] W.D. Davies, *The Gospel and the Land: Early Christianity and Jewish Territorial Doctrine* (Berkeley, CA: University of California Press, 1974), 4-5.

CHAPTER 1
[1] The terms "Palestine" and "Mandate Palestine" are used in this book synonymously, to designate that territory located between the Mediterranean Sea and the Jordan depression, and between Lebanon and the Sinai Peninsula. These boundaries for Mandate Palestine were established in 1920 under the League of Nations' mandate system. Palestine is used in a future sense on the front cover of this book.

[2] E.g., John F. Walvoord in *Things to Come: A Study in Biblical Eschatology*, J. Dwight Pentecost (1958; Grand Rapids: Zondervan, 1964), 75; Hal Lindsey, *The Rapture: Truth or Consequences* (New York: Bantam, 1983), 29-30.

[3] E.g., see Oswald T. Allis, *Prophecy and the Church* [1945] (n.p.: Presbyterian and Reformed, 1977), 32-36.

[4] E.g., Alfred Guillaume, "Zionists and the Bible," *From Haven to Conquest: Readings in Zionism and the Palestine Problem until 1948*, ed. Walid Khalidi (Beirut, Lebanon: The Institute for Palestine Studies, 1971), 26-27.

[5] W.D. Davies, *The Territorial Dimension of Judaism* (Berkeley, CA: University of California Press, 1982), xv.

[6] Quoted by Grace Halsell, *Prophecy and Politics: Militant Evangelists on the Road to Nuclear War* (Wesport, CN: Lawrence Hill, 1986), 150.

[7] Yehuda Elizur, "The Borders of Eretz Israel in Jewish Tradition," *Whose Homeland: Eretz Israel: Roots of the Jewish Claim*, ed. Avner Tomaschoff (Jerusalem: World Zionist Organization, 1978), 42.

[8] *Encyclopaedia Judaica*, 16 vols. (Macmillan: Jerusalem, 1972), 9:112.

[9] *Theological Wordbook of the Old Testament*, eds. R. Laird Harris, Gleason L. Archer, Bruce K. Waltke, 2 vols. (Chicago: Moody, 1980), 2:847.

[10] J. Alberto Soggin *Judges: A Commentary* in *The Old Testament Library*, tr. John Bowden (1979; rep., Philadelphia: Westminster, 1981), 23. Soggin claims all major contemporary commentators, except one, regard "not" as the correct reading in Jud 1.18. This view also correlates with vv. 19, 21, 27, 29-35 ("did not drive out," "did not take possession" or the like.)

As regards the word "valley," most authorities believe it refers to the Shephelah with its east-west valleys connecting to the coastal plain. The RSV, JB and NIV read "plain" instead of "valley." "Plain" makes better sense because chariots were only suited to relatively flat land. The Israelites, confined to the rugged hill country, had no use for chariots. If "plain" is the correct reading in v. 19, then "did not take" must also be correct in v. 18. Otherwise, the two verses would contradict. Accordingly, Judah did not take possession of any Philistine territory at this time.

CHAPTER 2

[1] Strabo, *Works*, XVI. iv, 18; Pliny, *Natural History*, V, xiii, 1.

[2] Gleason L. Archer, *A Survey of Old Testament Introduction*, rev. ed. (Chicago: Moody, 1974), 278. Some of the more prominent biblical references are: Gen 10.14; Deut 2.23; 1 Chron 1.12; Jer 47.4; Eze 25.16; Zeph 2.5; Amos 9.7.

[3] Yohanan Aharoni, *The Land of the Bible: A Historical Geography*, tr. A.G. Rainey (Philadelphia: Westminster, 1966), 251.

[4] Hanna E. Kassis, "Gath and the Structure of the 'Philistine' Society," *Journal of Biblical Literature*, vol. 84 (1965), 266-67.

[5] *The Zondervan Pictorial Encyclopedia of the Bible*, gen. ed. Merrill C. Tenney, 5 vols. (Grand Rapids: Zondervan, 1975), 4:767.

[6] E.g., Aharoni, *Land of the Bible*, 247, 251.

[7] Mordechai Gichon, "The History of the Gaza Strip: A Geo-political and Geo-strategic Perspective," *The Jerusalem Cathedra*, ed. Lee I. Levine, 3 vols. (Detroit, MI: Wayne State University Press, 1982), 2:283.

[8] Aharoni, *Land of the Bible*, 250-51.

[9] E.g., John Bright, *The History of Israel*, 3rd ed. (Philadelphia: Westminster, 1959), 176.

[10] Tenney, *Zondervan Pictorial*, 4:771-72.

[11] *Encyclopaedia Judaica*, 9:115.

[12] John Mauchline, ed., *New Century Bible: 1 and 2 Samuel* (Greenwood, S.C.: Attic Press, 1971), 233.

[13] William Gesenius, *A Hebrew and English Lexicon of the Old Testament* (Oxford: Clarendon, 1907), 52; Francis Brown, *The New Brown-Driver-Briggs-Gesenius Hebrew and English Lexicon with an Appendix Containing the Biblical Aramaic* (Peabody, MA: Hendrickson, 1979), 607.

[14] Hans Wilheim Hertzberg, *I and II Samuel: A Commentary*, tr. J.S. Bowden (London: SCM, 1964), 290.

[15] Kassis, "Gath and Philistine Society," 269.

[16] Peter R. Ackroyd, *The Cambridge Bible Commentary: The Second Book of Samuel* (Cambridge: University, 1977), 86.

[17] Bright, *History of Israel*, 199.

[18] Cited in Bright, *History of Israel*, 199n.

[19] K.A. Kitchen, "The Philistines," *Peoples of the Old Testament*, ed. D.J. Wiseman (Oxford: Clarendon, 1973), 64.

[20] Bright, *History of Israel*, 212.

[21] Yohanan Aharoni, *Land of the Bible*, 272, 275.

[22] Yohanan Aharoni and Michael Avi-Yonah, *The Macmillan Bible Atlas* (New York: Macmillan, 1968), 90.

[23] T.R. Hobbs, *2 Kings in Word Biblical Commentary*, 51 vols. (Waco, TX: Word, 1985), 13:253.

[24] James B. Pritchard, *Ancient Near Eastern Texts Related to the Old Testament*, 2nd ed. (Princeton, NJ: University Press, 1955), 288.

[25] Aharoni and Avi-Yonah, *Macmillan Bible Atlas*, 109.

[26] Gichon, "History of the Gaza Strip," 2:293.

[27] Aharoni and Avi-Yonah, *Macmillan Bible Atlas*, 111.

[28] E.g., Josephus, *Antiquities*, XIII, iv.4; xii.4; xiii.3.

29 Aharoni and Avi-Yonah, *Macmillan Bible Atlas*, 133.

30 Solomon Zeitlin, *The Rise and Fall of the Judean State: A Political, Social and Religious History of the Second Commonwealth*, 2 vols. (Philadelphia: Jewish Publication Society of America, 1962), 1:322, 326-27.

31 Aryeh Kasher, "Gaza During the Graeco-Roman Era," *Jerusalem Cathedra*, 2:65.

32 Tenney, *Zondervan Pictorial*, 3:42.

33 *Cambridge Ancient History*, 2nd ed., 12 vols. (Cambridge: University, 1954), 8:533.

34 Zeitlin, *Judean State*, 1:317.

35 Josephus, *Ant.*, XIII, xv, 4.

36 Josephus, *Ant.*, XIII, xiv, 2.

37 W.D. Davies, *The Territorial Dimension of Judaism* (Berkeley, CA: University of California Press, 1982), 62-63.

38 Josephus, *Ant.*, XIV, iv, 4.

39 Zeitlin, *Judean State*, 1:354.

40 Josephus, *Ant.*, XIV, v, 3.

41 Emil Schurer, *The History of the Jewish People in the Age of Jesus Christ (175 B.C.-A.D. 135)* [1885-1924], rev. ed., Geza Vermes, et al., 3 vols. in 4 (Edinburgh: T. & T. Clark, 1973), 2:94, 107.

42 E.g., Arnold J. Toynbee, *A Study of History*, 12 vols. (London: Oxford, 1954), 8:309.

CHAPTER 3

1 *Encyclopaedia Judaica*, 9:122.

2 Mordechai Naor, ed., *Ha'haganah* (Tel Aviv: Ministry of Defence of Publishing House, Israel, 1985), 7, 9.

3 Walid Khalidi, ed., *From Haven to Conquest: Readings in Zionism and the Palestine Problem until 1948* (Beirut, Lebanon: The Institute for Palestine Studies, 1971), xxii.

4 Quoted by Wilbur Crane Eveland, *Ropes of Sand: America's Failure in the Middle East* (London: W.W. Norton, 1980), 20.

5 Quoted by Ibrahim Abu-Lughod, "Retrieving Palestinian National Rights," *Palestinian Rights: Affirmation and Denial*, ed. Ibrahim Abu-Lughod (Wilmette, IL: Medina Press, 1982), 6.

6 Indebted to Wesley G. Pippert, *Land of Promise, Land of Strife* (Waco, TX: Word, 1988), 164.

7 Elizur, "Borders of Eretz Israel," 53.

8 Letter by Mr. Abba Eban to W.D. Davies in *Territorial Dimension of Judaism*, 114n27.

9 Zionist slogan quoted by Naor, *Ha' haganah*, 126.

10 Naor, *Ha' haganah*, 106.

11 Naor, *Ha' haganah*, 154.

CHAPTER 4

1 Livia Rokach, *Israel's Sacred Terrorism*, 3rd ed. (Belmont, MA: Association of Arab-American University Graduates, 1980), 8-9.

2 Hassan bin Talal (Crown Prince of Jordan), *Palestinian Self-Determination: A Study of the West Bank and Gaza Strip* (New York: Charles River Books, 1982), 36-37.

3 The term "Israeli(s)" is used herein as commonly understood, to identify Jewish citizens of the State of Israel. It more accurately refers to any citizen of Israel, whether Jewish or Arab Palestinian.

4 Sami Hadawi, *Crime and No Punishment: Zionist Israeli Terrorism 1939-1972* (Beirut, Lebanon: Near East Ecumenical Bureau of Information and Interpretation), 49.

5 Hadawi, *Crime and No Punishment*, 53.

6 Chaim Herzog, *The Arab-Israeli Wars: War and Peace in the Middle East* (New York: Random House, 1962), 214.

7 Jimmy Carter, *The Blood of Abraham* (Boston: Houghton Miflin, 1985), 94.

[8] Abdallah Frangi, *The PLO and Palestine*, tr. Paul Knight (London: Zed Books, 1983), 127.

[9] Quoted by Frangi, *The PLO and Palestine*, 198.

[10] Edward W. Said, et al., *A Profile of the Palestinian People*, 2nd ed. (Chicago: Palestine Human Rights Campaign, 1987), 12.

[11] Herzog (*Arab-Israeli Wars*, 254-55), President of Israel since 1983, recounts that during the Yom Kippur War of 1973, General Ariel Sharon displayed open mistrust and hostility toward the General Staff and his other divisional commanders. During the conflict, Sharon became guilty of insubordination by developing his own war strategy, which some Israelis hail as ingenious tactics. After Sharon would not desist from his own designs, General Gonen, in charge of the Sinai battle, requested that Sharon be relieved of his command. His request was not granted, perhaps due to the critical time in battle.

[12] Quoted by Frangi, *The PLO and Palestine*, 237.

[13] Cited by Arthur Hertzberg in "What's a Jew to Do?" *Americans for Middle East Understanding's Public Affairs Series* No. 28.

CHAPTER 5

[1] Rabbi Meir Kahane, *They Must Go* (New York: Grosset & Dunlap, 1981), 181.

[2] Richard J. Ward, et al., *The Palestine State: A Rational Approach* (Port Washington, NY: Kennikat Press, 1977), 61.

[3] Frangi, *The PLO and Palestine*, 13,16.

[4] Quoted by *The Middle East*, 6th ed. (Washington, D.C.: Congressional Quarterly, 1986), 18.

[5] Janet Abu-Lughod, "The Continuing Expulsions from Palestine: 1948-1985," *Palestine: Continuing Dispossession*, ed. Glenn E. Perry (Belmont, MA: Association of Arab-American University Graduates, Inc., 1986), 28.

[6] Israel Defence Census, November, 1967.

[7] Figures cited from Janet Abu-Lughod, "Continuing Expulsions," 23.

[8] Figures cited from Michael Roof, *Detailed Statistics on the Population of Israel by Ethnic and Religious Group and Urban and Rural Residences: 1950 to 2010* (Washington, D.C.: U.S. Bureau of the Census, 1984), 5.

[9] Yehoshafat Harkabi, "Israel's Moment of Truth," *Palestine Perspectives*, No. 34, (Mar/Apr 1988).

[10] Cited by Pippert, *Land of Promise*, 111.

[11] Ward et al., *The Palestine State*, 26.

[12] David Lamb, *The Arabs* (New York: Random House, 1987), 201; Muhammad Hallaj, "Mission of Palestinian Higher Education," *A Palestinian Agenda for the West Bank and Gaza*, ed. Emile A. Nakhleh, (Washington, D.C.: American Enterprise Institute for Public Policy Research, 1980), 60-61.

[13] Shassan Harb, "Labor and Manpower," *Palestinian Agenda*, ed. Nakhleh, 96.

[14] Shmuel Sandler and Hillel Frisch, *Israel, the Palestinians and the West Bank: A Study in Intercommunal Conflict* (Lexington, MA: Lexington Books, 1984), 157.

[15] Hassan bin Talal, *Palestinian Self-Determination*, 89.

[16] Annex to UN General Assembly Resolution 2625 (XXV), October 24, 1970, cited by Hassan bin Talal, *Palestinian Self-Determination*, 89-90.

[17] *The Houston Post*, November 14, 1987.

[18] Quoted in *The Middle East*, 5th ed. (Washington, D.C.: Congressional Quarterly, 1981), 5.

[19] Cited by Michael W. Suleiman, "World Public Opinion and the Question of Palestine," *Palestine: Continuing Dispossession*, ed. Perry, 87, n7.

[20] Quoted by Lamb, *The Arabs*, 214.

[21] Eveland, *Ropes of Sand*, 355.

[22] Quoted by Ibrahim Abu-Lughod, *Palestinian Rights*, 69.

[23] Carter, *Blood of Abraham*, 120.

[24] Quoted by Eveland, *Ropes of Sand*, 353.
[25] *The Houston Post*, May 29, 1988.
[26] Carter, *Blood of Abraham*, 58.
[27] *The Houston Post*, December 25, 1988.
[28] *The Houston Post*, December 21, 1989.

CHAPTER 6
[1] *The Encyclopedia Americana: International Edition*, 30 vols. (New York: Americana, 1972), 2:151,
[2] David Lamb, *The Arabs* (New York: Random House, 1987), 222.
[3] Interview with George Habash in *The Israel-Arab Reader: A Documentary History of the Middle East Conflict*, rev. ed., eds. Walter Laqueur and Barry Rubin (New York: Penguin, 1970), 500.
[4] *The Houston Post*, June 10, 1988.
[5] Frangi, *PLO and Palestine*, 96-97.
[6] Frangi, *PLO and Palestine*, 103.
[7] Interview with Yasser Arafat in *Israel-Arab Reader*, 376.
[8] Quoted by Lamb, *Arabs*, 216.
[9] *The Houston Post*, May 2, 1989.
[10] Abraham Sela, "The PLO, the West Bank, and Gaza Strip", *Jerusalem Quarterly*, No. 8 (Summer 1978), 69.
[11] *Israel-Arab Reader*, 510-11.
[12] *Israel-Arab Reader*, 513-14.
[13] *Israel-Arab Reader*, 514-18.
[14] Lamb, *Arabs*, 216.
[15] *The Houston Post*, February 7, 1989.
[16] *The Houston Post*, February 7, 1989.

CHAPTER 7
[1] *The Houston Post*, November 28,1989.
[2] *The Houston Post*, February 17, 1990.
[3] See Hadawi, *Crime and No Punishment*, 63-66.
[4] Pippert, *Land of Promise*, 79-80.
[5] Carter, *Blood of Abraham*, 129.
[6] Frangi, *The The PLO and Palestine*, 65, 71.
[7] Frangi, *The PLO and Palestine*, 65.
[8] Frangi, *The PLO and Palestine*, 70-71.
[9] Frangi, *The PLO and Palestine*, 72.
[10] Hadawi, *Crime and No Punishment*, 63-64.
[11] Hadawi, *Crime and No Punishment*, 36-37.
[12] Toynbee, *Study of History*, 8:289-90.
[13] *Encyclopedia Americana*, 3:605.
[14] Begin's 1977 Platform of the Likud Coalition.
[15] Carter, *Blood of Abraham*, 42.
[16] Herzog, *Arab Israeli Wars*, 21.
[17] Hadawi, *Crime and No Punishment*, 48.
[18] Menachem Begin, *The Revolt: Story of the Irgun* (New York: Henry Schuman, 1951), 162.
[19] *Journal of Palestine Studies*, Vol. 1, No. 4 (Summer 1972), 142-46.
[20] Herzog, *Arab Israeli Wars*, 75.
[21] Eveland, *Ropes of Sand*, 352.
[22] Quoted from *Hehazit* (summer 1943) in *Palestine Perspective* (March/April 1988).
[23] Quoted from *Hehazit* (summer 1943) in *Palestine Perspective* (March/April 1988).
[24] Quoted from Sharett's dairy (p. 33) in Rokach, *Israel's Sacred Terrorism*, xviii.
[25] *The Houston Post*, March 3, 1985.
[26] *The Houston Post*, February 17, 1990.

CHAPTER 8

[1] Beth Spring, "Palestinian Christians: Caught in a War of Two Rights," *Christianity Today,* April 18, 1986.

[2] The National Council of Churches of Christ in the U.S.A.'s *Middle East Panel Report: A Study Document* (New York: Fellowship of Reconciliation, 1980), 4.

[3] Eugene T. Fisher, "The Holy See and the State of Israel: The Evolution of Attitudes and Politics," *Journal of Ecumenical Studies* (Spring 1987), Vol. 24, No. 2, 197.

[4] *L'Osservatore Romano,* September 14, 1987.

[5] Robert L. Brashear, "Corner-stone, Stumbling Stone: Christian Problems in Viewing Israel," *Union Seminary Quarterly Review,* Vol. 38, No. 2 (1983), 212.

[6] Allan Solomonow, ed., *Where We Stand: Offical Statements of American Churches on the Middle East Conflict,* Introduction by Charles Angell (New York: Middle East Consultation Group, 1977), 7-8.

[7] Since antiquity, many Jewish rabbis have embraced the dual Messiah theory as that which they think best satisfies biblical messianic prophecies. It is believed that one Messiah, a normal human being, referred to as Messiah ben Joseph, will fulfill scriptures depicting Messiah's sufferings. The other Messiah, called Messiah ben David, will fulfill the many scriptures indicating Messiah's deliverance of Israel and His reign as King. Proponents of this view are uncertain whether or not the second Messiah will be a superhuman, divine person.

[8] See Robert L. Wilken, "The Restoration of Israel in Biblical Prophecy," *To See Ourselves As Others See Us,* eds. Jacob Neusner and Ernest S. Fredrichs (Chico, CA: Scholars, 1985), 450-51; Leroy Edwin Froom, *The Prophetic Faith of Our Fathers,* 4 vols. (Washington, D.C.: Review and Herald, 1950).

[9] Philip Schaff, *History of the Christian Church* [1918], 8 vols. (Grand Rapids: Eerdmans, 1985), 2:614.

[10] See *The Link* (November 1983), Vol. 16, No. 4., 3-7.

[11] Quoted in *The Link* (November 1983), Vol. 16, No. 4, 7.

[12] Figures by Halsell, *Prophecy and Politics,* 139.

[13] Cheryl A. Rubenberg, "Palestinian Human Rights Under Israeli Rule," *Church and Society* (March/April 1987), 10.

[14] Wilbur M. Smith, *Egypt and Israel coming Together?,* Foreword by Kenneth Taylor (1957 rep.; Wheaton, IL: Tyndale, 1978), vii.

[15] Lindsey, *Late Great,* 139-40.

[16] Lindsey, *Late Great,* 140; John F. Walvoord with John E. Walvoord, *Arma-geddon: Oil and the Middle East Crisis* (Grand Rapids: Zondervan, 1974), 114.

[17] Cited by Colin Chapman, *Whose Promised Land?,* rev. ed. (Tring, England: Lion, 1985), 206.

[18] Cited by Halsell, *Prophecy and Politics,* 178.

[19] Halsell, *Prophecy and Politics,* 45.

[20] Halsell, *Prophecy and Politics,* 67.

[21] Quoted by Halsell, *Prophecy and Politics,* 66-67.

[22] Halsell, *Prophecy and Politics,* 55-58.

[23] Halsell, *Prophecy and Politics,* 121.

[24] Quoted by Halsell, *Prophecy and Politics,* 65.

[25] Lynn Bozich Shetzer, "For the Peace of Jerusalem," *The Church and Society* (March/April 1987), 78.

[26] Jerry Falwell, ed., *The Fundamentalist Phenomenon: The Resurgence of Conservative Christianity* (New York: Doubleday, 1981), 215.

[27] Falwell, *Fundamentalist Phenomenon,* 216.

[28] Pippert, *Land of Promise,* 209-10.

[29] Arthur Hertzberg, "Zionism and the Jewish Religious Tradition," *The Jerusalem Colloquium on Religion, Peoplehood, Nation and Land,* eds. Marc H. Tanenbaum and R.J. Zwi Werblovsky (Jerusalem: Truman Research Institute of Hebrew University, 1972), 174.

[30] Quoted by Chapman, *Whose Promised Land?*, 166.

[31] Charles Caldwell Ryrie, *Dispensationalism Today* (Chicago: Moody, 1965), 105-09.

[32] In Rev 17.9-10 the KJV disassociates the seven kings from the seven mountains with the words, "And there are seven kings." On this basis many past expositors have interpreted the seven mountains literally, identifying the so-called seven-hilled city of Rome as the location of the harlot Babylon, a supposed ecclesiastical system. Since the Vatican is located in Rome, they have concluded that the Catholic Church is that harlot. However, most modern versions, e.g., RSV, NASB, JB, NEB and NIV, read, "and they are seven kings," or the like. Accordingly, the harlot does not sit on the seven-hilled city of Rome but on seven mountains which are symbolic of the seven kings.

[33] Edwin Yamauchi, *Foes from the Northern Frontier* (Grand Rapids: Baker, 1982), 20.

[34] The author's forthcoming book, *Babylon Is Coming*, includes a thorough exposition of Eze 38-39. It refutes this Russian interpretation, showing that Gog is the Antichrist.

[35] C.F. Keil and F. Delitzsch, *Commentary on the Old Testament*, 10 vols. (rep. Grand Rapids: Eerdmans, 1983), 1:22. Cf. p. 32.

CHAPTER 9

[1] Quoted by Talal, *Palestinian Self-Determination*, 125.

[2] Quoted by Talal, *Palestinian Self-Determination*, 124.

[3] "Definition of Aggression," General Assembly Resolution 331 (XXIX), December 14, 1974. However, Julius Stone (*Israel and Palestine Assault on the Law of Nations* [Baltimore, MD: John Hopkins University Press, 1981], 52), one of the world's foremost authorities on international law, argues against this definition.

[4] *A Palestinian State: The Case Against*, (Jerusalem: Israel Information Center, 1979), 5.

[5] Carter, *Blood of Abraham*, 45.

[6] Carter, *Blood of Abraham*, 207.

[7] *The New York Times*, February 24, 1983.

[8] *The Worcester Telegram*, September, 9, 1982.

[9] *The Houston Post*, February 2, 1983.

[10] *The Seattle Post-Intelligencer*, May 18, 1988.

[11] *The Washington Post*, May 23, 1989.

[12] Cited by Pippert, *Land of Promise*, 238-40.

CHAPTER 10

[1] Pippert, *Land of Promise*, 176.

[2] Tenney, *Zondervan Pictorial*, 5:247.

[3] Cited by the Congressional Research Service in *The West Bank-Gaza Economy: Problems and Prospects* (Washington: U.S. Government, 1980), 46.

[4] Quoted by Mitchell Bard, "Can Israel Withdraw," *Commentary*, Vol. 85 (April 1988), 31.

[5] Ward, et al., *The Palestine State*, ix.

[6] Don Peretz, "Forms and Projections of a Palestinian Entity," *The Palestine State*, 84.

[7] *The Houston Post*, April 6, 1988.

[8] See the twelve surveys of Louis Guttman, taken in Israel between 1973 and 1978, cited by Sandler and Frisch (*Israel, the Palestinians and the West Bank*, 129).

[9] Quoted by Said, *A Profile of the Palestinian People*, 4.

[10] Indebted to Kahane, *They Must Go*, 233-38.

CHAPTER 11

[1] E.g., J. Dwight Pentecost, *Things To Come: A Study in Biblical Eschatology* (1958; Grand Rapids: Zondervan, 1964), 46-47; against J. Barton Payne, *Encyclopedia of Biblical Prophecy: The Complete Guide to Scriptural Predictions and Their Fulfillment* (New York: Harper & Row, 1973), 121-26.

[2] Payne, *Encyclopedia of Biblical Prophecy*, 139.

[3] M. Friedlander, *The Commentary of Ibn Ezra on Isaiah*, 2 vols. in 1 (New York: Philip Feldheim, 1873), 1:59.

[4] In 2 Thes 2.8 the apostle Paul strongly alludes to Isa 11.4 as Messianic. While Isaiah gives a general description that Messiah "will slay the wicked," Paul individually identifies "the wicked" as "that lawless one"—the final Antichrist—whom Jesus will destroy at His coming in glory.

[5] The more reliable MT has "again" while the LXX retains only "the second time." Together, as in the NASB, they are redundant. This variance has caused some critical scholars to reject the contention that Isaiah here predicts a future Messianic regathering.

[6] John N. Oswalt, *The Book of Isaiah: Chapters 1–39* (Grand Rapids: Eerdmans, 1986), 288. Oswalt, however, views Israel as taking only the slopes of Philistia.

[7] E.g., Keil and Delitzsch, *Commentary on the OT*, 7:291; Solomon B. Freehof, *Book of Isaiah* (New York: Union of American Hebrew Congregations, 1972), 78.

[8] John Calvin, *Commentary on the Prophet Isaiah*, tr. William Pringle, 4 vols. (rep.; Grand Rapids: Eerdmans, 1958), 1:393. See also Keil and Delitzsch, *Commentary on the OT*, 7:291.

[9] Joseph Addison Alexander, *Commentary on the Prophecies of Isaiah* [1846], 2 vols. in 1 (Grand Rapids: Zondervan, 1971), 1:261.

[10] Edward J. Young, *The Book of Isaiah: The English Text, with Introduction, Exposition, and Notes*, 3 vols, (Grand Rapids: Eerdmans, 1965), 1:401. Young says of v. 14, "What Isaiah is here describing cannot, of course, be understood in a literal sense . . . to take place in Palestine" (p. 399). Young gives no reasons for this dismissal. Such outright rejection of a literal interpretation of Israel in OT prophecies is more excusable of earlier expositors than one in 1965, after modern Israel had been a state for eighteen years.

[11] J.N. Darby, one of the early Plymouth Brethren teachers, and C.I. Scofield contributed more than any others to the rise of premillennialism over the past 150 years. Their "dispensational premillennialism" includes a pretribulational "rapture" of the church, seven years before Jesus' second coming to the earth. This view is to be distinguished from "historic premillennialism," believed by its adherents to be the position of the early church, in which all events concerning Jesus' return, including the rapture, are placed at the end of the Tribulation.

[12] William Kelley, *An Exposition of the Book of Isaiah* [1871], 4th ed. (Minneapolis: Klock & Klock, 1979), 149-50.

[13] W.E. Vine, *Isaiah: Prophecies, Promises, Warnings* (rep.; Grand Rapids: Zondervan, 1971), 49-50.

[14] E.H. Plumptre, "Isaiah," *A Biblical Commentary for English Readers: Job to Isaiah*, ed. Charles John Ellicott (New York: E.P. Dutton and Co., n.d.), 455.

[15] Payne, *Encyclopedia of Biblical Prophecy*, 295. Cf. p. 664.

CHAPTER 12
[1] Tribulation often refers in Scripture to Satan-inflicted persecution of God's people. The term, "the Tribulation," appears herein to distinguish it from all previous periods of tribulation, which have been less severe and/or less widespread. That is why it is called in the NT, "the great tribulation" (Mt 24.15; Rev 7.14). In the OT the same period is called "the time of Jacob's distress" (Jer 30.7; cf. Dan 12.1). The Tribulation lasts three and a half years. It begins with an act in the rebuilt temple in Jerusalem, when the regular sacrifice is removed and replaced by "the abomination of desolation." The Tribulation ends at the coming of Messiah in glory (Dan 9.27; 11.31-33; 12.11; Mt 24.15). Dispensationalists arbitrarily designate Daniel's entire 70th week, which lasts seven years, as the Tribulation and distinguish its latter half as "the great tribulation" (Dan 9.25-27; Rev 7.14). But Jesus used both terms interchangeably (Mt 24.21, 29), showing that they identify the same time.

[2] E.g., Payne, *Encyclopedia of Biblical Prophecy*, 408. Cf. p. 104.

[3] See Isa 32.15; Eze 39.29; Zech 12.10, which depict Messianic conditions. In Ac 2.17-21 the apostle Peter quotes Joel 2.28-32 and reckons its fulfillment to be on that

day of Pentecost. Luke does not say that the heavenly signs occurred, an omission strongly suggesting that they did not. Also, the Spirit's outpouring was selective, coming only upon those few disciples, not all mankind. Thus, that day of Pentecost was only a partial fulfillment of Joel 2.28-32. The universal outpouring still awaits the inauguration of the Messianic kingdom. Then, Moses' wish will come true, "that all the LORD's people [would become] prophets, that the LORD would put His Spirit upon them!" (Num 11.29).

⁴ Merrill F. Unger, *Unger's Bible Handbook: An Essential Guide to Understanding the Bible* (Chicago: Moody, 1966), 404. Unger regards the entire contents of Joel 2-3 as referring to the latter days.

⁵ E.g., Payne, *Encyclopedia of Biblical Prophecy*, 410.

⁶ E.g., 1 Macc 3.41; 2 Macc 8.11, 25; Josephus, *Ant.*, XII, vii, 3.

⁷ Robert Chisholm, "Joel," *Bible Knowledge Commentary: Old Testament*, John F. Walvoord and Roy Zuck, gen. eds. (Wheaton, IL: Victor, 1985), 1422.

⁸ A.C. Gaebelein, *The Prophet Joel: An Exposition* (New York: "Our Hope," 1909), 150-51.

CHAPTER 13

¹ Charles Lee Feinberg, *The Minor Prophets* [1951] (Chicago: Moody, 1976), 221.

² Feinberg, *Minor Prophets*, 225.

³ Unger, *Unger's Bible Handbook*, 428.

⁴ Josephus, *Wars*, VI, 7, 3.

⁵ E.g., Keil and Delitzsch, *Commentary on the OT*, 10:144.

⁶ H.A. Ironside, *Notes on the Minor Prophets* (New York: Loizeaux Bros., n.d.), 299. Ironside interprets Philistia, in vv. 4-7, allegorically as corrupt Christianity. But he adds, "a more complete fulfillment will take place in the last days."

⁷ *Theological Wordbook of the Old Testament*, ed. Harris et al., 1:258.

⁸ John D.W. Watts, *The Books of Joel, Obadiah, Jonah, Nahum, Habakkuk and Zephaniah* in *The Cambridge Bible Commentary: New English Bible* (India: CUP, 1975), 167-68; Keil and Delitzsch, *Commentary on the OT*, 10:141.

⁹ E.g., Rav Uzi Kelcheim, "Our Moral Title to the Land of Israel—in the Writings of Ramban (Nahmanidus)," *Whose Homeland*, ed. Tomaschoff, 60.

¹⁰ Keil and Delitzsch, *Commentary on OT*, 10:378.

CHAPTER 14

¹ Many scholars suppose multiple authorship of Regardless, Zechariah because chs. 1-8 and 9-14 differ in content and style. Zechariah is considered herein as a literary unit, providing maximum value in comparing its sections.

² David Baron, *The Visions and Prophecies of Zechariah* (Grand Rapids: Kregel, 1918), 297-99; Charles Lee Feinberg, *God Remembers: A Study of the Book of Zechariah* (New York: American Board of Missions to the Jews, 1965), 160, 163; Frederick A. Tatford, *The Prophet of the Myrtle Grove: An Exposition of the Prophecy of Zechariah* (London: Henry E. Walter, Ltd., 1971), 101.

³ Keil and Delitzsch, *Commentary on the OT*, 10:331-32. Although Keil interprets a future fulfillment of much of this passage, in accordance with his allegorizing method, he finds that fulfillment in the church rather than in a literal, earthly Israel.

⁴ Josephus, *Ant.*, XI, viii, 5.

⁵ Rex Mason, *The Books of Haggai, Zechariah and Malachi* in *The Cambridge Bible Commentary on the New English Bible* (Cambridge: University, 1977), 87.

⁶ Quoted by Feinberg, *God Remembers*, 46.

⁷ Merrill F. Unger, *Zechariah: Prophet of Messiah's Glory* (Grand Rapids: Zondervan, 1963), 159; Tatford, *Prophet of the Myrtle Grove*, 101.

⁸ A.C. Gaebelein, *Studies in Zechariah*, 8th ed. (New York: "Our Hope," 1911), 83. Gaebelein held the distinction of being the only contributing editor for both the "old" and "new" *Scofield Reference Bible*.

[9] Ironside, *Minor Prophets*, 380.

[10] Feinberg, *God Remembers*, 153.

[11] See Keil and Delitzsch, *Commentary on the OT*, 10:325.

[12] E.g., Charles Caldwell Ryrie, *The Ryrie Study Bible: New American Standard Translation* (Chicago: Moody, 1976), 1423.

[13] *New Scofield Bible*, 971; also Feinberg, *God Remembers*, 169, 172; Ironside, *Minor Prophets*, 394.

[14] Feinberg, *God Remembers*, 172.

APPENDIX A

[1] Aharoni and Avi-Yonah (*The Macmillan Bible Atlas*, 51) place the Avvites between Gaza and the Wadi el Arish.

[2] George Adam Smith, *The Historical Geography of the Holy Land*, 26th ed. (New York: Harper and Brothers, 1894), 169.

[3] E.g., Smith, *Historical Geography of the Holy Land*, 172.

[4] Aharoni, *The Land*, 246.

[5] Aharoni and Avi-Yonah, *Macmillan Bible Atlas*, 49.

[6] Alassandra Nibbi, *The Sea Peoples and Egypt* (Park Ridge, NJ: Noyes Press, 1975), 3-4, 35-48.

[7] Nibbi, *Sea Peoples and Egypt*, 10.

[8] Nibbi, *Sea Peoples and Egypt*, 4-5, 48-58.

[9] Aharoni, *The Land*, 245.

[10] Nibbi (*Sea Peoples and Egypt*, 112) cites expert Yadin in *The Art of Warfare in Biblical Lands*, 339-40.

[11] Nibbi, *Sea Peoples and Egypt*, 73, 103.

[12] Aharoni, *The Land*, 246.

[13] Nibbi, *Sea Peoples and Egypt*, 81-82, 100.

[14] Michael Avi-Yonah, ed., *Encyclopedia of Archaeological Excavations in the Holy Land*, 4 vols. (Englewood Cliffs, NJ: Prentice-Hall, 1975), 1:125.

[15] Avi-Yonah, *Archaeological Excavations*, 1:125.

[16] Cited by Amihai Mazar, "The Emergence of the Philistine Material Culture," *Israel Exploration Journal*, Vol. 35, Nos. 2-3 (1985), 102.

[17] Cited by G. Ernest Wright, "Fresh Evidence for the Philistine Story," *The Biblical Archaeologist*, Vol. 29, No. 3 (September 1966), 71.

[18] Aharoni, *The Land*, 251.

[19] Aharoni, *The Land*, 248.

APPENDIX B

[1] "Arabia" is used herein to denote only the Arabian Peninsula, and "Arabian" refers only to an inhabitant, or former inhabitant, of Arabia, having a long genealogy of descendants who lived in Arabia.

[2] Israel Eph'al, *The Ancient Arabs: Nomads on the Borders of the Fertile Crescent, 9th-5th Centuries B.C.* (Jerusalem: Magnes Press, 1982), 6.

[3] E.g., Israel Eph'al, " 'Ishmael' and 'Arab(s)': A Transformation of Ethnological Terms," *Journal of Near Eastern Studies* (October 1976), Vol. 35, No. 4, 227.

[4] E.g., Bernard Lewis, *The Arabs in History*, 4th rev. ed. (New York: Harper & Row, 1966), 12.

[5] Eph'al, *Ancient Arabs*, 9.

[6] Edward Atiyah, *The Arabs* (Beirut, Lebanon: Lebanon Bookshop, 1955), 35.

[7] Atiyah, *The Arabs*, 7.

[8] Lewis, *Arabs in History*, 14.

[9] Quoted by Joan Peters, *From Time Immemorial: The Origins of the Arab-Jewish Conflict over Palestine* (New York: Harper & Row, 1984), 148.

[10] British Foreign Office publication No. 60, quoted by Peters, *From Time Immemorial*, 157.

[11] Quoted by Peters, *From Time Immemorial*, 156.

[12] Lewis, *Arabs in History*, 15.

[13] Eph'al, "Transformation of Ethnological Terms," 225.

[14] Keil and Delitzsch, *Commentary on the OT*, 1:220, 265.

[15] *The Koran: Translated into English from the Original Arabic*, tr. George Sale (London: Frederick Warne, n.d.), 438, n6.

[16] Eph'al, *Ancient Arabs*, 234. Eph'al, however, regards the genealogy of Ishmael and others in Genesis as Jewish midrash (unhistorical).

[17] Tenney, *Zondervan Pictorial*, 3:48.

[18] Josephus, *Ant.*, I, xii, 4.

[19] Eph'al, "Transformation of Ethnological Terms," 234. Josephus (*Ant.*, I, xii, 2; II, ix, 3; II, iii, 3) refers to the Arabs as Ishmaelites, which Eph'al attempts to dismiss (p. 233.).

[20] David K. Shipler, *Arab and Jew: Wounded Spirits in a Promised Land* (New York: Times Books, 1986), 152.

[21] This is providing that Ps 83 was written before this time, as generally supposed.

[22] Eph'al, "Transformation of Ethnological Terms," 227.

[23] Doron Mendels, *The Land of Israel as a Political Concept in Hasmonean Literature: Recourse to History in Second Century B.C. Claims to the Holy Land* (Tubingen: Mohr, 1987), 147-51.

[24] Keil and Delitzsch, *Commentary on the OT*, 1:171.

[25] Eph'al, *The Ancient Arabs*, 232.

[26] Eph'al, *The Ancient Arabs*, 233.

APPENDIX C

[1] Laqueur and Rubin, eds., *The Israel-Arab Reader*, 125-28.

APPENDIX F

[1] Carter, *Blood of Abraham*, 144.

[2] *Bibliotheca Sacra* (October 1961), Vol. 138, No. 552, 309.

[3] Quoted by Chapman, *Whose Promised Land?*, 193-94.

[4] The words "God's promised regathering" refer herein to God's final regathering, not the predicted return of the Babylonian exiles in the 5th century B.C. (e.g., Isa 44.28; 48.20; Jer 25.11; Dan 9.2).

[5] E.g., Lindsey, *Late Great*, 49. Charles Lee Feinberg (*The Prophecy of Ezekiel: The Glory of the Lord* [Chicago: Moody, 1969], 207) shows otherwise.

[6] E.g., Lindsey, *Late Great*, 41, 50; Ryrie, *Ryrie Study Bible*, 1284.

[7] Feinberg, *Ezekiel*, 212.

[8] Many dispensationalists claim that the 144,000 Jews in Rev 7.4 will evangelize the world during the Tribulation, resulting in the redeemed multitude of v. 9 (e.g., Lindsey, *Late Great*, 99-100). Some further suppose that these Jews will stir a spiritual awakening in Israel during the Tribulation. This interpretation is based solely on the juxtaposition of the two visions, a weak hermeneutic. Furthermore, it is contrary to a clear and recurrent theme in the biblical prophets: Israel will succumb to apostasy and idolatry in the latter days (Deut 31.29; Isa 29.13-14; 31.6-7; Amos 9.8-11; Zeph 3.18), as will the rest of the world (Mt 24.12-13; 2 Thes 2.3; 2 Tim 3.1-5).

SCRIPTURE INDEX
(Includes Intertestamental Literature)

258

AUTHOR INDEX

SUBJECT & PERSON INDEX